IMAGES
*of America*

# STEARNS COUNTY MINNESOTA

IMAGES
*of America*

# STEARNS COUNTY MINNESOTA

Lee M.A. Simpson

ARCADIA
PUBLISHING

ISBN 978-0-7385-0833-7

Published by Arcadia Publishing
Charleston, South Carolina

Printed in the United States of America

Library of Congress Catalog Card Number: 00107785

For all general information contact Arcadia Publishing at:
Telephone 843-853-2070
Fax 843-853-0044
E-mail sales@arcadiapublishing.com
For customer service and orders:
Toll-Free 1-888-313-2665

Visit us on the Internet at www.arcadiapublishing.com

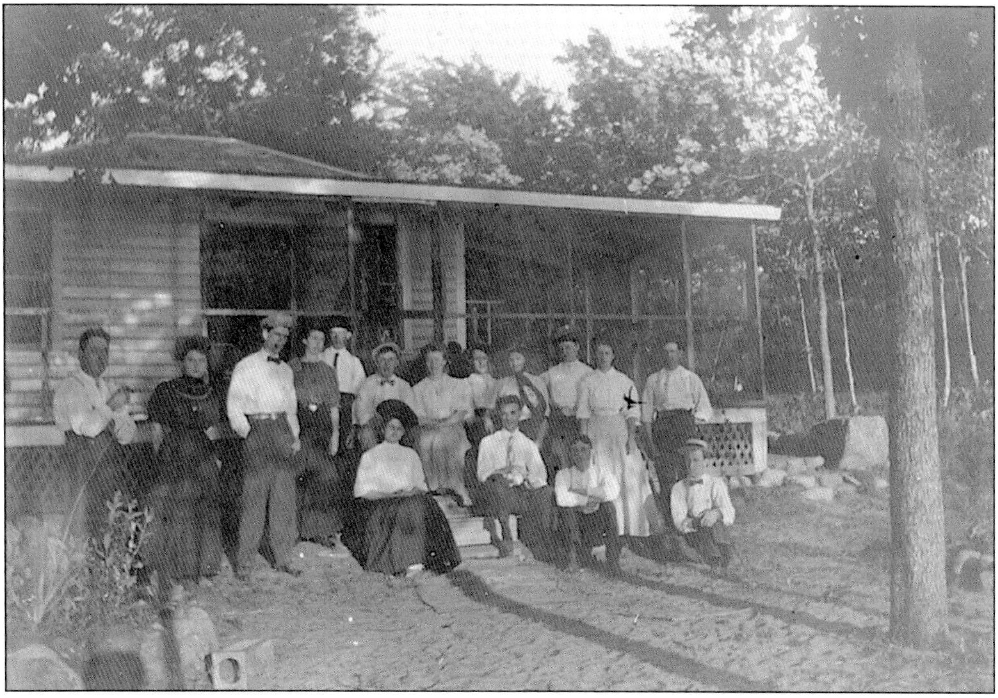

Shady Nook Cottage at Avon on the shores of Upper Spunk Lake, 1907. (Courtesy of Richard Kelly.)

# Contents

# ACKNOWLEDGMENTS

Numerous people have contributed information and materials for this book. I owe a debt of gratitude to my research assistants Dennis Green and Kari Brixius, both of whom spent many hours at the Stearns History Museum helping to identify the people and the places in the photographs and postcards that follow. The text of this book relies heavily on information gathered from the Stearns History Museum in St. Cloud. I am particularly grateful to John Decker and Bob Loomel for their assistance. The Stearns History Museum is a top local history museum and those interested in the history of Stearns County should head there first for more information on the county. I have also used William Bell Mitchell's *History of Stearns County* (1915), articles from the many Stearns county newspapers, and the oral histories of Stearns county residents.

The collection of images in this book comes from a variety of public and private sources. A special thanks goes to the Central Minnesota Historical Center and the University Archives at St. Cloud State University for access to their collections. One of the key private donors to this project was Richard Kelly of St. Cloud. He granted me unlimited access to his personal postcard collection. The variety of images in these postcards reflects the diverse activities of residents of Stearns County. They also demonstrate the importance of booster activities for all businesses and cities within the county. Other contributors to the photos in this book include the Hunstiger family, Kari Brixius, Tim O'Hara, Charlie Grafft, Don Hofsommer, Jenny Giambruno, Roy Bernick, the Gaetz family, and Dave Lindmeier. Their personal collections help put a face on Stearns County.

# INTRODUCTION

*Images of America: Stearns County, Minnesota,* embodies the coalescence of local history and national history. It is an exploration of a single county in the American Midwest that retains a unique character yet experienced all of the larger forces of national history: immigration, economic fluctuations, technological innovation, war and peace, and political change. The images of Stearns County show us who we were and who are as we have redefined ourselves in the way we live, work, play, study, worship, and contend with our natural environment.

Stearns county is situated a short distance south of the geographic center of Minnesota, on the west side of the Mississippi River. It is the largest county in the southern half of the state, and in 2000, the county ranked seventh in population and 14th in size of the 87 counties in the state. The total area of the county is approximately 1,394 square miles, most of which is dominated by agriculture. The county is the home of 30 cities and 35 townships. The largest city, St. Cloud, has a population of 60,362 and serves as the county seat. El Rosa, the smallest incorporated town, has a population of 75, and lies on the western edge of the county. While St. Cloud serves as the primary business and political center for the county, the many smaller cities and towns in the county serve important functions as service centers for surrounding agricultural and recreational areas. Stearns County's newest municipality, the City of Ventura, named in honor of Governor Jesse Ventura, officially became a city on May 2, 2000.

Reflecting the broader trends of western American history, the region that became Stearns County experienced all of the growing pains of the onslaught of white migration. The land was originally home to the Ojibwe and Dakota Indians, most of whose descendants were removed to reservations in northern Minnesota. Although white exploration of the area began with the Lewis and Clark expedition of 1805, white men could not legally acquire title to land in the area until 1847. Immigration began as a trickle but picked up in 1854 when a large number of German Catholics decided to make the county their home. The influx of immigrants led the state legislature to establish Stearns County as a territorial government on February 20, 1855. The legislation initially put forth the name of Stevens County to honor Governor Isaac I. Stevens who had explored the area in 1853; however, the name Stearns was chosen instead to honor Charles Thomas Stearns, a member of the Territorial Council who had been a key player in securing legislation establishing the county as an independent political entity. He moved to St. Cloud the following year where he became a prominent innkeeper. His Stearns Hotel became the original building on the St. Cloud State University campus.

The history of Stearns County has been well documented by many historians, and this book is not an effort to recreate what has already been done. What follows, however, is unique. First, its pictorial format brings the history of the county alive. Residents and non-residents will be able to see first hand how this county has changed over time. Second, the use of postcards in this collection is significant. Postcards played an important role as booster material for the cities and towns of Stearns County. Economic growth and development can only occur if people move into a community. These postcards sold the county as a place of thriving businesses and recreational opportunities, but also as a county of homes, churches, and schools. Third, I have tried, where appropriate, to place events in Stearns County in a wider historical perspective. Regional and national events and developments helped shape the lives of county residents and the physical appearance of its towns and cities.

Many of the buildings pictured in this collection no longer exist, and others are at risk as the pressures for growth and modernization increase in the 21st century. I hope this book will help remind current residents of the value of their county's past and the benefits that come from preserving it. I hope, too, that it will help introduce new residents and visitors to a vibrant county and perhaps explain how things got to be the way they are today.

# *One*

# Main Street

Like their sister cities throughout the American West, Stearns County cities in many respects were "instant cities." In less than a generation, a region virtually untouched by the white man could claim all the trappings of "civilization." Schools, churches, newspapers, county, town and township government, businesses, and farms, dotted the landscape. Although the county continues to retain its rural feel today, its cities form the heart and soul of the county. Whether unincorporated township, town, or city, each community has served a specific rural constituency.

The county seat, St. Cloud, serves as the principle city for both the county and for central Minnesota as a whole. Today it is a city of over 60,000 with a thriving economy. Residents from the surrounding countryside venture into the city for jobs, shopping, and entertainment on a scale not available in the county's smaller towns and townships. Established in 1853 and incorporated in 1856, St. Cloud is actually the product of the merging of three distinct communities: Upper Town platted in 1853 by Tennessee fur trader Sylvanus P. Lowry, Middle Town platted in 1855 by John L. Wilson, and Lower Town platted in 1856 by George Fuller Brot. Wilson gave his plat the name St. Cloud after the suburb in Paris, France, where the emperor Napoleon had a summer palace. Each community had its own ethnic character, streets, ferry crossings, churches, schools, and stores that they retained even after consolidating in 1856 to gain more political power and to share common services and facilities.

The county's second largest city is Sauk Centre, located approximately 30 miles northeast of St. Cloud. Sauk Centre is best known as the hometown of writer Sinclair Lewis and as the model for the towns of Gopher Prairie in *Main Street* and Zenith in his novels *Babbit* and *Arrowsmith*. Primarily a service center for the surrounding agricultural area, Sauk Centre had ambitions for growth in the early 1900s that continue today as the city tries to take advantage of its location on Interstate 94.

The growth and development of all of the cities of Stearns County relied on selling the city, the county, the region, and the state. As relatively young cities in 1900, residents—like Sinclair Lewis' fictional George Babbitt—boosted their cities because their economic livelihood depended on it. In this vein, almost every business in a town paid for the printing of picture postcards of their business on the main street of town. Many businesses also paid for postcards of city attractions such as parks, lakes, and modern city services. The postcards that follow were a more subtle form of booster activity than the blatant boastfulness Babbitt engaged in. Instead, claims of city greatness were backed up by a photographic image. As historical resources, they have a profound legacy in revealing the history of Main Street, Stearns County.

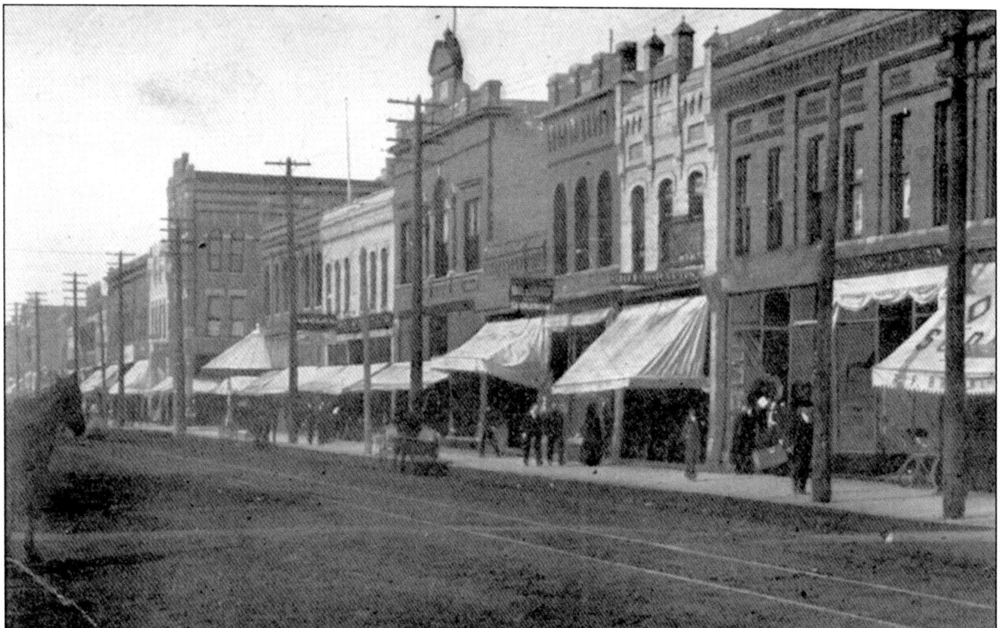

Pedestrians meander down St. Germain Street, St. Cloud, *c.* 1910. St. Germain was the main street for St. Cloud and the heart of the business district until the opening of the Crossroads Mall on the western edge of the city in 1965. (Courtesy of Richard Kelly.)

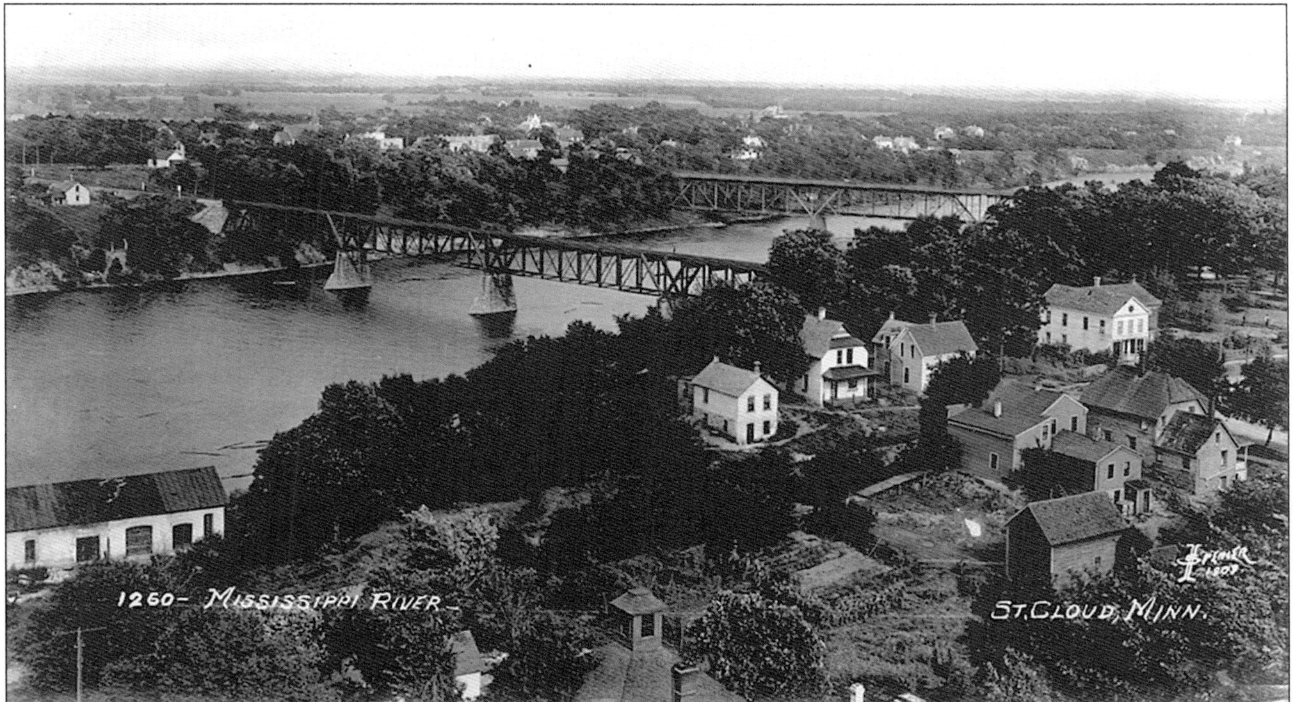


Above is an aerial view of St. Cloud looking northeast across the Mississippi River *c.* 1910. The bridge in the foreground is the St. Germain Street Bridge and the bridge in the background is the Great Northern Railroad Bridge. Note the open farm country in the background; St. Cloud is still rural at this time. (Courtesy of Richard Kelly.)

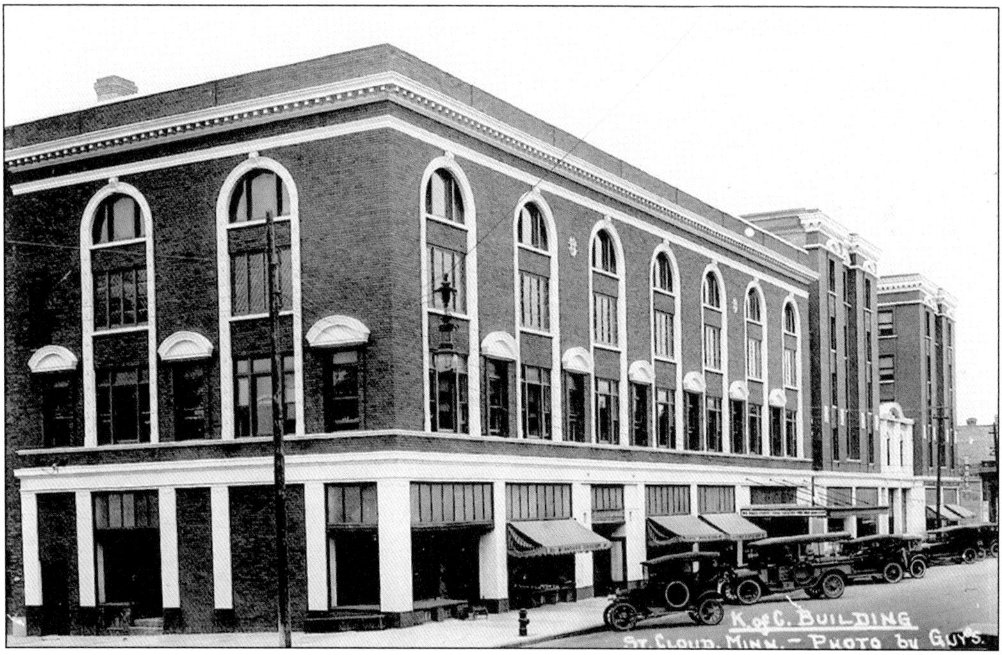


The top view of the 900 block of St. Germain Street, c. 1920, looks east and shows the Knights of Columbus building. The bottom view looks west and shows the Breen Hotel and Pharmacy. This block currently houses the historic Paramount Theater, which was refurbished in the late 1990s to create the Paramount Arts District. The Breen Hotel was turned into the Germain Towers Apartments. (Courtesy of Richard Kelly.)

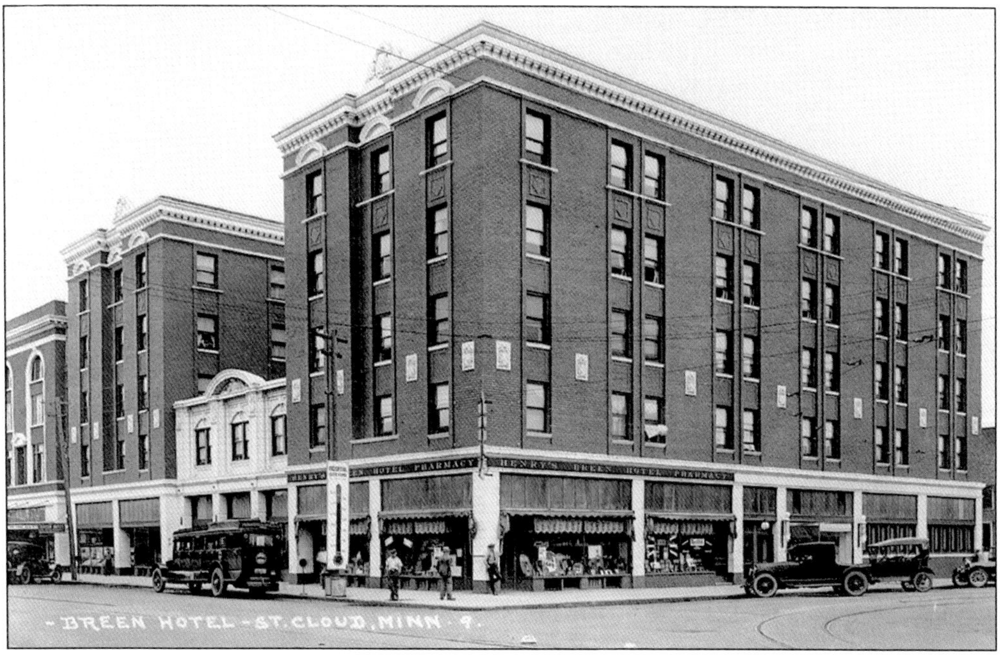

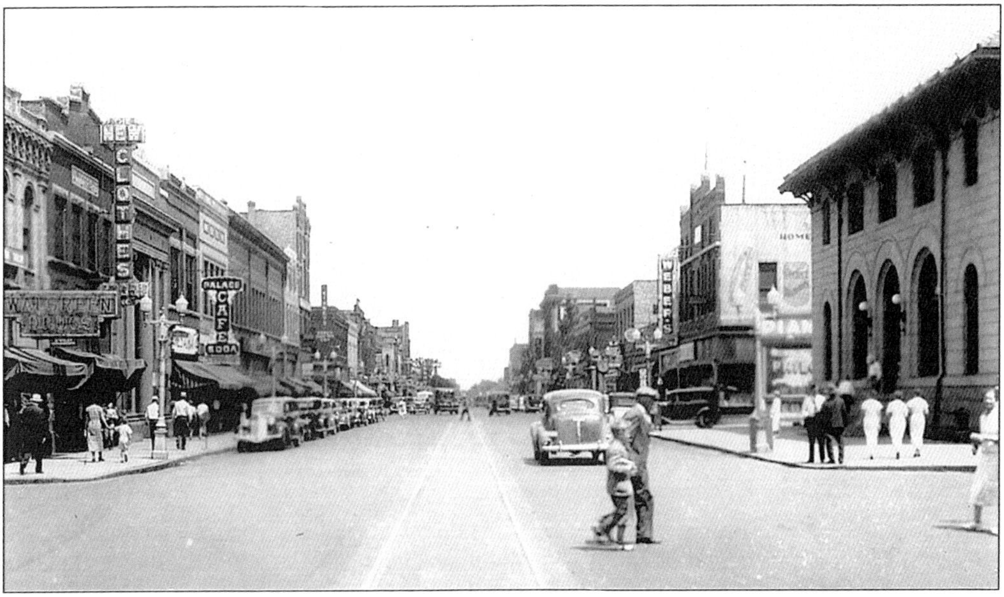


"Main Street, St. Cloud" reads this postcard from the 1940s. This view looks east down St. Germain Street. The building that housed both the post office and the federal building is in the right foreground. The trolley tracks down the center of the street were abandoned in 1936. (Courtesy of Richard Kelly.)

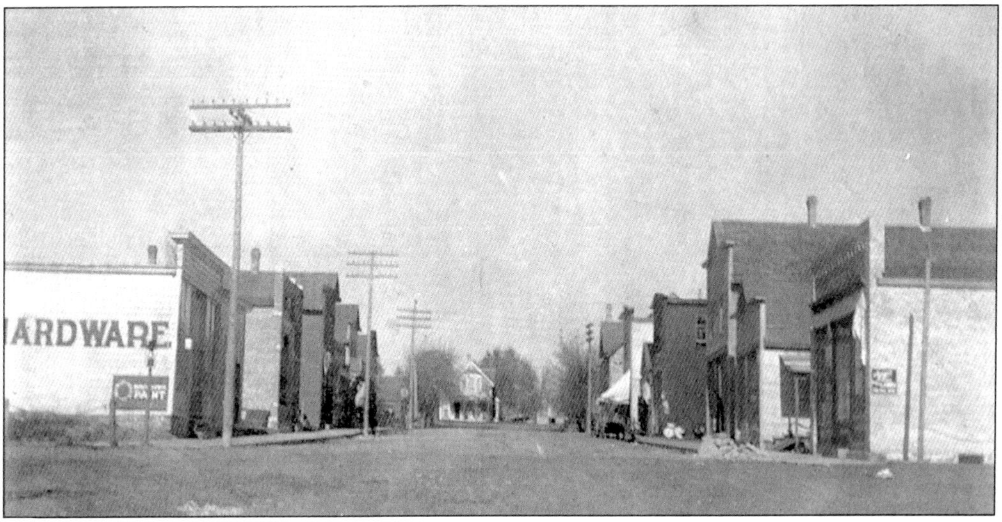


Pictured above in this 1908 image is Main Street, Kimball. Established in 1886 and incorporated in 1892, the community got its start when the Soo Line Railroad was built in 1886. Its proper name is Kimball Prairie. The city's name was never legally changed to Kimball and all city documents must have Kimball Prairie on them. Located in southern Stearns County, rural Kimball experienced the technological revolution of electricity and telephone of the late 19th and early 20th centuries. (Courtesy of Richard Kelly.)

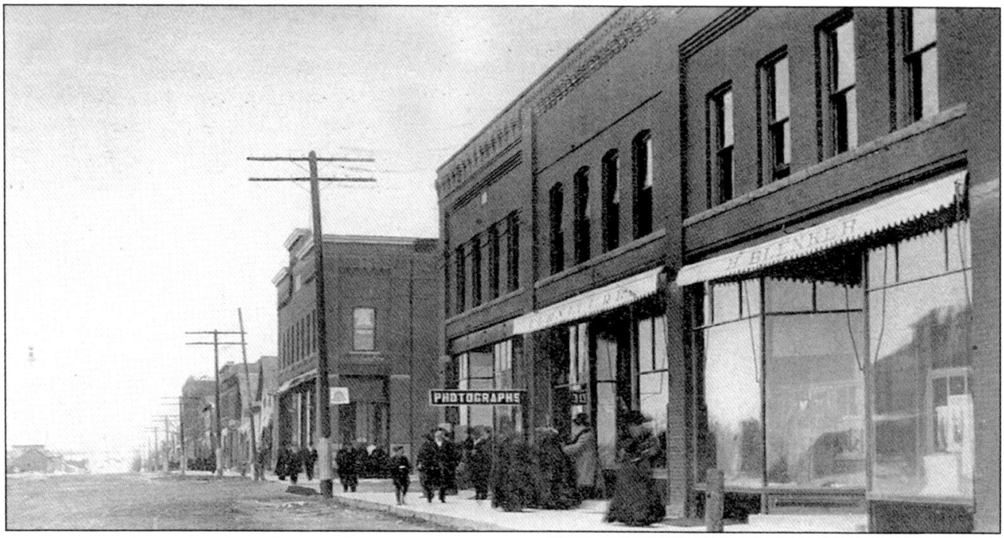


Incorporated in 1890, Albany boasted a thriving business district where pedestrians could window shop on Main Street by 1910. This postcard was produced for Henry J. Blenker as an advertisement for his furniture shop. (Courtesy of the Central Minnesota Historical Center.)

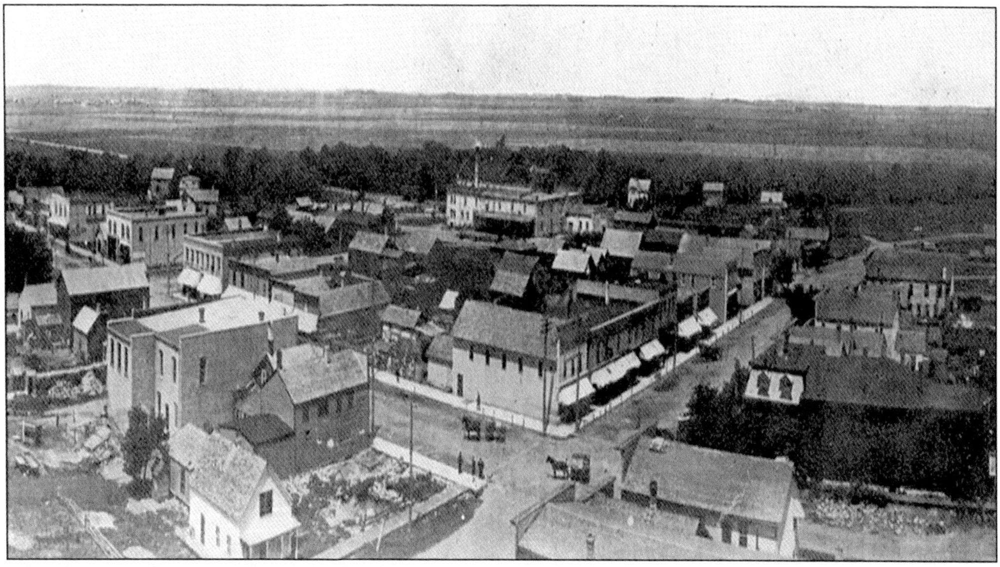

The thriving business district of Paynesville is shown above in this 1913 image. Named after Edwine E. Payne, the town was incorporated in 1887. Approximately eight blocks wide, the Paynesville downtown provided important commercial services to farmers in the southeastern county. (Courtesy of the Central Minnesota Historical Center.)

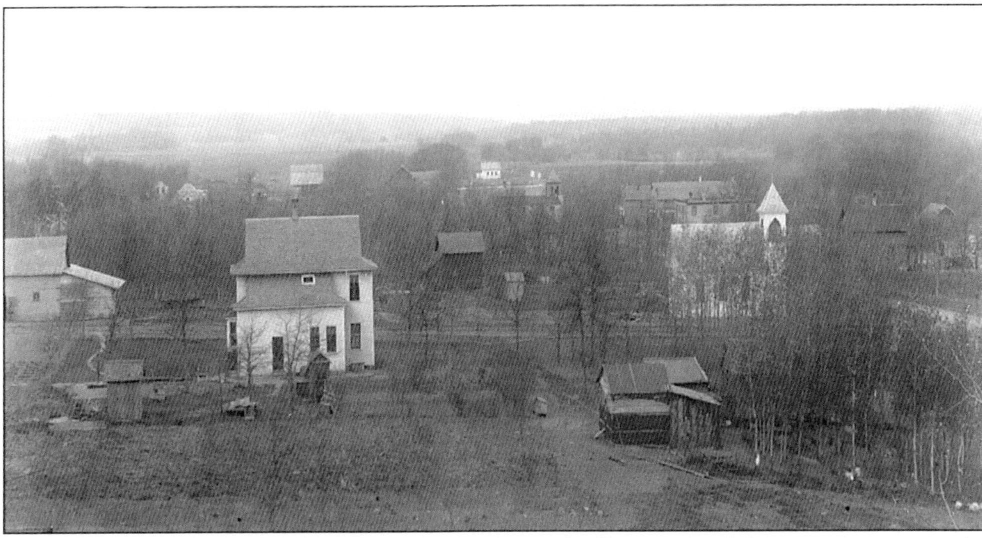

Established in 1865 and incorporated in 1903, Rockville is named for its numerous rocky formations. It became an important granite producing community in the early 20th century. (Courtesy of the Central Minnesota Historical Center.)

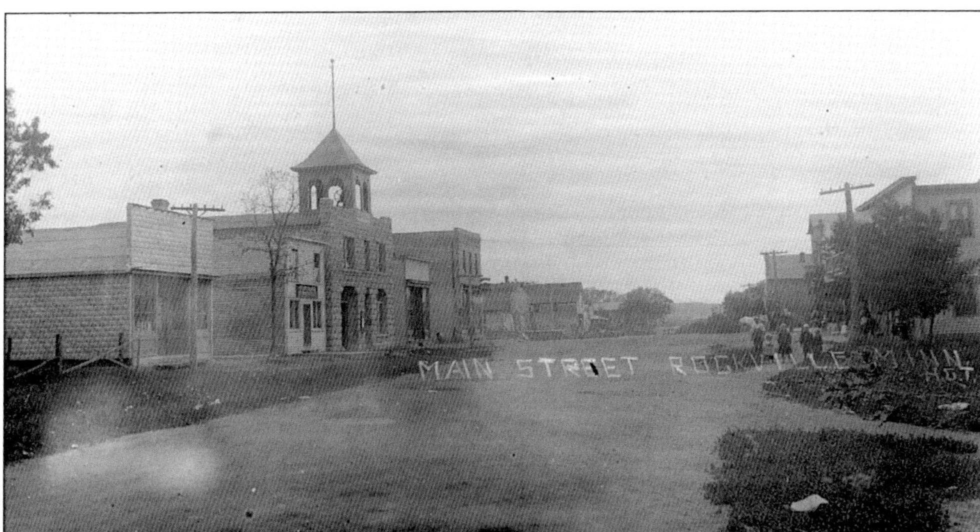


Main Street, Rockville, is seen in this *c.* 1912 image. Located just 20 miles west of St. Cloud, Rockville could not compete for economic dominance of the county. Nonetheless, the town boasted a bank, two blacksmiths, an ice cream shop, and a lumber mill by the 1910s. (Courtesy of the Central Minnesota Historical Center.)

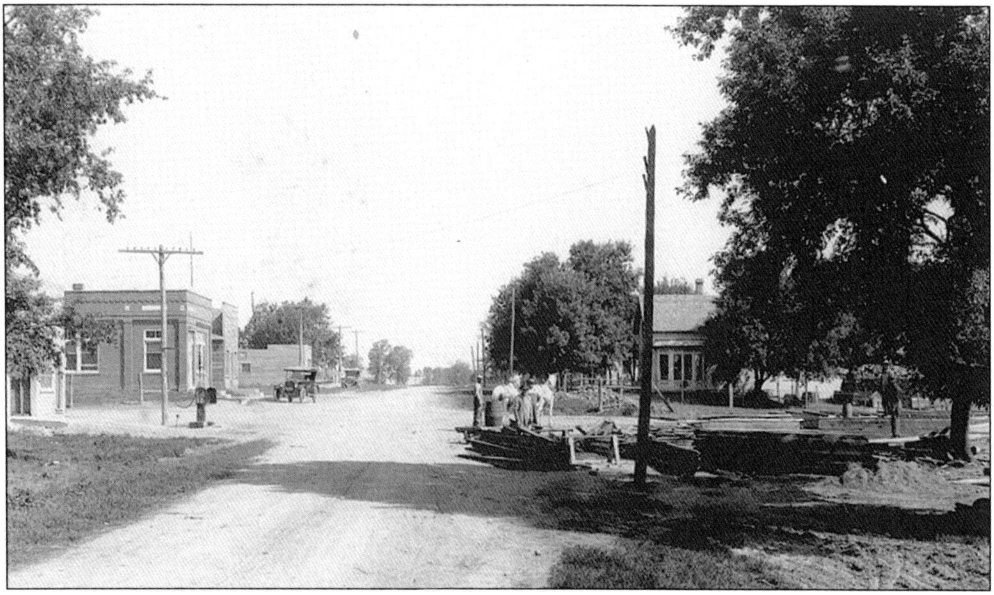

These two views show the growth of Fairhaven Township in southeastern Stearns County. The top picture, postmark dated 1922, indicates this is a growing farming community. Note the horses and the pile of lumber on the right-hand side of the photo. One year later, the lumber pile has become a building and automobiles have replaced the horses. Fairhaven has arrived as a village of substance. (Courtesy of Richard Kelly.)

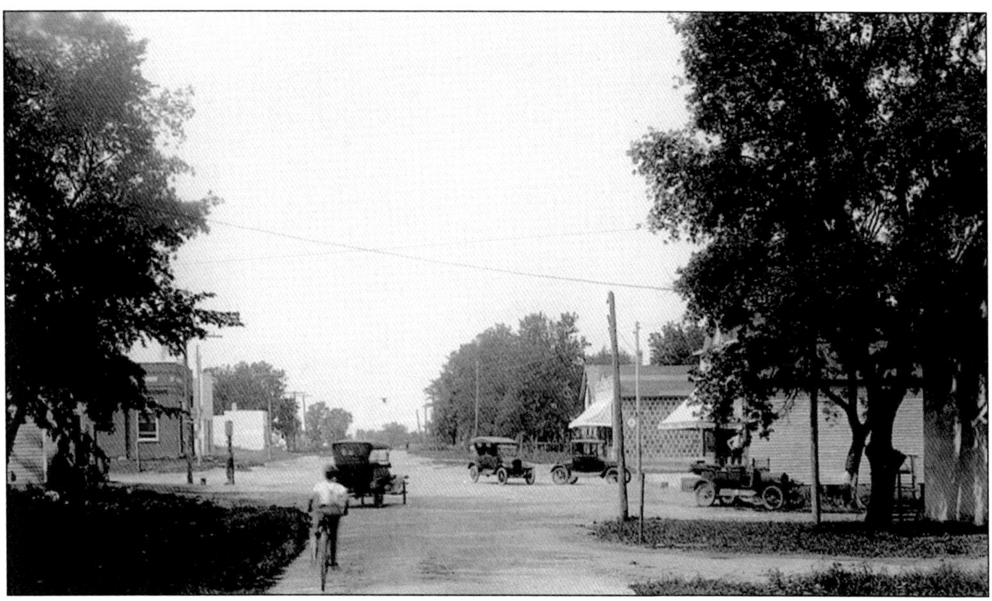

# *Two*

# FRIENDS AND FAMILIES

In 1915, historian William Bell Mitchell wrote, "It is indeed in its men and women, rather than in its factories and commerce, its grains and vegetables, its live stock and fruits, that Stearns County takes its greatest pride. From her cities, from her villages, and from her farms have gone forth those who have taken an important part in the activities of the world, and who, whether in commerce or diplomacy, in the professions or in the trades, have maintained that steadfastness of purpose, and staunchness of character, that mark true Stearns County men and women wherever they may be found."

The images that follow are not of those who left the county to make their mark on the world; rather, they capture the essence of the people who stayed behind and carved out a life from the granite and the farmland of the county. These are the faces of a cross-section of the people who made Stearns County home. They are people united by common causes, shared interests, and often by blood or by marriage. Any gathering of strangers in the county soon finds that, often, intimate connections bind them together.

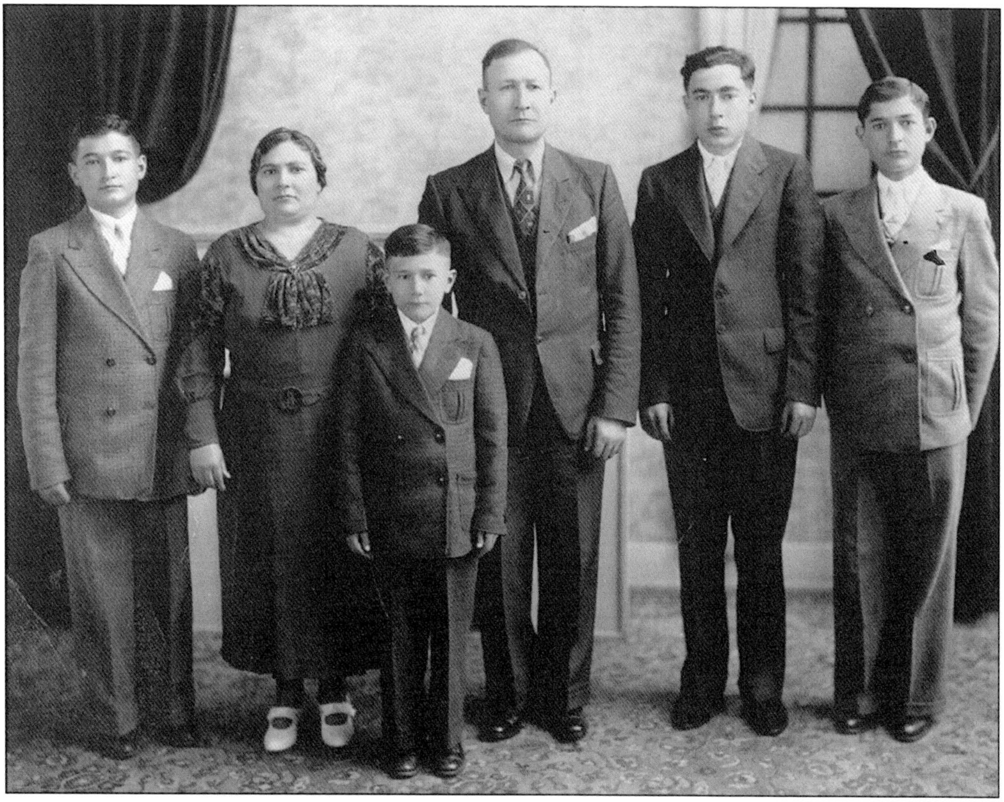

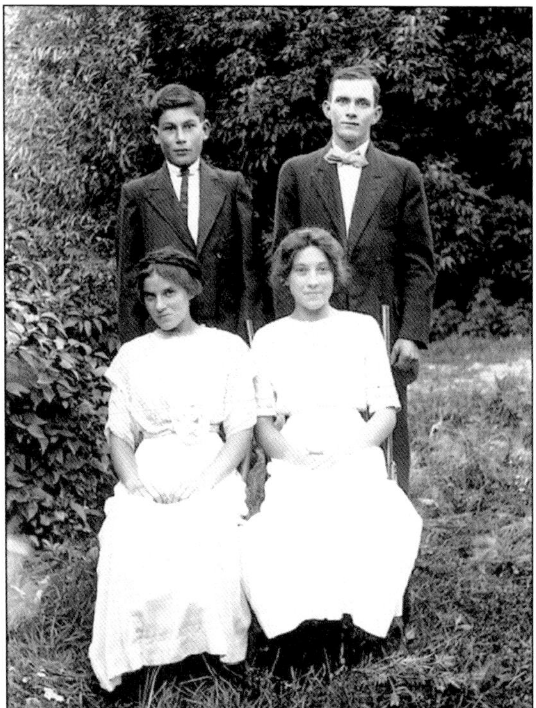

The Giambruno family posed for this family portrait in 1937. From left to right: Anthony, Vita, Frank, Stephen, Peter, and Louis. (Courtesy of Jenny Giambruno.)

William, John, Marion, and Isabel Alexander, the youngest of Henry and Margret Alexander's six children, pose for a family portrait in Rockville, c. 1912. In 1898, the year John was born, Henry became the sole owner of the Rockville Granite Company. (Courtesy of the Central Minnesota Historical Center.)

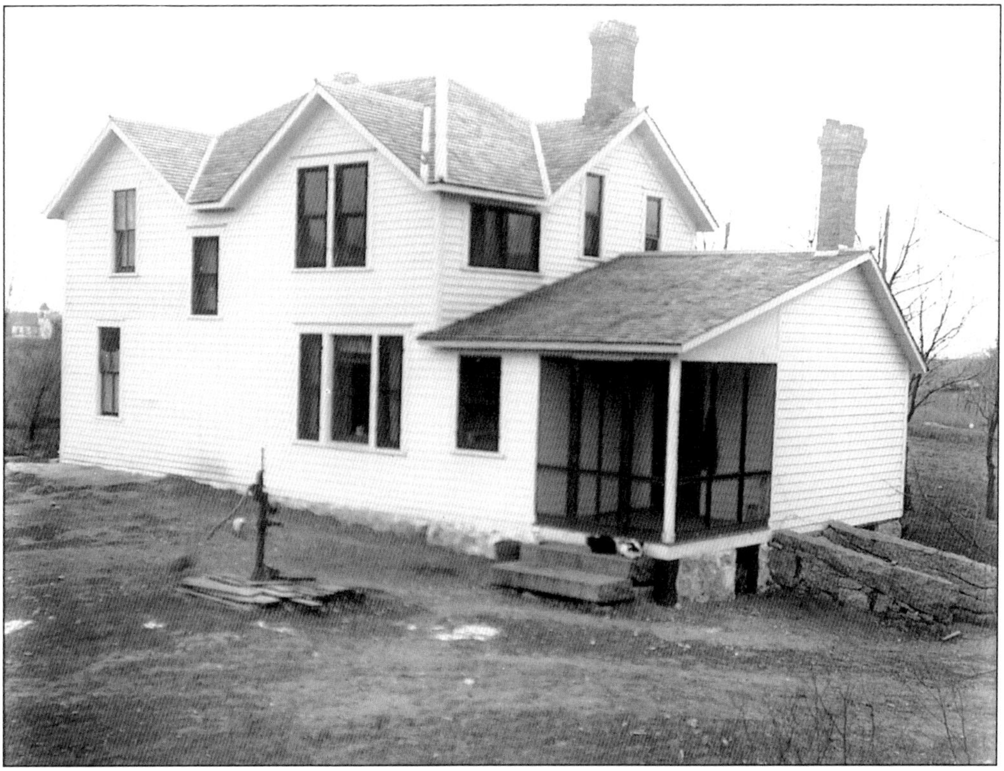

Above is the Alexander family home in Rockville, c. 1912. Notice the pump outside indicating this house did not have indoor plumbing. The house also shows the many additions typical of Midwestern homes in this period. Additions usually reflected the birth of another child. (Courtesy of the Central Minnesota Historical Center.)

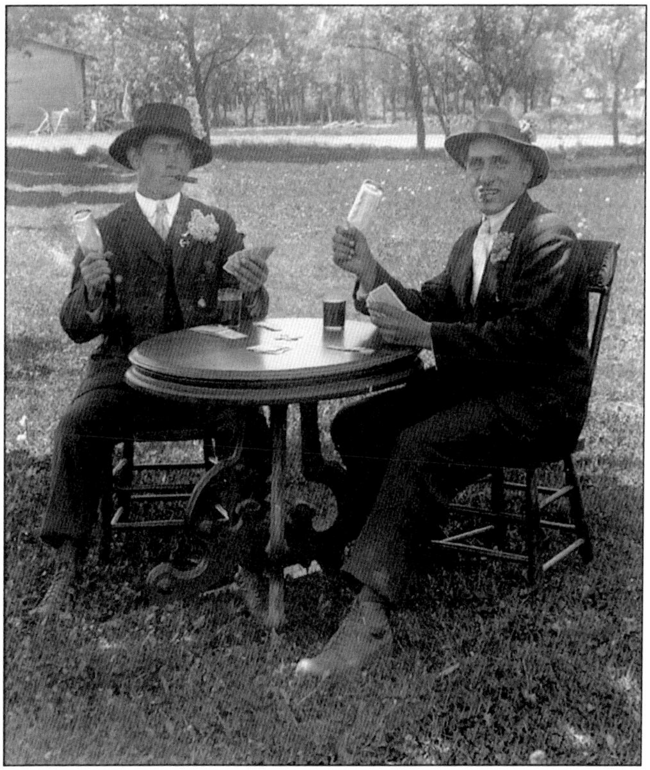

William Schultz and ? Ziolkoski ham it up for the camera in Rockville, c. 1912. (Courtesy of the Central Minnesota Historical Center.)

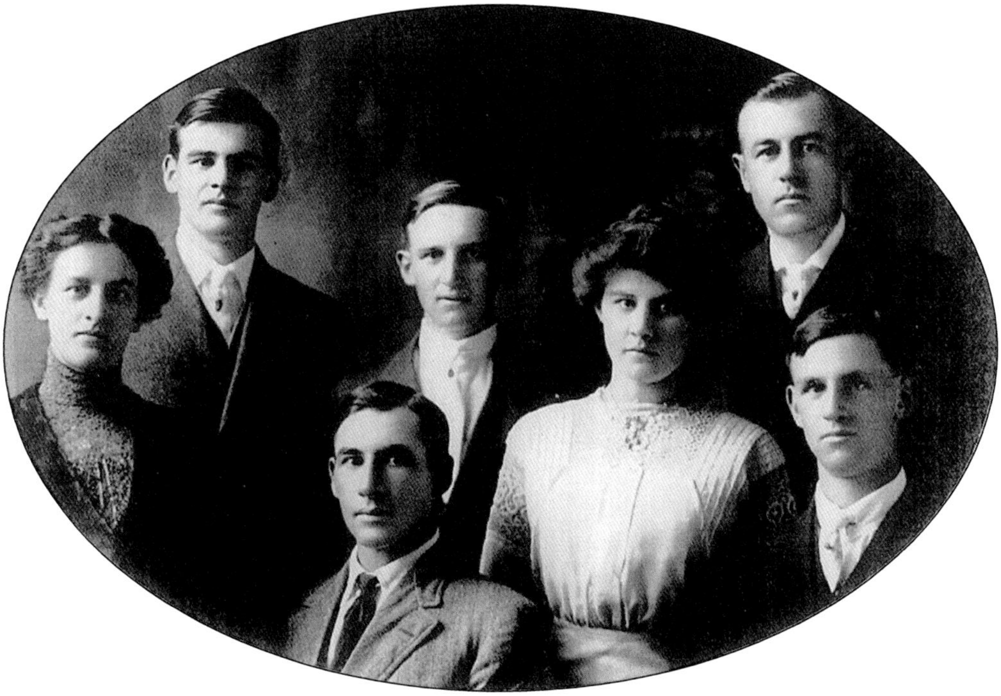

The family of Joseph and Augusta (Schroeder) Hunstiger *c.* 1917., are pictured, clockwise from top left: Mayme, Bernard, Anthony, Frank, Leo, Sebina, and Joseph. The Hunstigers first settled in Stearns County in 1880. (Courtesy of the Hunstiger family.)

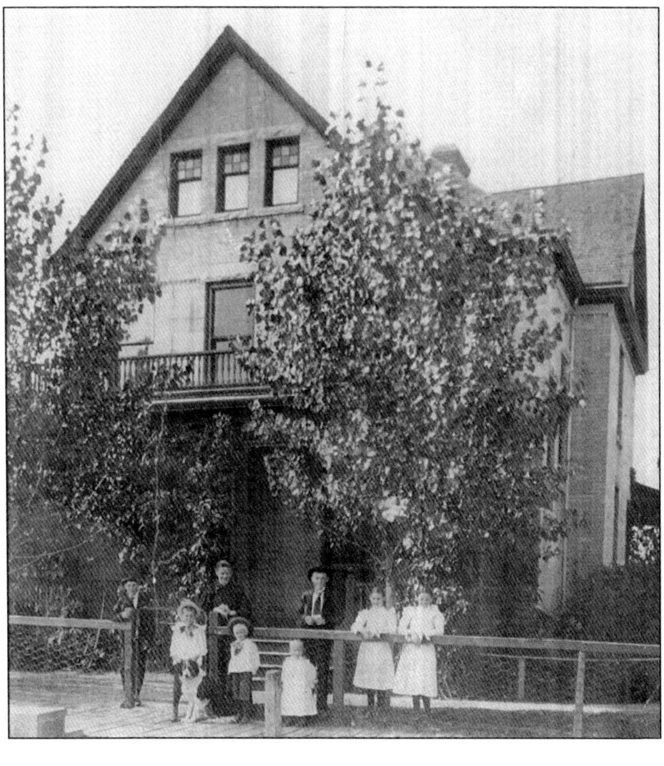

The Hunstiger homestead located at Twelfth Avenue and First Street North in St. Cloud, *c.* 1892. From left: Joe, Ben, Augusta, Anthony, Leo, Frank, Sebina, and Mayme. (Courtesy of the Hunstiger family.)

Anthony and Martha (Meyer) Hunstiger pose for their wedding portrait, c. 1920. (Courtesy of the Hunstiger family.)

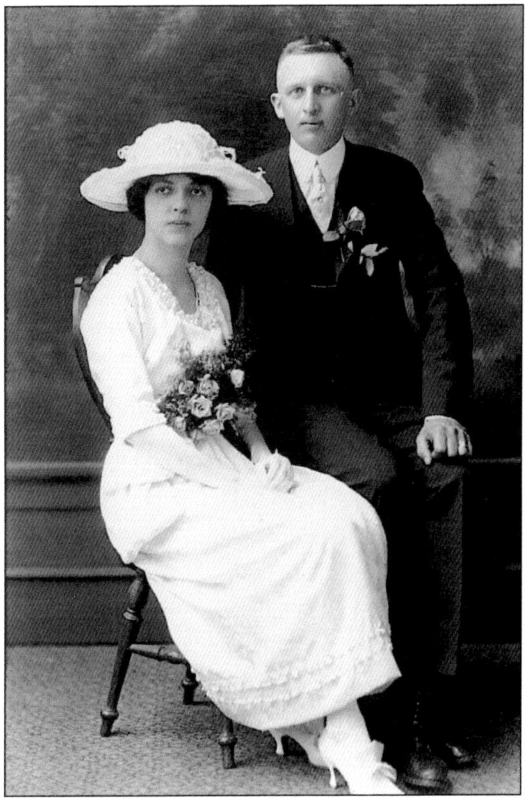

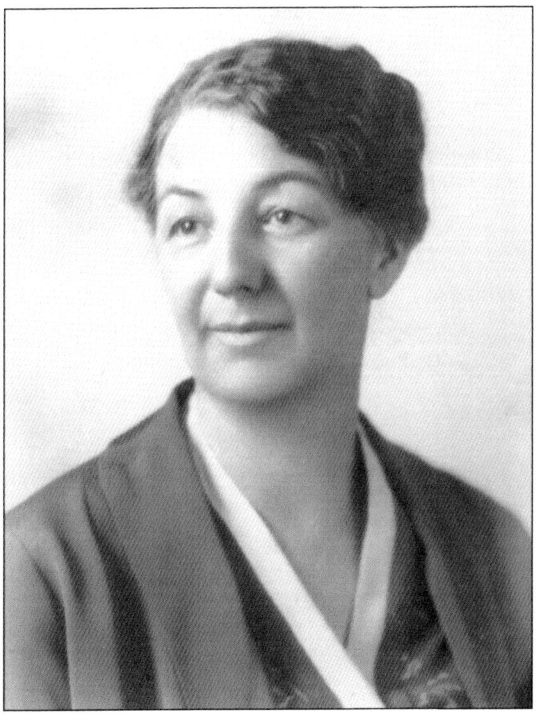

Miss Ethel Graves served as president of the St. Cloud College Club in 1928–29. This club was the precursor to the American Association of University Women. (Courtesy of the Central Minnesota Historical Center.)

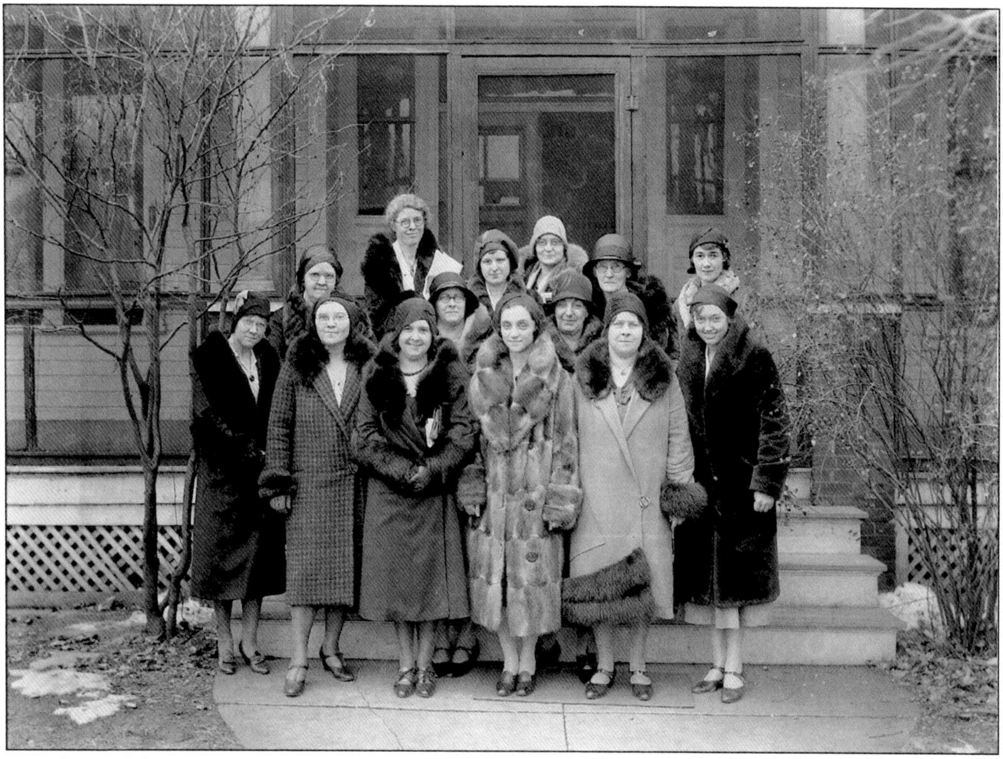

Members of the St. Cloud College Club pose in 1931. Many of these women were members of the Riverview faculty at the St. Cloud Normal School. (Courtesy of the Central Minnesota Historical Center.)

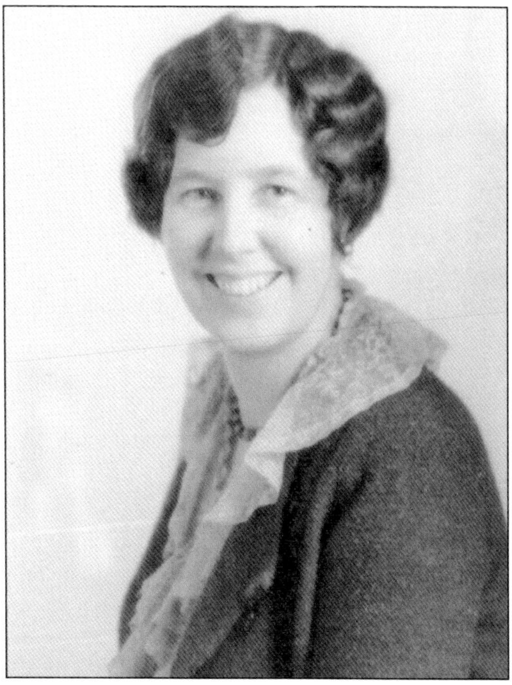

Mrs. Leslie Zeleny served as president of the College Club at St. Cloud from 1934–35. (Courtesy of the Central Minnesota Historical Center.)

Mathilda and Harry Burns of St. Cloud are shown here in 1926. Harry was a prominent St. Cloud lawyer. (Courtesy of Jenny Giambruno.)

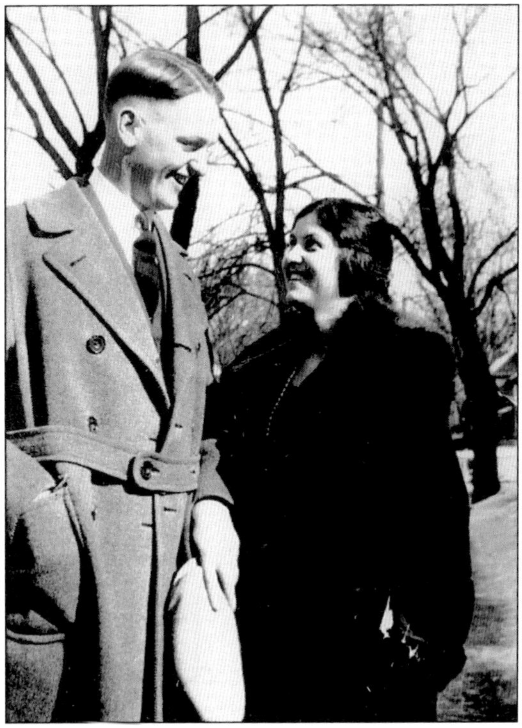

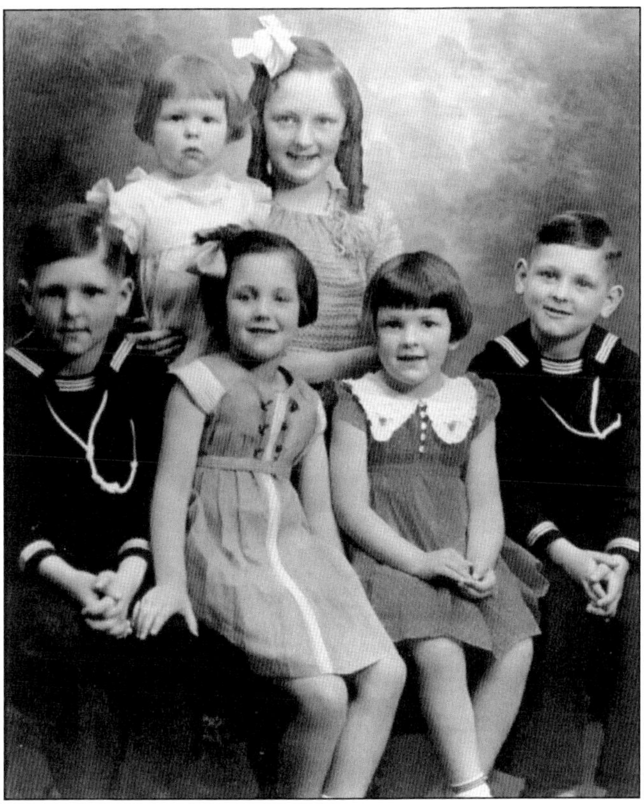

The children of Mathilda and Harry Burns pose for this 1936 portrait. Front row, left to right: Terrence, Nancy, Colleen and John; Back row: Kathleen and Margaret. (Courtesy of Jenny Giambruno.)

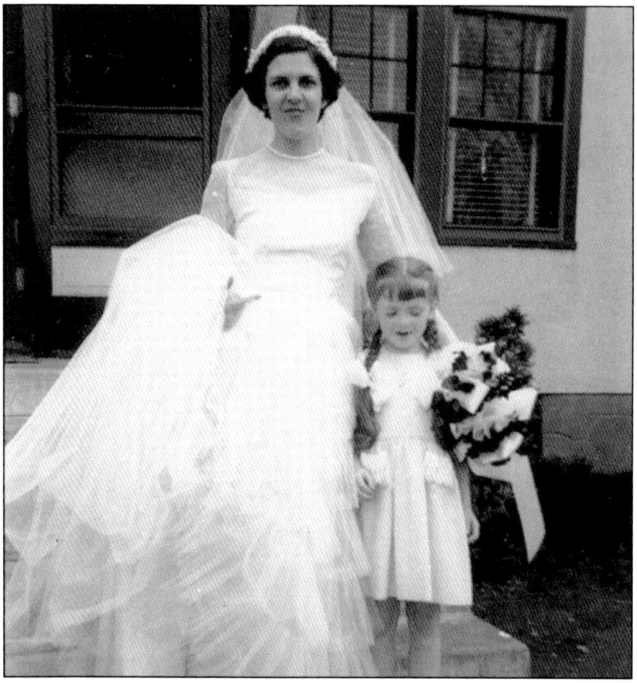

Colleen Burns poses with Dorothy Schneider before Colleen's wedding to Richard Rawlings, May 2, 1953. (Courtesy of Jenny Giambruno.)

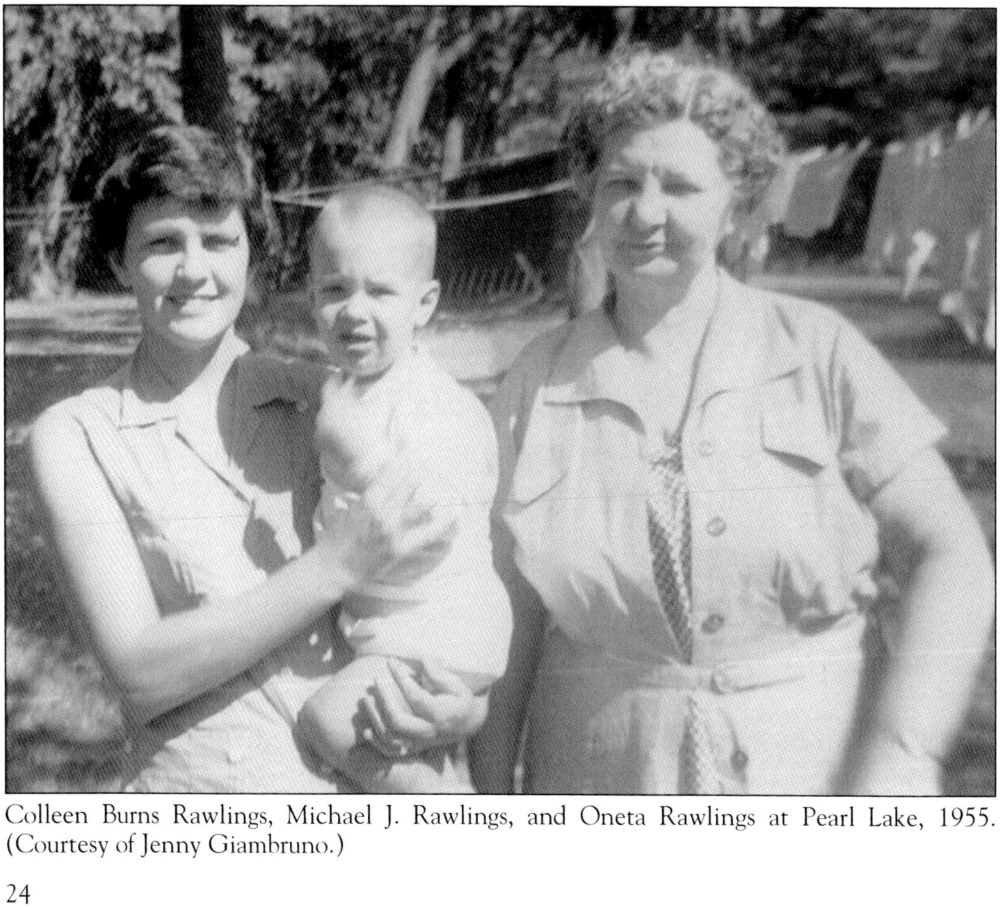

Colleen Burns Rawlings, Michael J. Rawlings, and Oneta Rawlings at Pearl Lake, 1955. (Courtesy of Jenny Giambruno.)

Richard Rawlings and his son Michael ham it up for the camera with Aunt Margaret Burns Lytle, on a trip to southern California, c. 1955. Margo was Mike's godmother. "Mr. Hollywood" reads the caption. (Courtesy of Jenny Giambruno.)

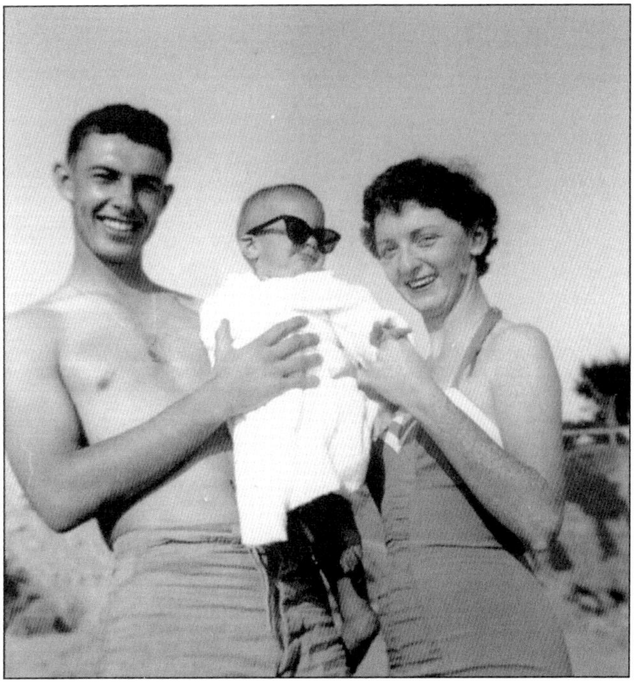

The children of Richard and Colleen Rawlings clown for the camera at Christmas, 1964. Michael, Terry, David, Kristi, Amy, and Jenny. (Courtesy of Jenny Giambruno.)

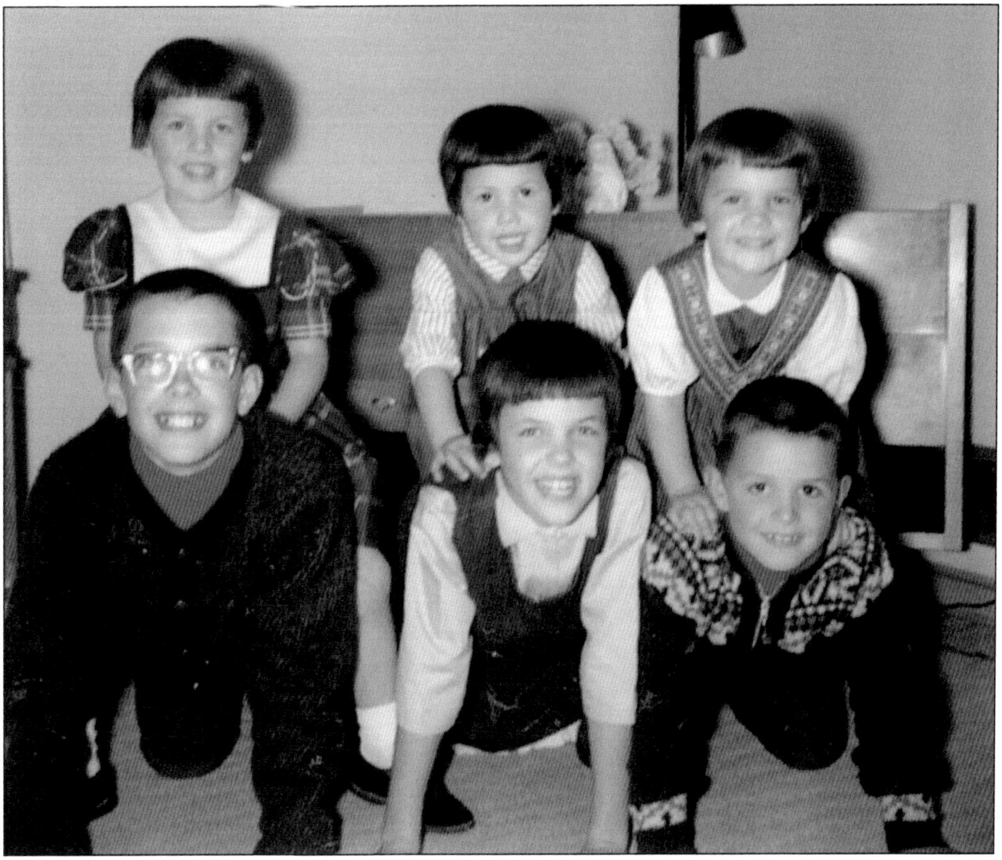

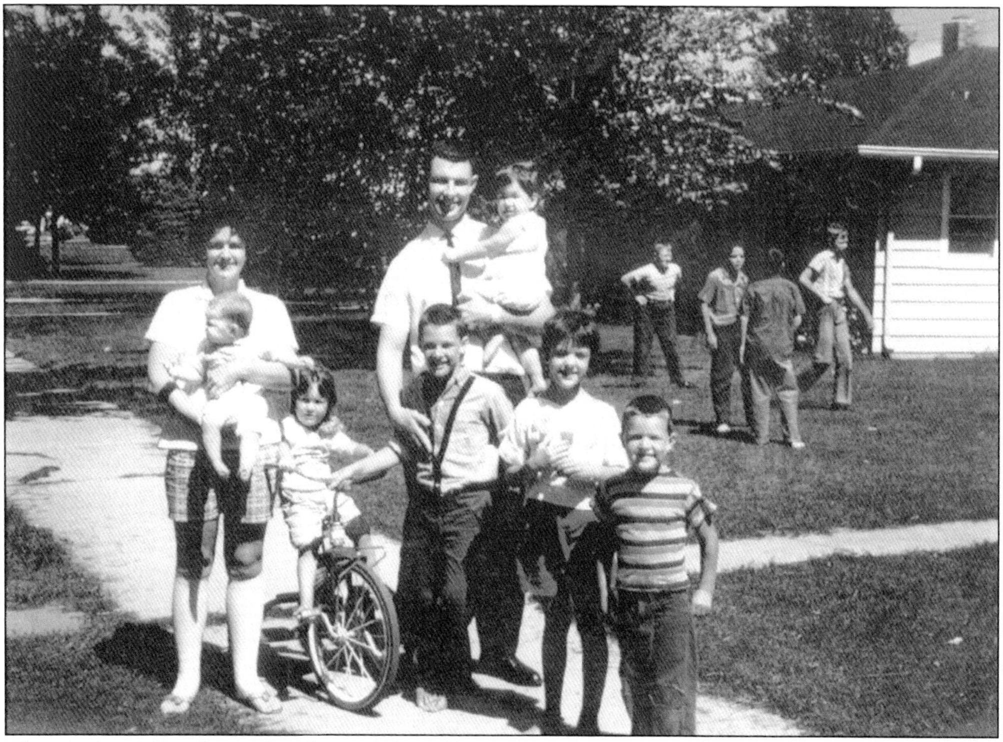

The Richard Rawlings family and friends enjoy a warm summer day in St. Cloud, 1962. Michael, Terry, David, Kristi, Amy, and Jenny are with their parents Colleen and Richard. (Courtesy of Jenny Giambruno.)

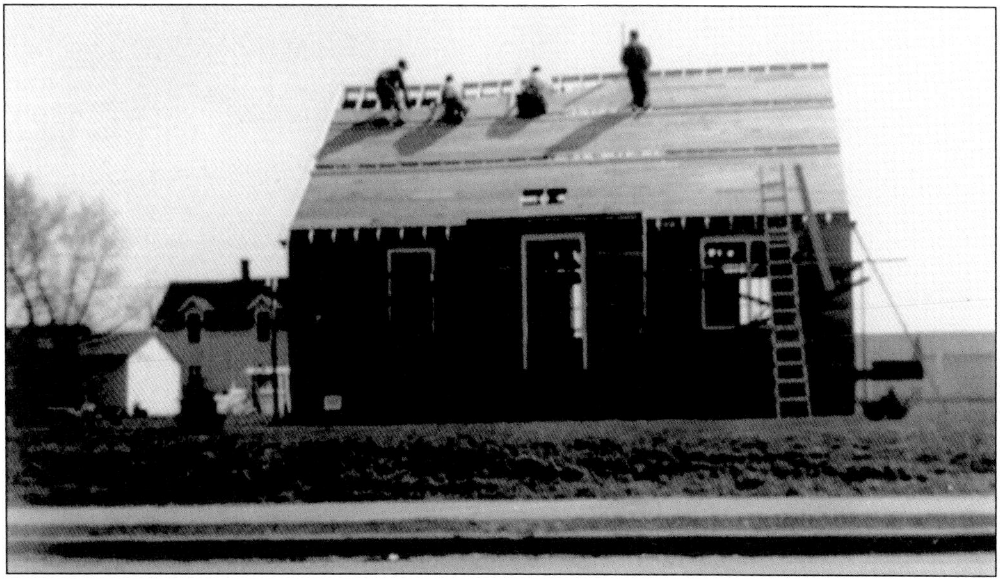

The Brixius family home is shown above under construction in 1953. The home on Ninth Street North in St. Cloud took four years to build, during which time the family lived in the basement. The length of time it took to build the home and the living arrangements of the family were fairly typical for Stearns County families. (Courtesy of Kari Brixius.)

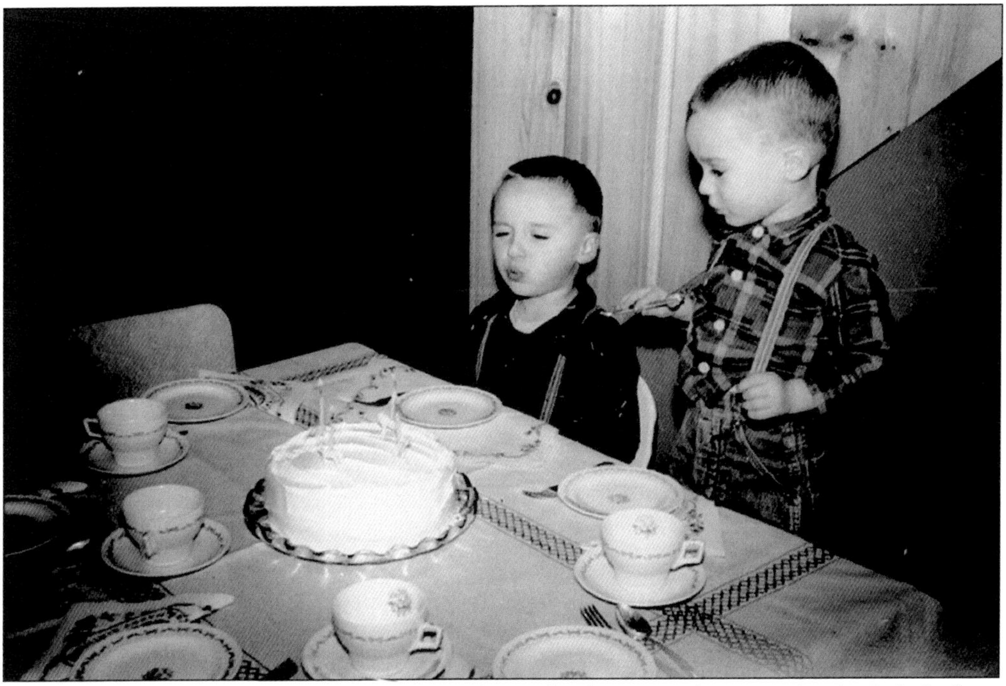

Albert A. Brixius celebrates his fourth birthday in his basement home with a little help from his brother Andrew in 1954. (Courtesy of Kari Brixius.)

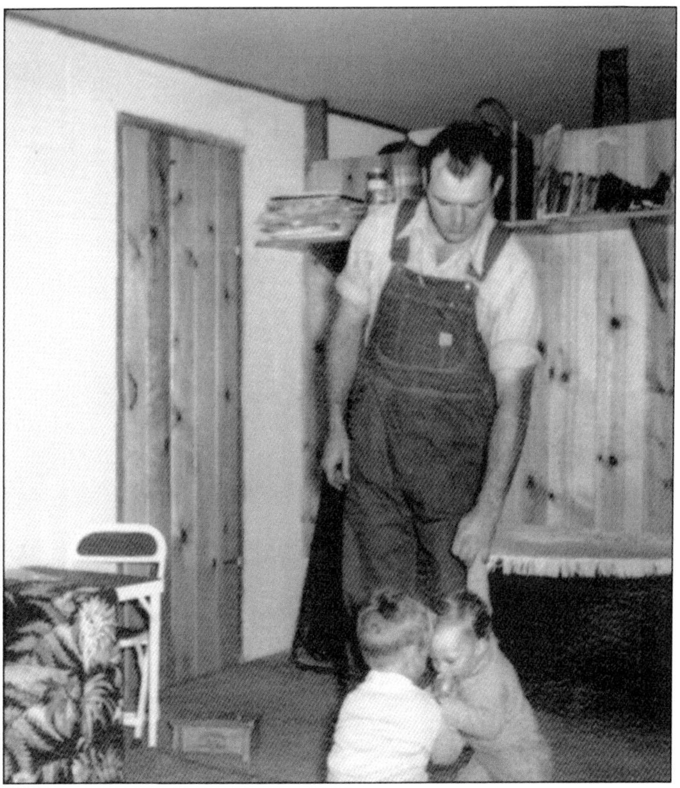

Despite the cramped quarters, Albert C. Brixius still found room enough to play with his children Albert A. and Andrew in 1952. (Courtesy of Kari Brixius.)

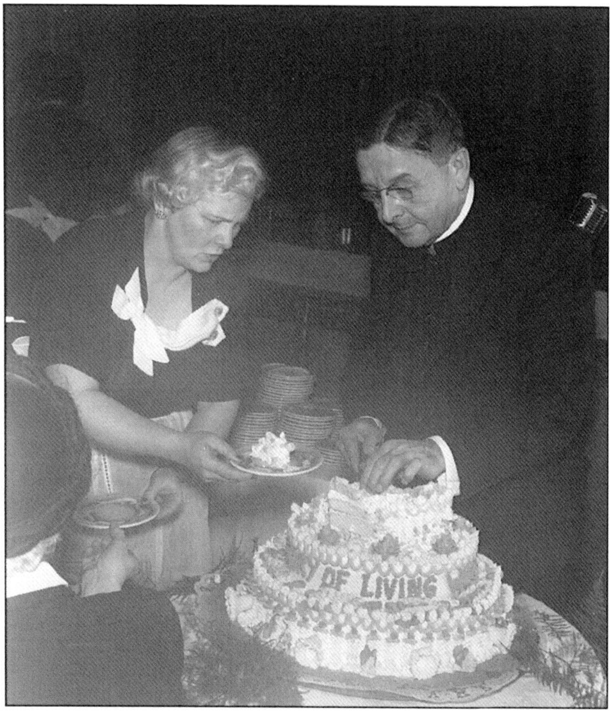

Mrs. Marion Zapp, wife of St. Cloud banker Eddie Zapp, serves cake at the centennial celebration of Father Pierz's arrival in the area in 1952. With her is bishop Peter Bartholome. Mrs. Zapp was a native of Minneapolis, but was married in Holy Angels Church in St. Cloud, and lived in the city until her death in 1999. She is survived by seven children. (Courtesy of the Central Minnesota Historical Center.)

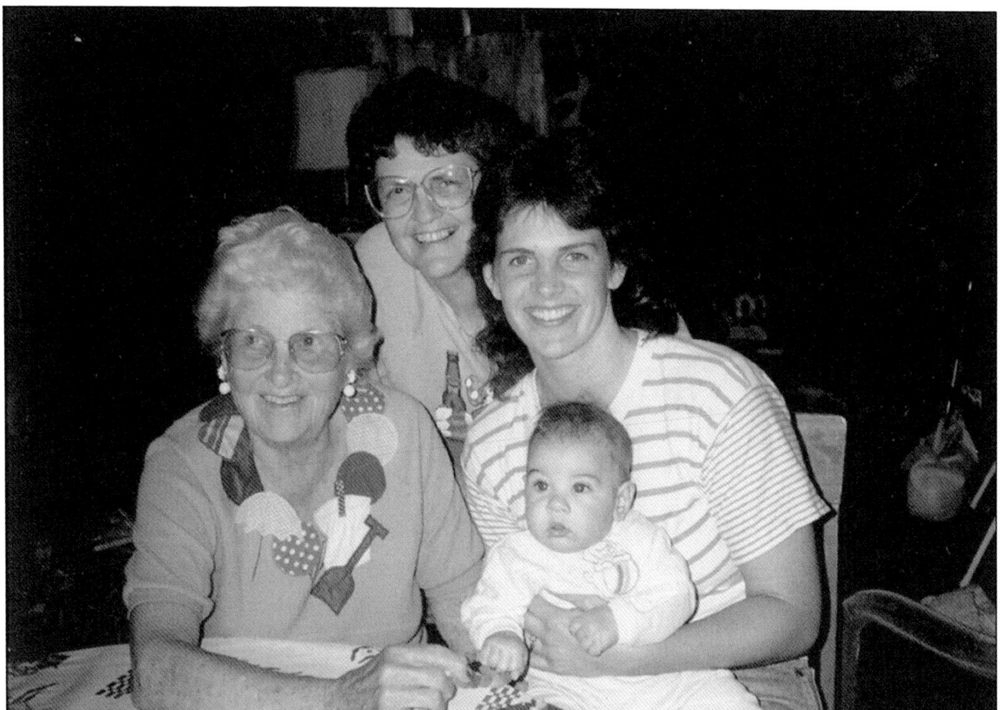

Representing the importance of strong family ties, four generations pose in this 1990 portrait. Mathilda Burns, Colleen Burns Rawlings, Jenny Rawlings Giambruno, and Adam Giambruno. (Courtesy of Jenny Giambruno.)

# *Three*

# ALL IN A DAYS WORK

Although primarily a rural county, Stearns County residents have found a variety of ways of making a living. In addition to farming, county residents have earned a living in the granite, milling, lumber, and tourist industries. Perhaps most important to the county are the many independent businesses that have provided services for county residents.

For many years, granite represented the major industry for the county. Situated on a massive granite shelf, the St. Cloud area is the second largest granite producing area in the United States. St. Cloud granite is used mainly for building construction and for stone monuments, but it also has been milled into mixing blades for candy making, acid vats for chemical plants, and jewelry. The granite industry was such an important part of the economy for St. Cloud that the city officially adopted the title of "Granite City" in 1913. The industry weathered the Great Depression of the 1930s through the grace of government contracts and today the Cold Spring Granite Company in Cold Spring is the world's largest producer of granite and an important part of the county's economic growth and development.

As a county of rivers, Stearns County has also been the home to a thriving grain milling industry. As early as 1885, water-powered mills could be found at Holdingford, Le Sauk, St. Joseph, St. Cloud, Rockville, Cold Spring, Melrose, Sauk Centre, St. Augusta, Clearwater, Fairhaven, and Paynesville. The Melrose Mill contained six pair of "run" millstones, which produced 25,000 barrels of flour a year. Until 1880, workers worked 10 to 12-hour shifts and the top price for a barrel of flour was approximately $6.00. Most grain is now shipped out of the county for milling.

Waterpower also fueled the timber industry in the county. Sawmills and lumberyards could be found in St. Cloud, Rockville, and most other cities on or near a river. Logs were harvested from the forests of northern Minnesota during the winters and then sent down the rivers in spring. Each logging company would brand their own wood to know which ones were theirs as they floated down the rivers. Lumber mills retrieved the logs, cut them, and sold them to homebuilders and to cities to be used for sidewalks. When railroad tracks stretched into northern Minnesota, trains began carrying more timber. Today no real lumbering takes place in Stearns County.

Other residents have made their living in perhaps more unique ways. In 1917 Samuel Pandolfo dreamed of the Granite City becoming a booming automobile manufacturing city. He built his Pan Motor Works on 47 acres of land on the edge of St. Cloud. Approximately 750 cars were built at the site from 1917 to 1922. Visionary that he was, he also built housing for his workers adjacent to the plant. These bungalows were connected to the factory by a series of tunnels so that workers would have no weather excuse for not coming to work. The Pan Motor Works was short lived, however, when Mr. Pandolfo was run out of town on charges of fraud.

Catering to the county's German Catholic residents, breweries started to appear in the area in the 1850s. Breweries flourished until prohibition outlawed the businesses in 1918. Today, the only surviving large brewery in the area is Gluek Brewing Company in Cold Spring. With the proliferation of "micro" breweries in the 1990s, the brewing industry is enjoying a resurgence with the success of O'Hara's and the Granite City Brewing Company in St. Cloud.

Servicing the citizens of Stearns County required thriving business districts in all communities. Butchers, bakers, druggists, and dry goods merchants helped each community create a Main Street like those described by Sinclair Lewis. Prior to the 1960s and the building of Crossroads Center in St. Cloud, main streets provided the only shopping for Stearns County residents. Since 1965, all of Stearns County's cities have struggled to maintain their downtown business districts and avoid the pitfall of urban decay.

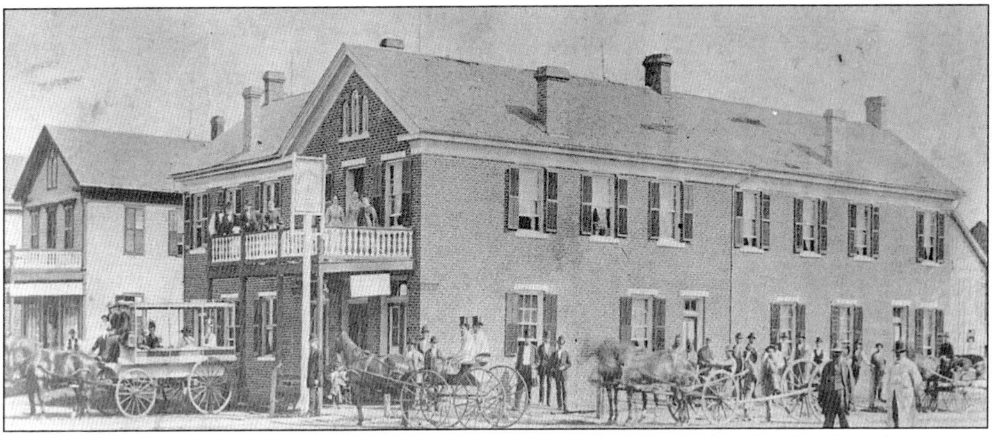

Providing visitors with lodging is one of the first signs of city growth. The St. Cloud Hotel in downtown St. Cloud, c. 1870, represents the city's early efforts to achieve city stature. (Courtesy of the Central Minnesota Historical Center.)

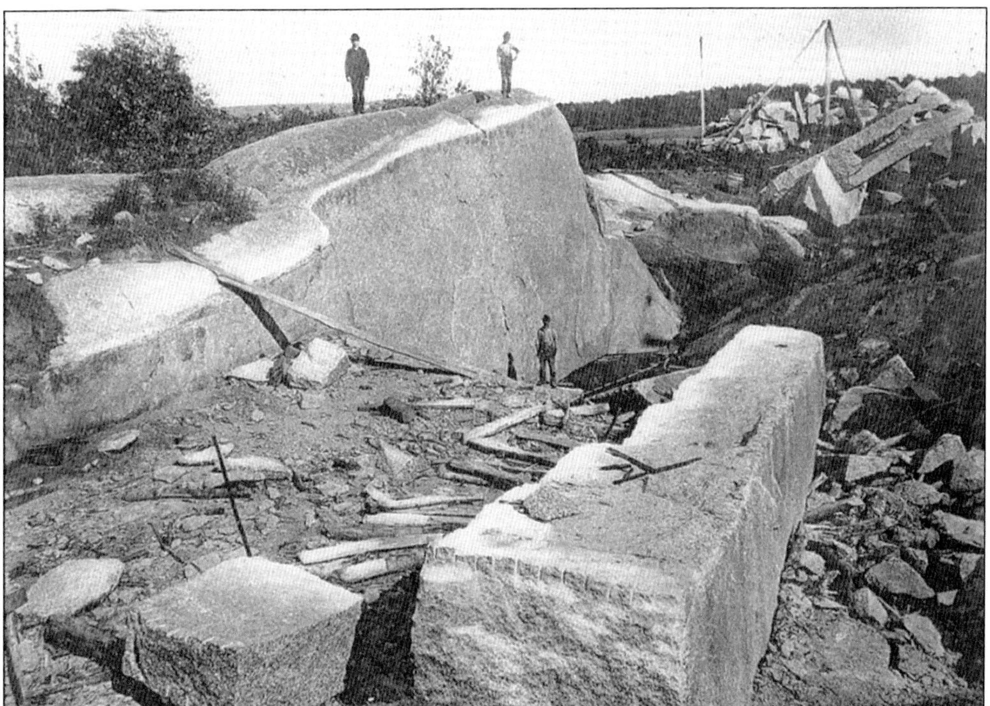

"The Granite City," St. Cloud, states this postcard from the early 1920s. W.J. and G.O. Holes pioneered the St. Cloud granite business when they opened the first quarry in 1868 at the present site of the Minnesota Correctional Facility. By 1920 nearly 50 concerns and shops in St. Cloud produced granite products. (Courtesy of Richard Kelly.)

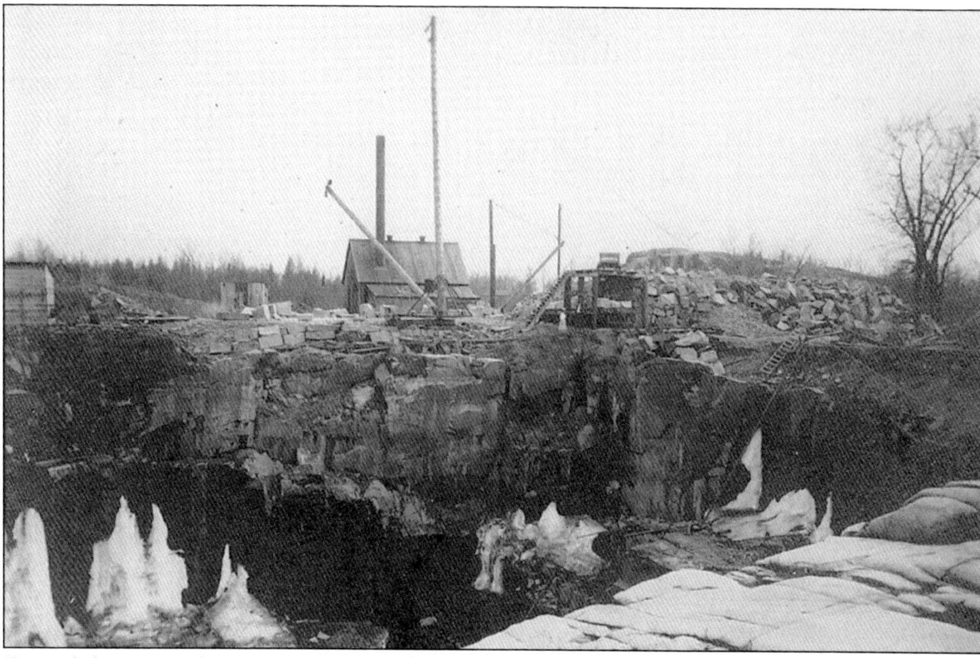

One of about two dozen quarries in and around St. Cloud, the Simmers and Campbell Granite Quarry was located in St. Cloud Township, southwest of Waite Park. This 1907 postcard shows how this industry scars the landscape. Simmers and Campbell gained experience in the granite industry as partners with Henry Alexander in the Rockville Granite Company. Alexander bought the other two out in 1898. (Courtesy of Richard Kelly.)

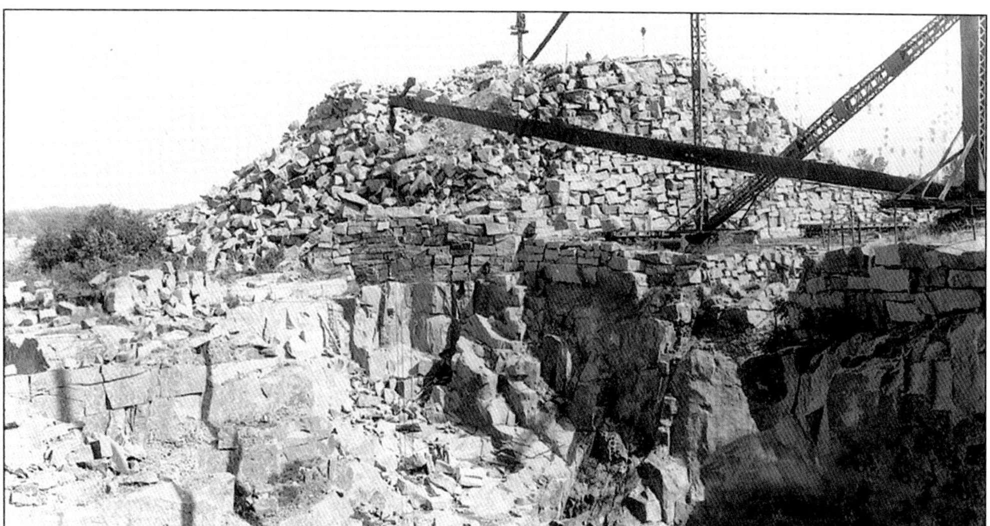

North Star Quarry in northwest St. Cloud is pictured above c. 1930. The Great Depression caused many small concerns to go out of business. The larger companies survived on government contracts, especially in supplying granite for WPA projects. (Courtesy of Richard Kelly.)

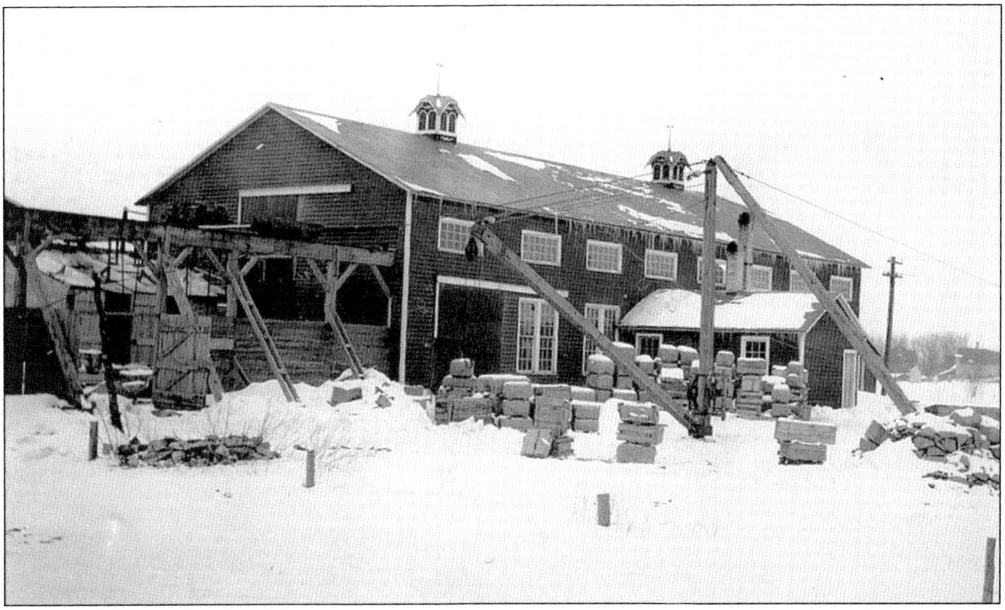

First organized in 1904 in St. Cloud by Charles P. Ahlgren, Emil Hagquist, and Frank Exckstrom, the Granite City Granite Company Millworks quarried "Superior Gray" and "Superior Red" granite exclusively for monuments. The local plant closed in 1973, but the company continues to operate under the same name in Delano, MN. The company used picture postcards of its facility to notify customers of completed orders. (Courtesy of Richard Kelly.)

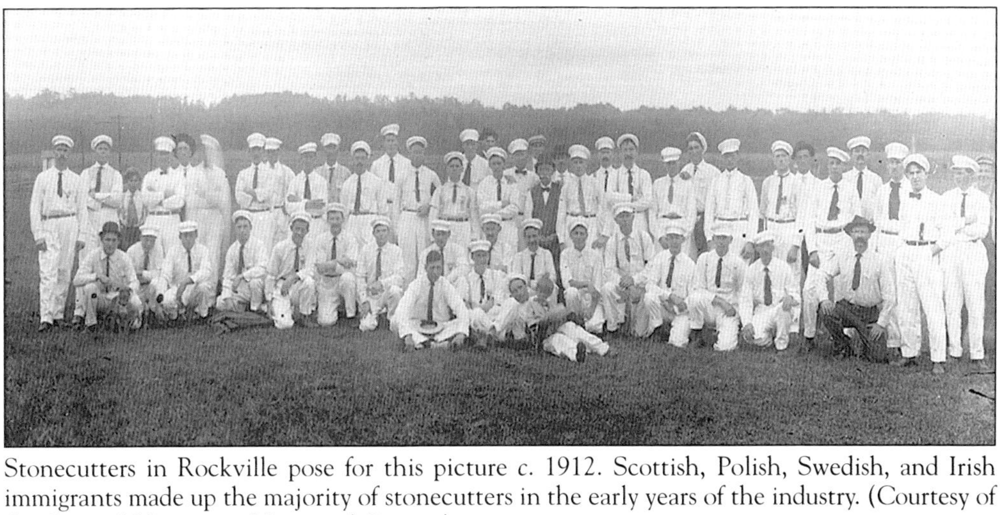

Stonecutters in Rockville pose for this picture c. 1912. Scottish, Polish, Swedish, and Irish immigrants made up the majority of stonecutters in the early years of the industry. (Courtesy of the Central Minnesota Historical Center.)

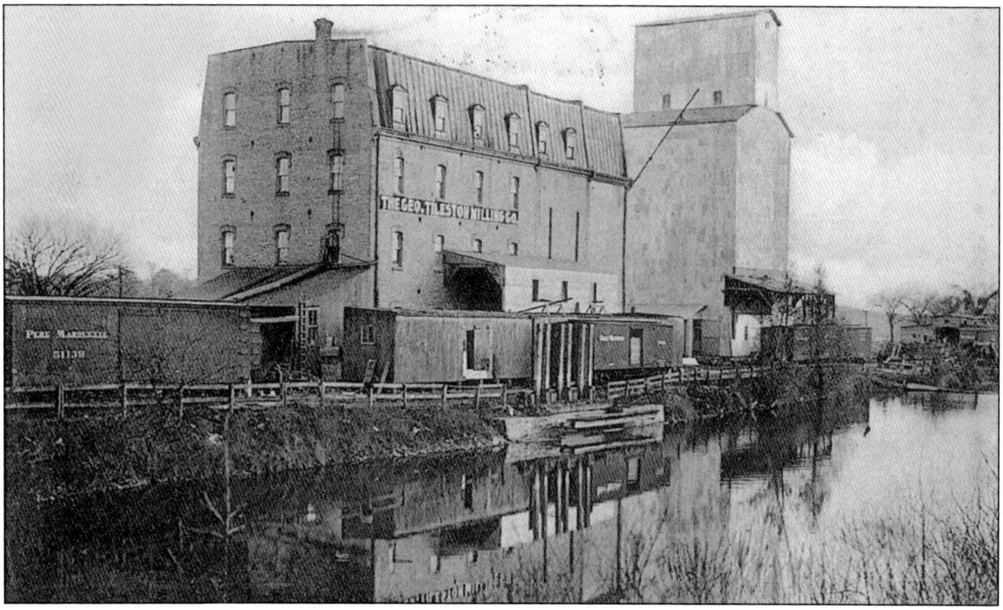

The George Tileston Milling Company of St. Cloud was widely known as one of the important interior milling concerns in the region in the early 20th century. This postcard shows the company's mill and new elevator in 1911. The mill burned down in 1915, but the galvanized steel grain elevator was recycled into hangars at Whitney Field Airport. (Courtesy of Richard Kelly.)

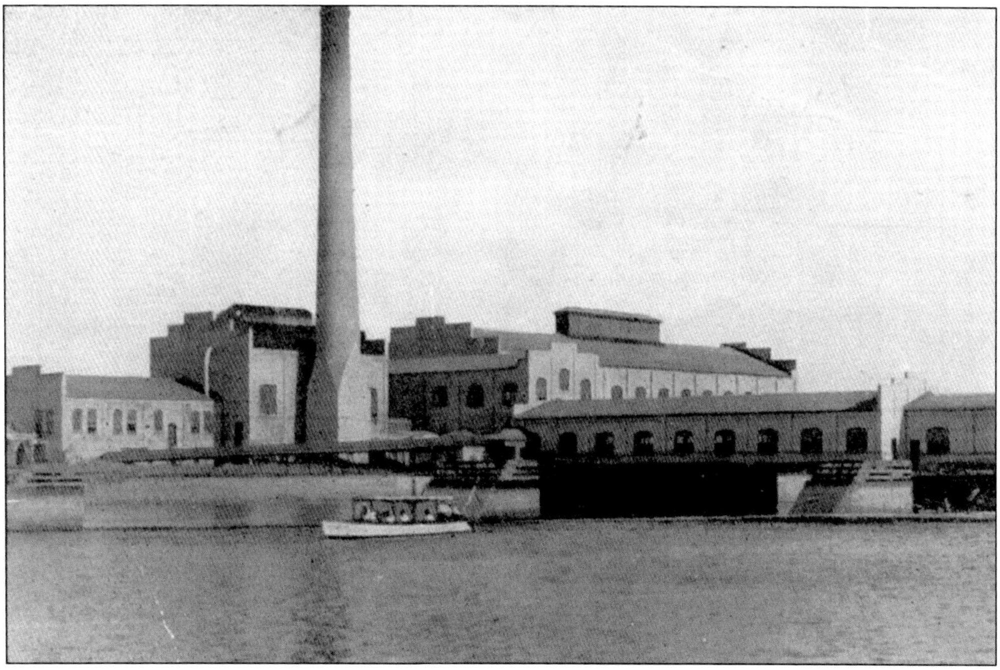

Dams along the Mississippi provided a cheap source of power for the Watab Paper and Pulp Mills, Sartell, c. 1920. Work began on the dam in 1905 and finished in 1908. The mill was finished in 1907. In 1946 it became the St. Regis Paper Mill and in 1984 became part of Champion International Corporation. (Courtesy of Richard Kelly.)

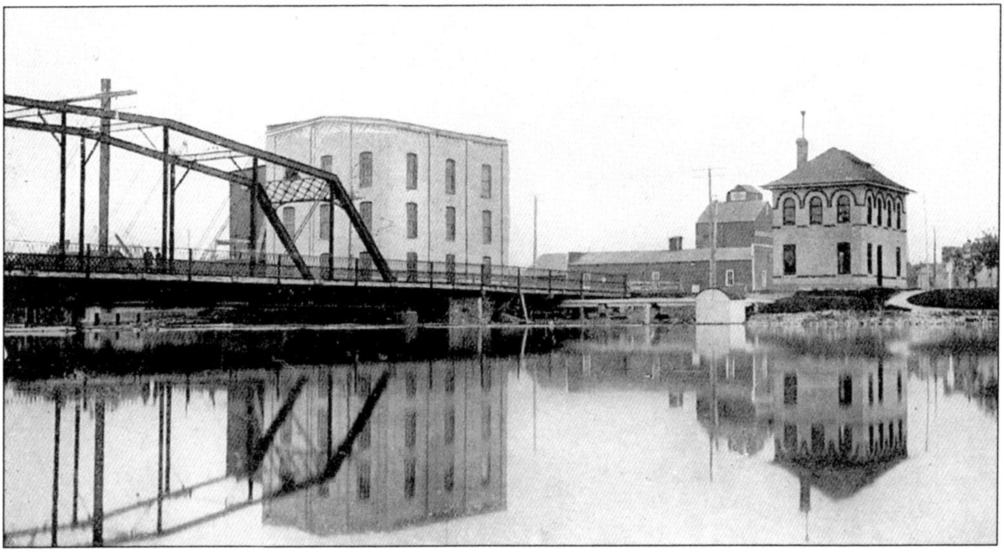

Although Sauk Centre's main claim to fame is as the birthplace of author Sinclair Lewis, the Central Minnesota Power and Milling Company provided jobs for many residents and ground local wheat into flour. This particular post card was sent to Spokane, Washington in January 1907. The notation on the card reads, "Plenty below zero!—Doesn't look like this now." (Courtesy of Richard Kelly.)

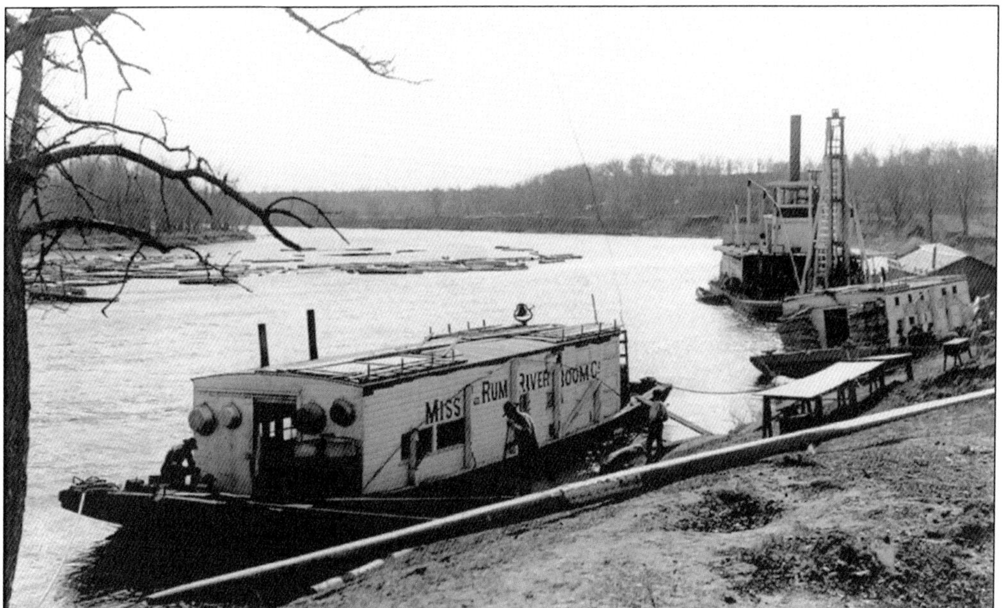

The Mississippi River Boom Company provided an important service to the logging industry in St. Cloud in 1908. This logging outfit helped remove the logs from the river and prepare them for transport to the sawmill. (Courtesy of Richard Kelly.)

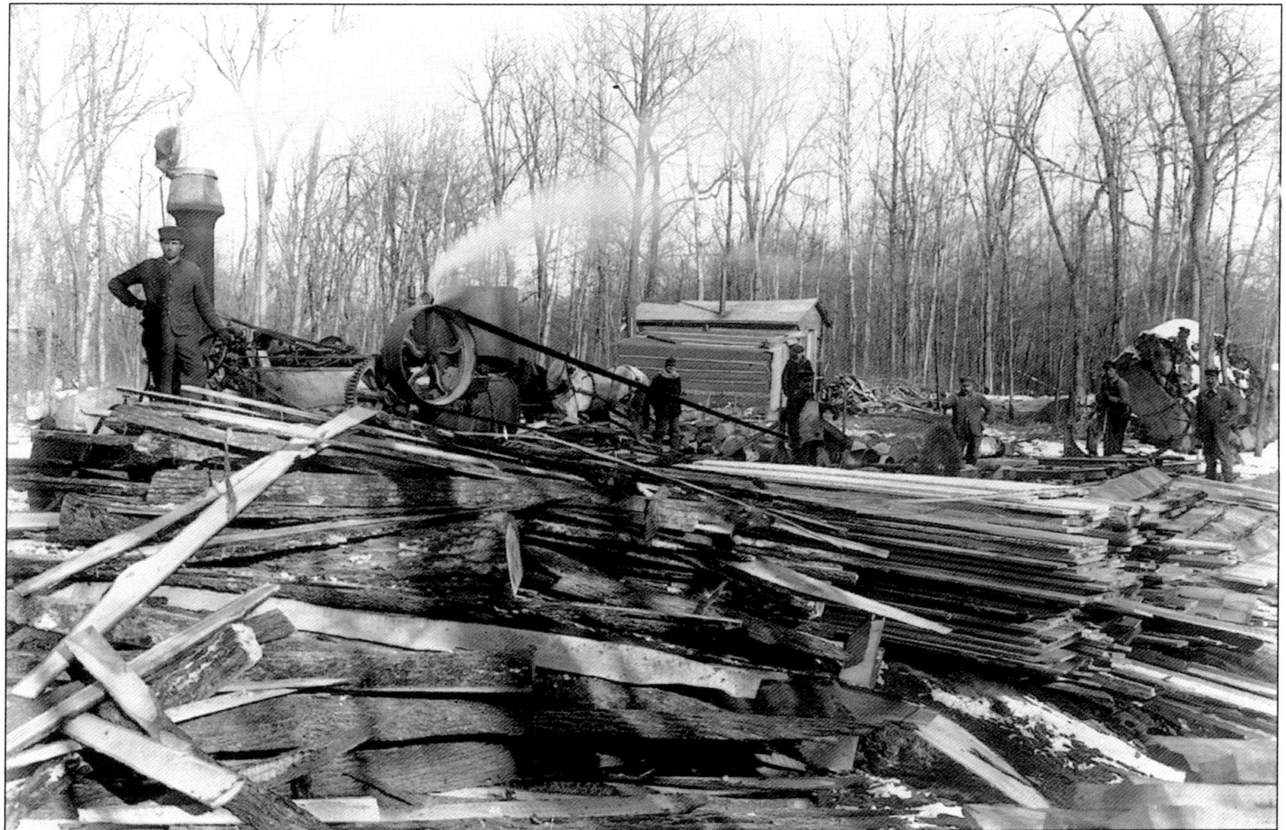

An average worker in a sawmill would work an 11-hour day in 1880. The consumer could buy lumber between 1870 and 1880 for about 1 to 2¢ per foot. These workers pose at the William Gohman sawmill in Rockville, *c.* 1912. (Courtesy of the Central Minnesota Historical Center.)

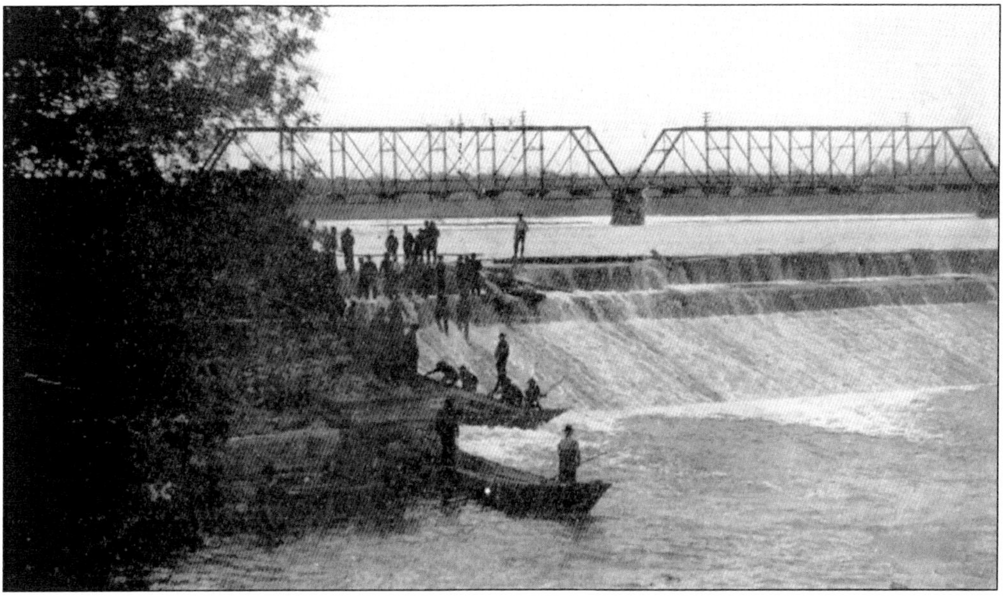

Here are two views of log drivers at work on the Mississippi River at St. Cloud, 1910. The bottom picture shows up close the dangers of this work as drivers struggled to work around dams and other rapids along the river. Almost all logging and lumber mills were placed on or near rivers or lakes and they required plenty of land for storage of logs. (Courtesy of Richard Kelly.)

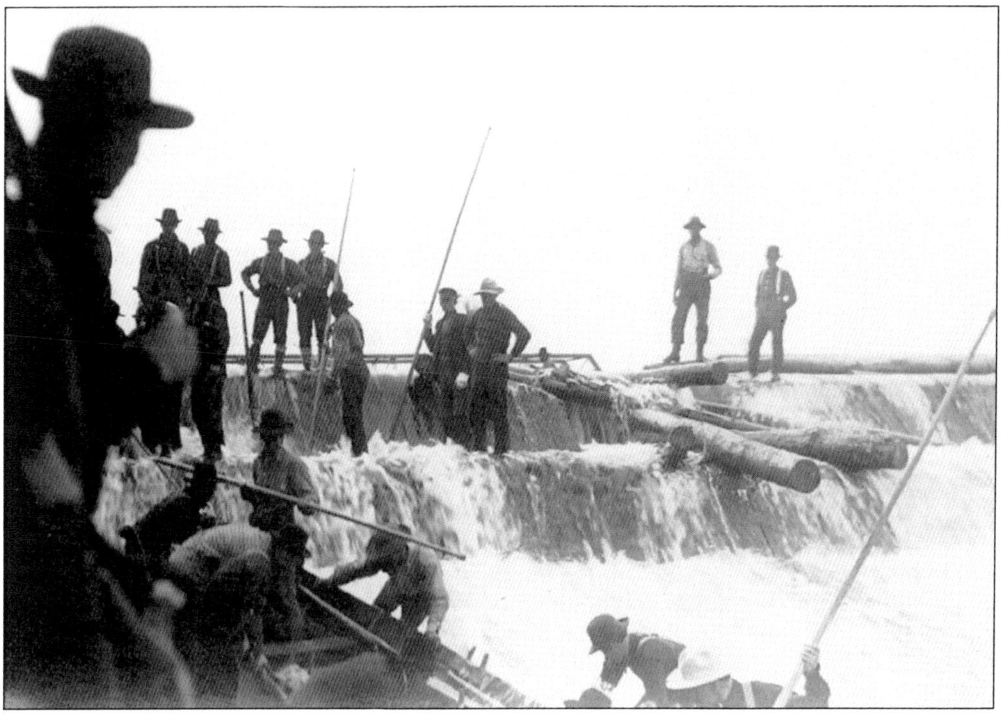

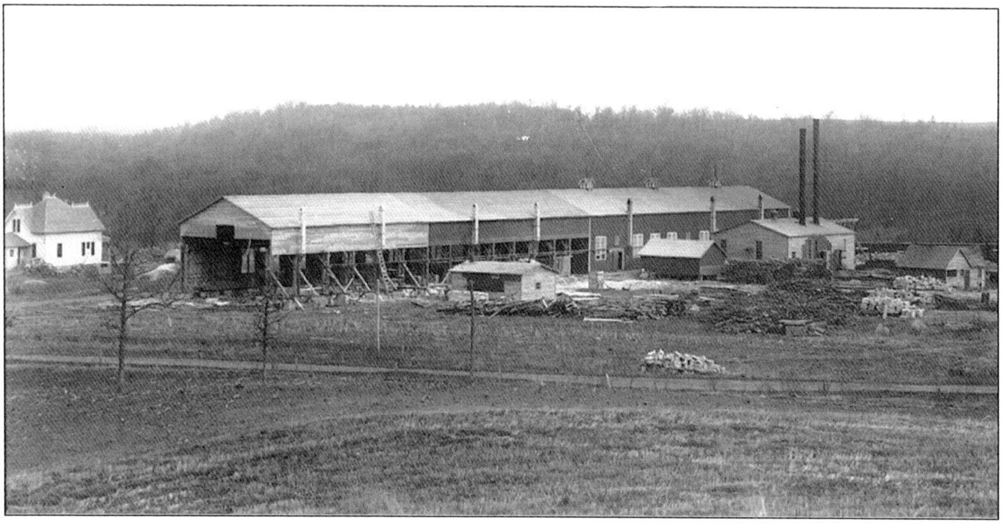

The opening of the Rockville Lumber Company, c. 1913, facilitated building in Rockville. The yard operated from 1913 to 1988. It was originally built by Al Rothstein in partnership with an Eden Prairie man. The company sold lumber, cement, lime, and brick. (Courtesy of the Central Minnesota Historical Center.)

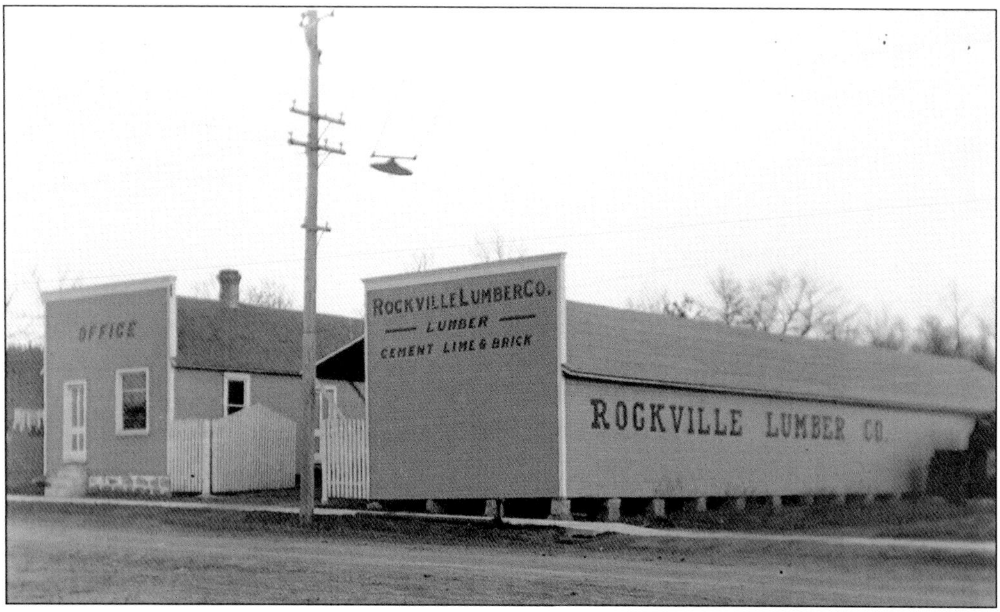

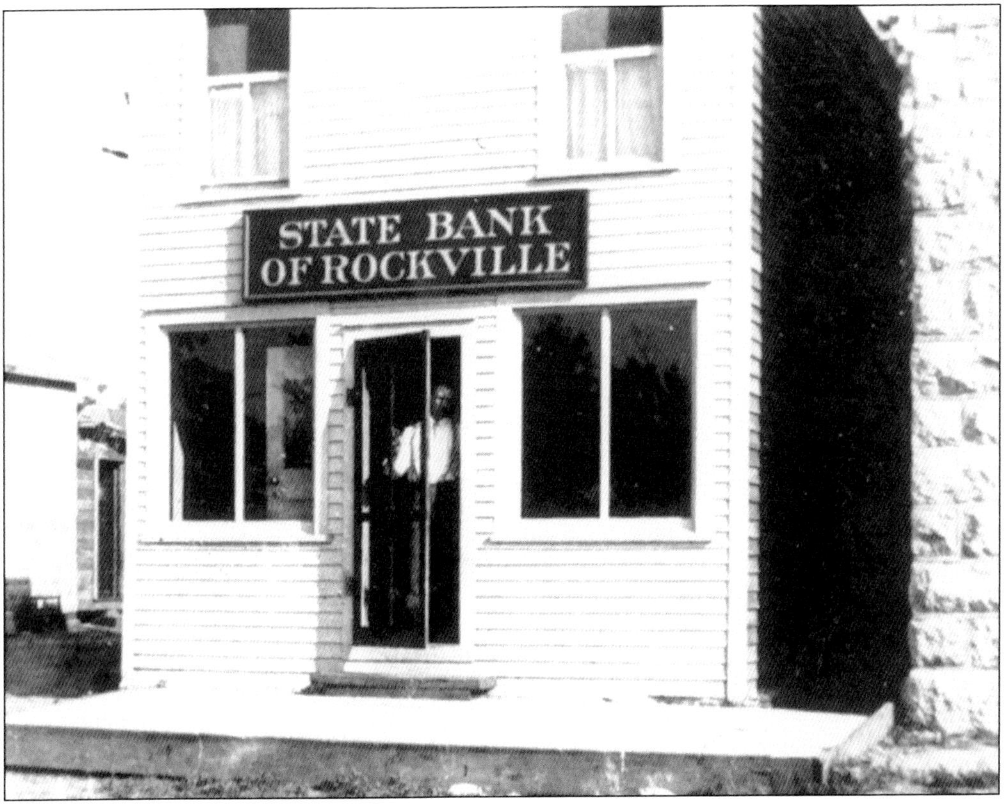


A booming granite industry helped support the State Bank of Rockville, c. 1910. (Courtesy of the Central Minnesota Historical Center.)

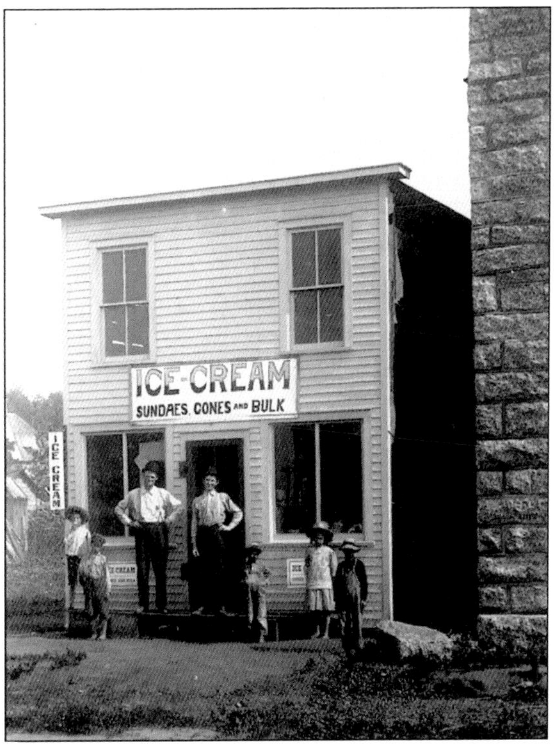


Nothing could be better on a hot summer day than an ice cream cone at the ice cream shop in Rockville, c. 1910. (Courtesy of the Central Minnesota Historical Center.)

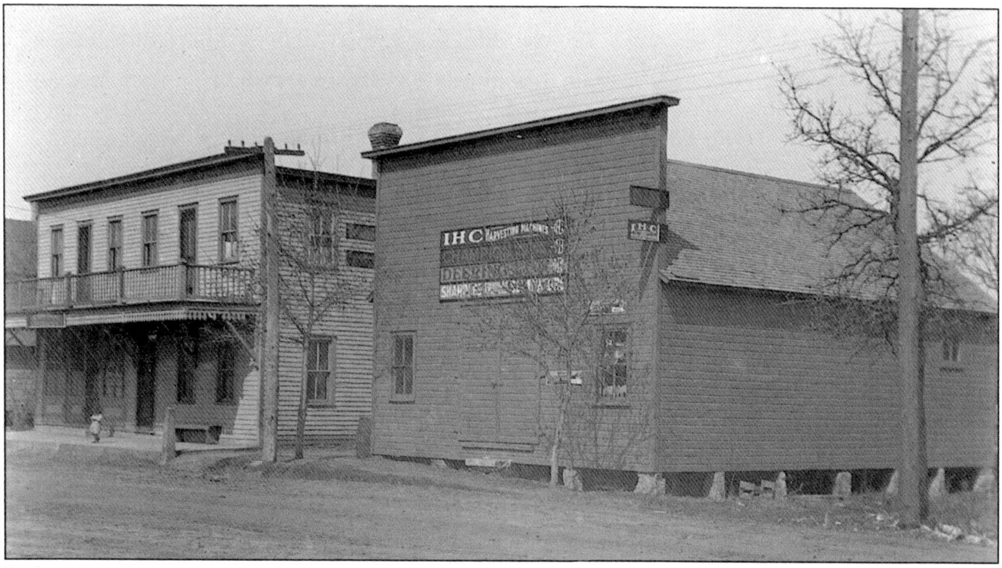


Indicating a continued reliance on horsepower, Rockville supported two blacksmith shops c. 1910. (Courtesy of the Central Minnesota Historical Center.)

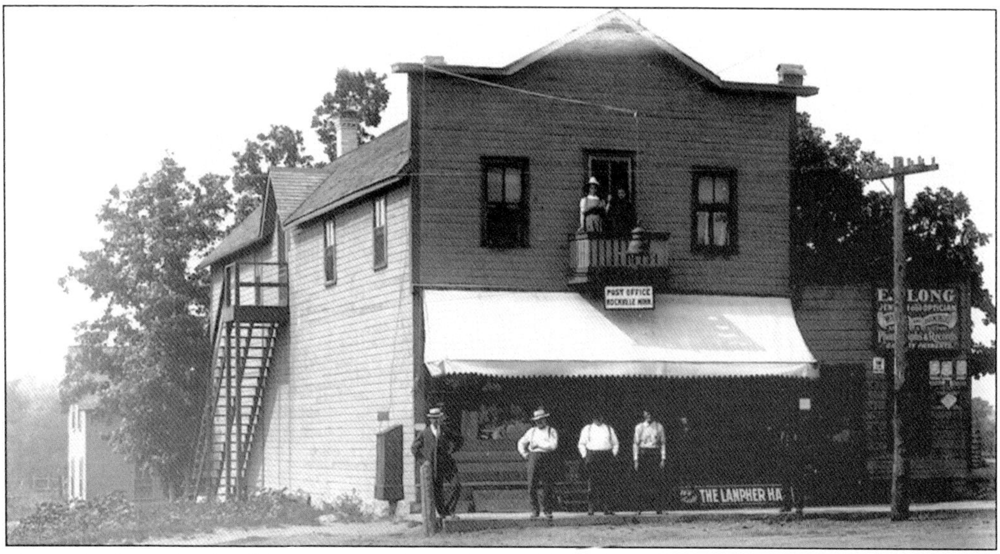


Pictured above is the Weisman Brothers General Merchandise on Main Street, Rockville, c. 1910. Like many small towns around the country, the general store also served as the post office. When the building burned in 1941, the Weisman's ran the post office out of their living quarters. (Courtesy of the Central Minnesota Historical Center.)

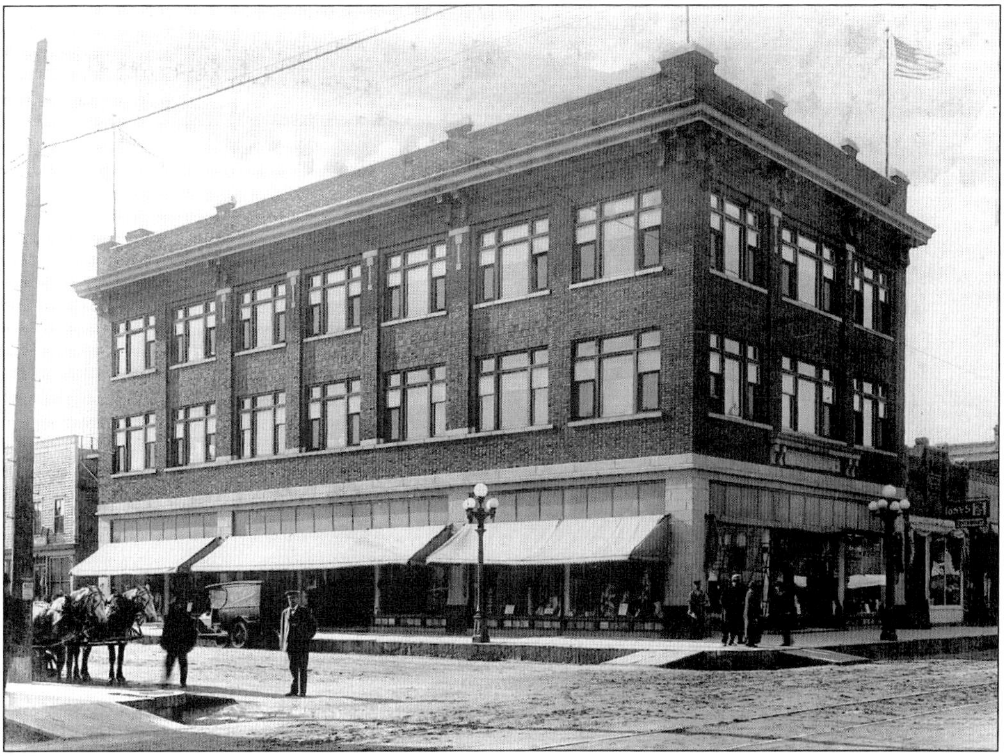

In the late 19th century, department stores altered the urban landscape by catering to women shoppers. Fandel's Department Store came to downtown St. Cloud in 1900. Located in the 600 block of St. Germain Street, the building was torn down in the early 1980s to make room for the Herberger's department store and the Centre Square development. This photo shows the store about 1915. (Courtesy of the Central Minnesota Historical Center.)

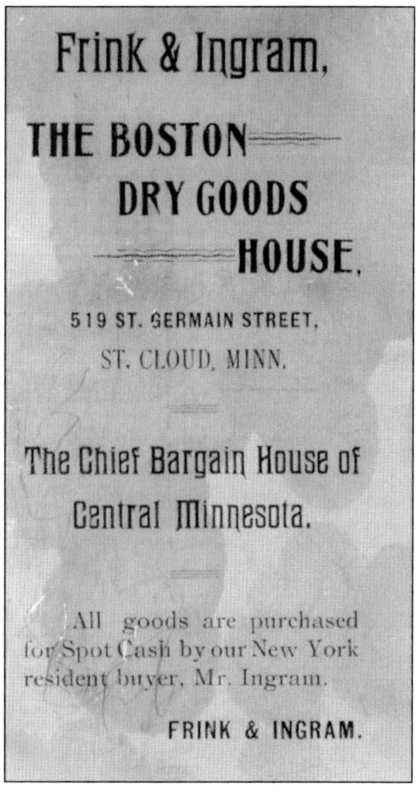


Several St. Cloud businesses advertised in this "Lightning Calculator and Business Men's Pocket Companion," from 1893. They included the Frink & Ingram Dry Goods Store and the Fred Price Men's Clothing Store. (Courtesy of Richard Kelly.)

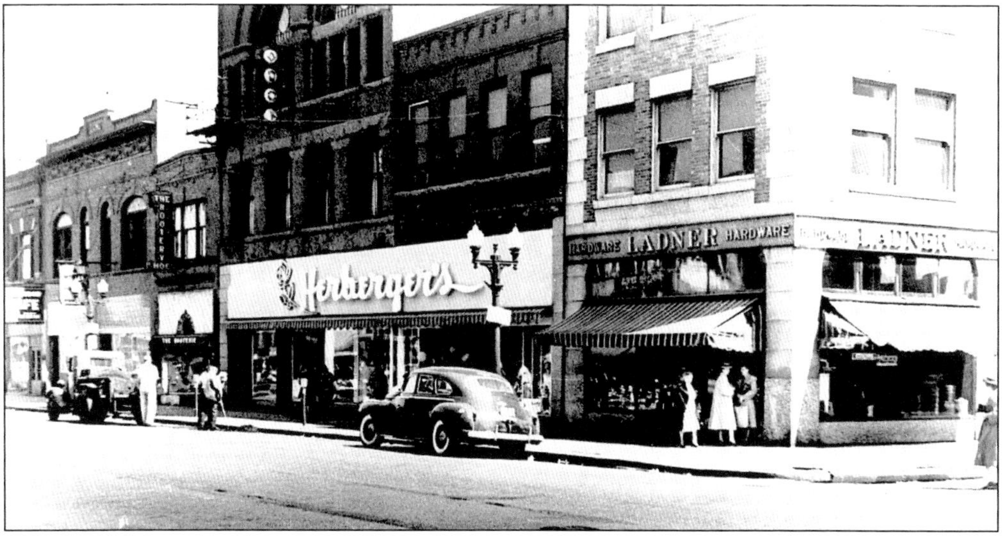


Herberger's opened in downtown St. Cloud in 1927, bringing competition to Fandel's. Located in the 500 block of St. Germain Street. This building is currently home to the Masonic Temple. This photo dates from the late 1940s. (Courtesy of the Central Minnesota Historical Center.)

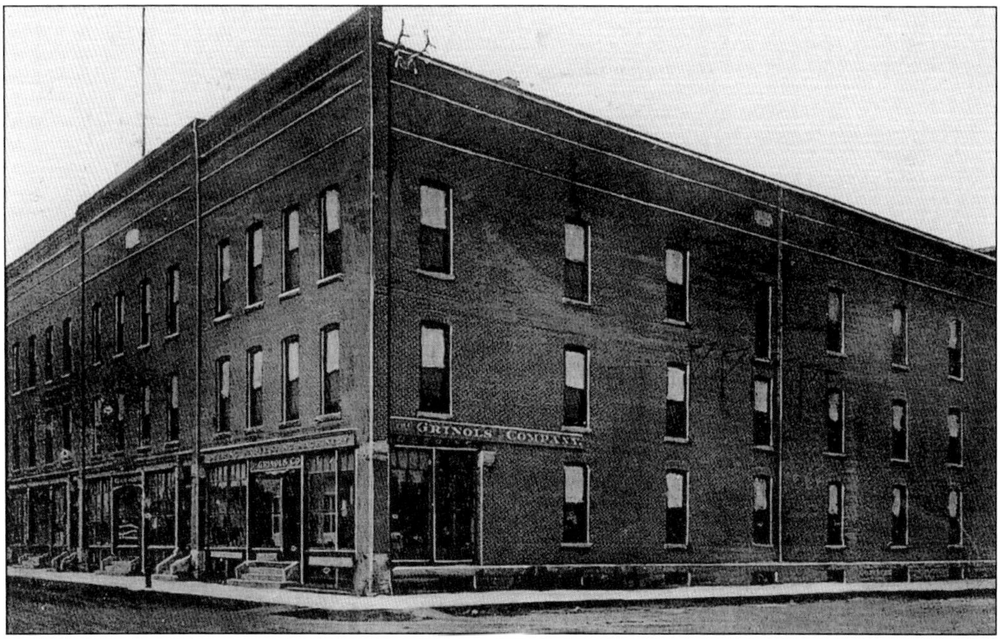


The Carter Building, First Street North, St. Cloud in 1911, was built as a basic warehouse. This building has housed a variety of businesses including a business college, a machine shop, a pharmacy, and currently a senior citizen's residence. (Courtesy of Richard Kelly.)

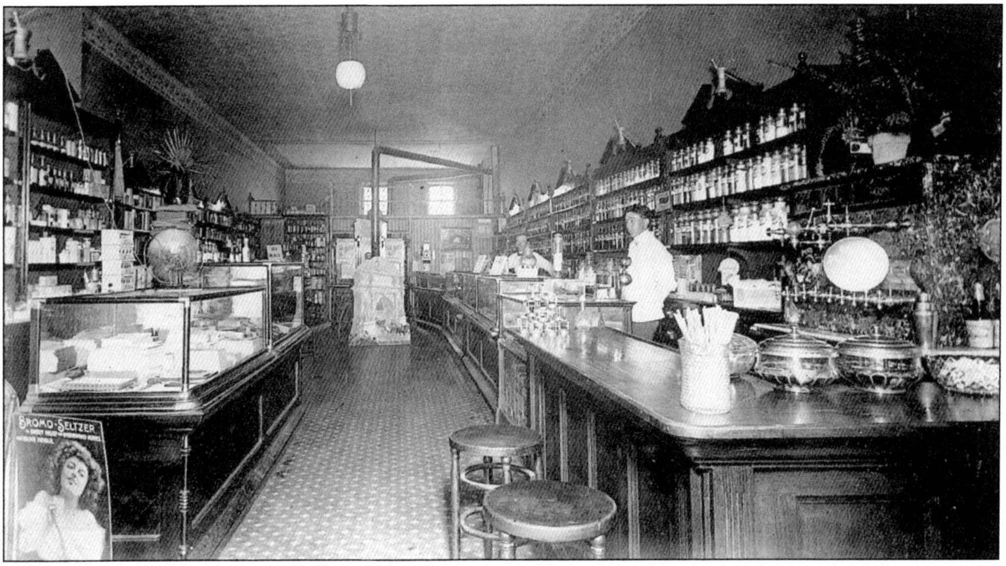


The above image shows the interior of the Carter building drug store in St. Cloud, *c.* 1900. Like most drug stores, this served as soda fountain and dry goods store as well as pharmacy. (Courtesy of the Central Minnesota Historical Center.)

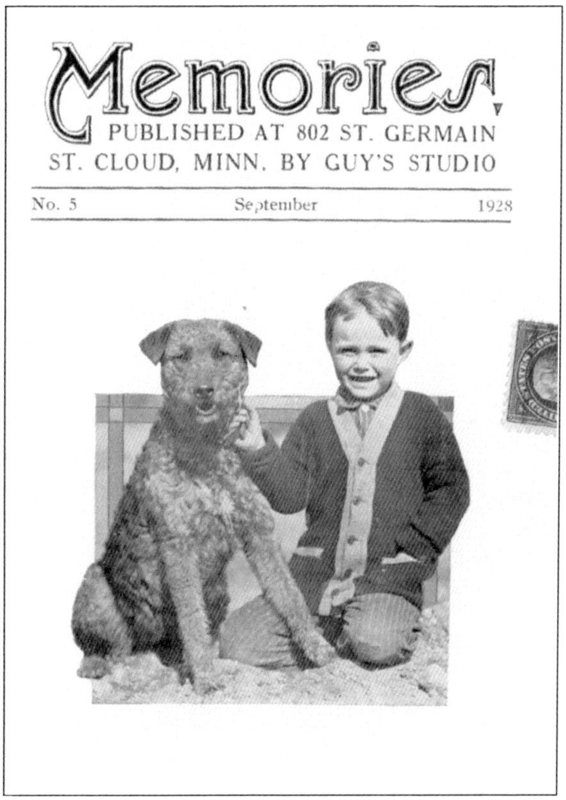


"Memories" by Guy's Studio, 802 St. Germain Street, St. Cloud, 1928 is shown to the right. Collie Guy opened his studio in what had once been his father's jewelry store. This advertisement sells his work with children.

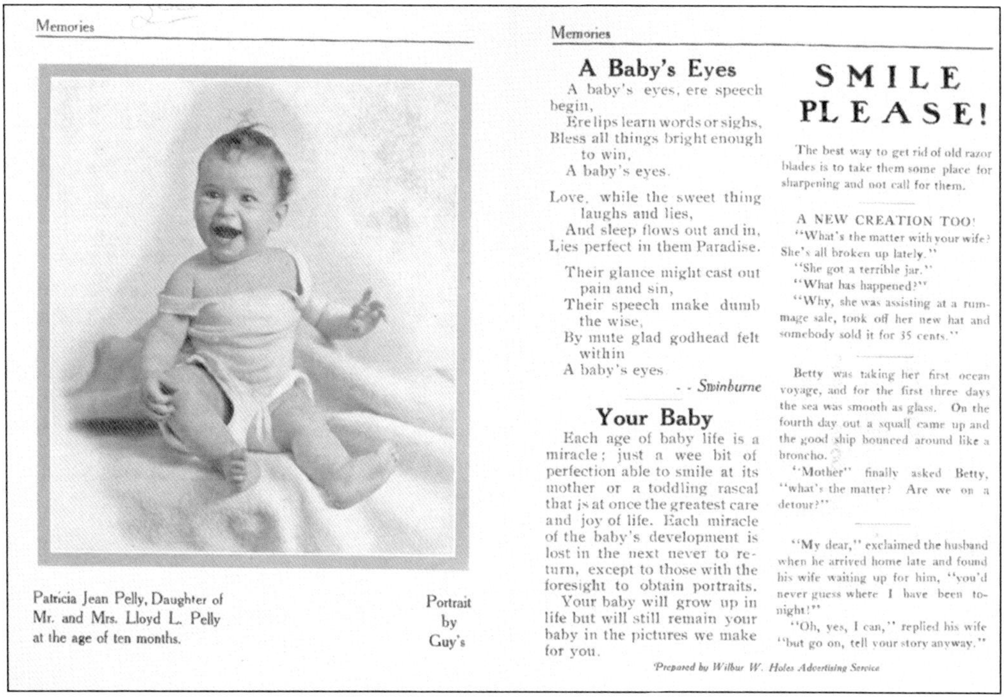

Memories

Patricia Jean Pelly, Daughter of Mr. and Mrs. Lloyd L. Pelly at the age of ten months.

Portrait by Guy's

Memories

## A Baby's Eyes

A baby's eyes, ere speech begin,
Ere lips learn words or sighs,
Bless all things bright enough to win,
A baby's eyes.

Love, while the sweet thing laughs and lies,
And sleep flows out and in,
Lies perfect in them Paradise.

Their glance might cast out pain and sin,
Their speech make dumb the wise,
By mute glad godhead felt within
A baby's eyes.

- - *Swinburne*

## Your Baby

Each age of baby life is a miracle; just a wee bit of perfection able to smile at its mother or a toddling rascal that is at once the greatest care and joy of life. Each miracle of the baby's development is lost in the next never to return, except to those with the foresight to obtain portraits.

Your baby will grow up in life but will still remain your baby in the pictures we make for you.

## SMILE PLEASE!

The best way to get rid of old razor blades is to take them some place for sharpening and not call for them.

A NEW CREATION TOO!

"What's the matter with your wife? She's all broken up lately."

"She got a terrible jar."

"What has happened?"

"Why, she was assisting at a rummage sale, took off her new hat and somebody sold it for 35 cents."

Betty was taking her first ocean voyage, and for the first three days the sea was smooth as glass. On the fourth day out a squall came up and the good ship bounced around like a broncho.

"Mother" finally asked Betty, "what's the matter? Are we on a detour?"

"My dear," exclaimed the husband when he arrived home late and found his wife waiting up for him, "you'd never guess where I have been to-night!"

"Oh, yes, I can," replied his wife "but go on, tell your story anyway."

*Prepared by Wilbur W. Holes Advertising Service*

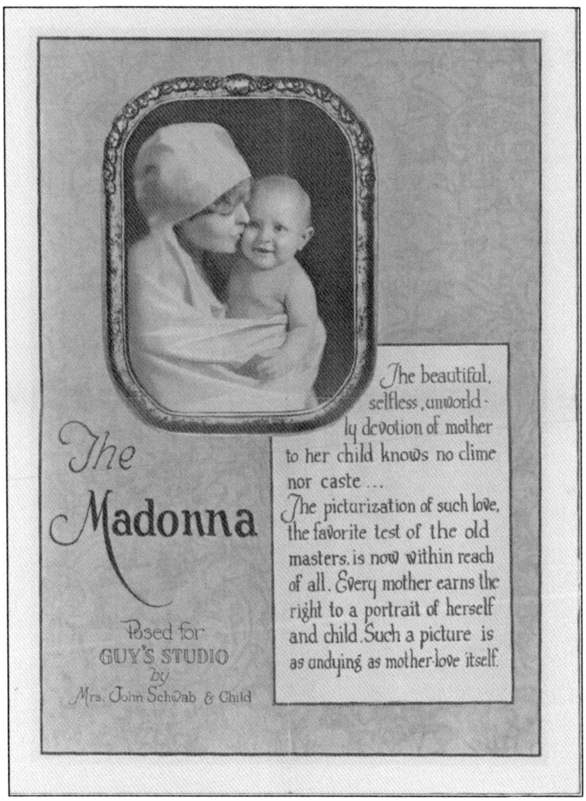


In addition to private sittings, this studio photographed much of the city for postcards throughout the 1910s and 1920s. (Courtesy of Richard Kelly.)

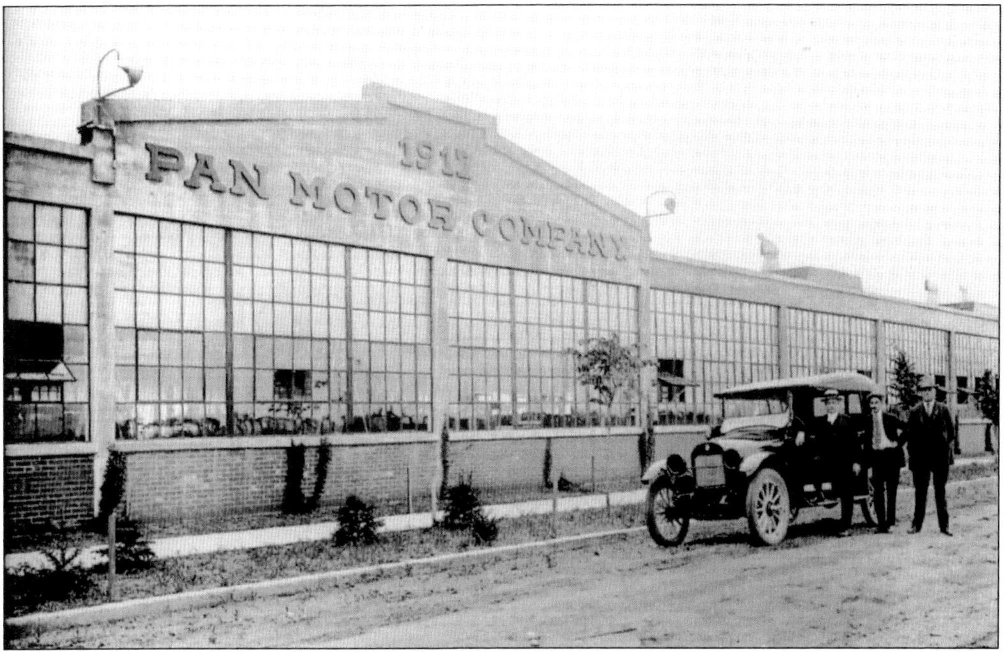


At the time these photos were taken c. 1910, the Pan Motor Company Works existed well outside St. Cloud. Today the factory building houses the Frigidaire factory on Thirty-Third Avenue North.

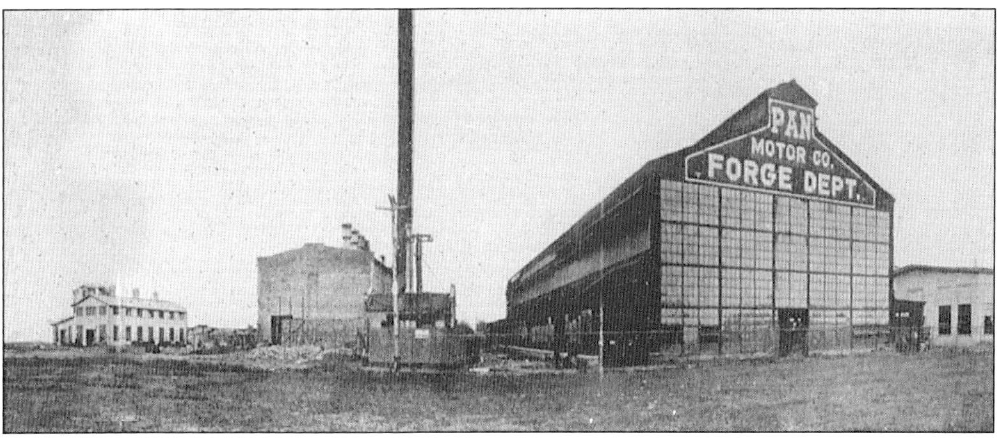

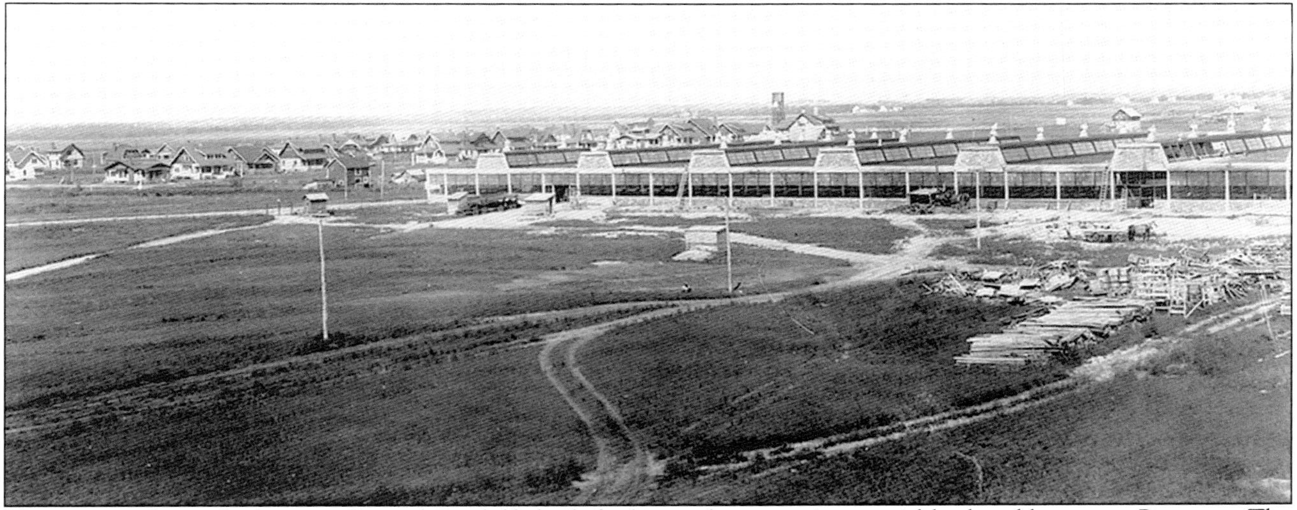

This picture shows the housing Samuel Pandolfo built for his workers creating a neighborhood known as Pantown. The homes seen in the back left of the picture still exist today. The Pantown Historic District is currently being created to protect this neighborhood. (Courtesy of Roy Bernick and Richard Kelly.)

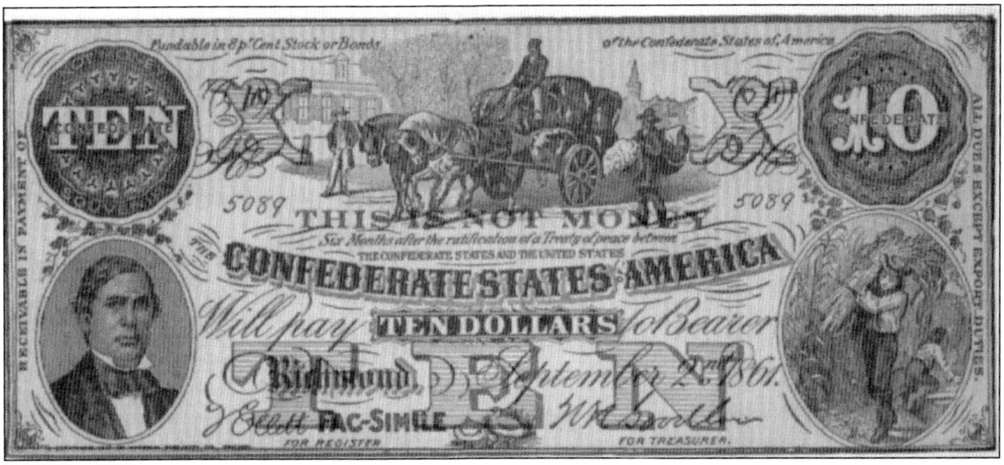


The J.P. Callahan Furniture Company of St. Cloud advertised for business in 1890. This circular shows the continued influence of the Civil War on American society. (Courtesy of Richard Kelly.)

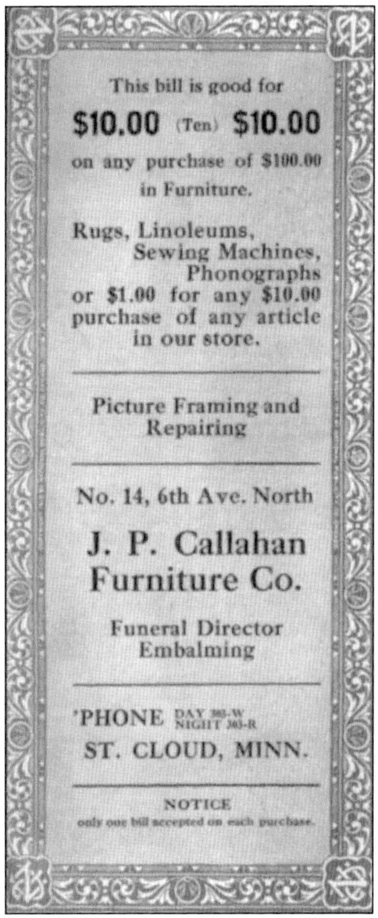

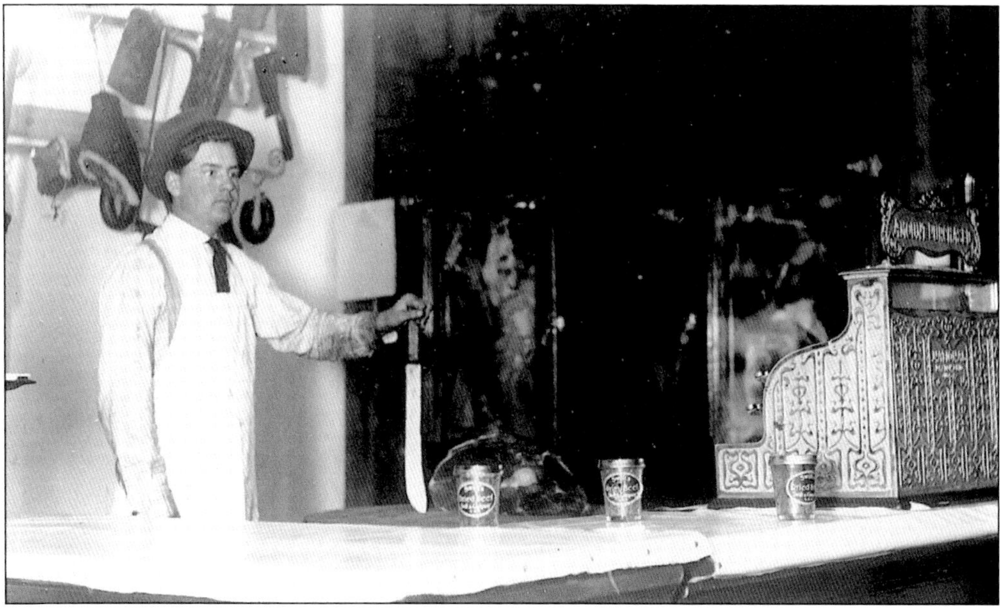

Butchers catered to both rural and urban residents in Stearns County. This view shows the interior of the Rockville butcher shop, c. 1900. (Courtesy of the Central Minnesota Historical Center.)

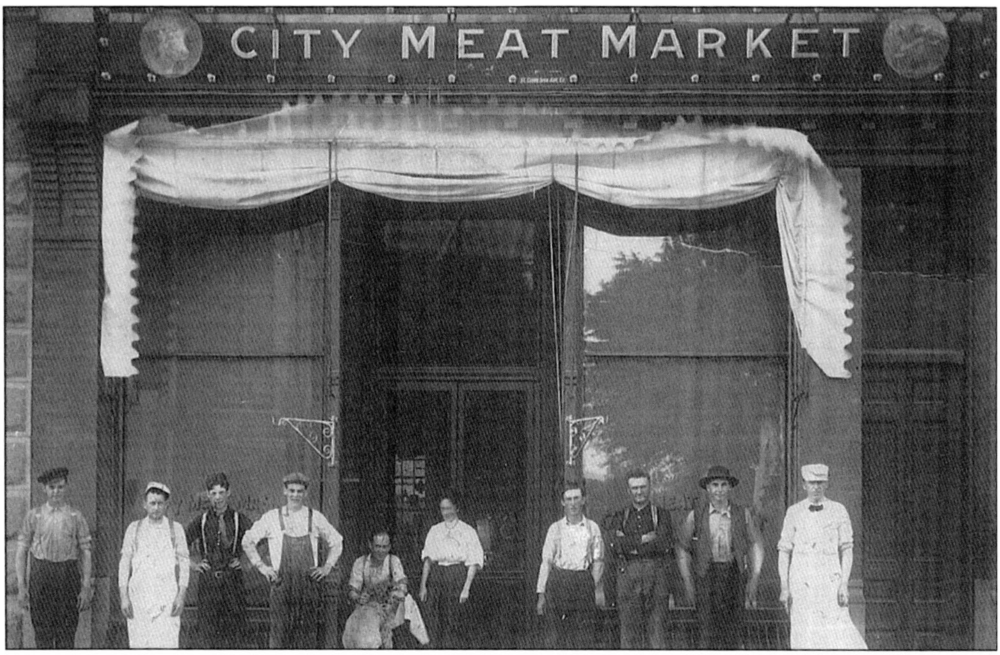


The City Meat Market owned by the Joseph Hunstiger Company was located in the 800 block of St. Germain Street, St. Cloud. Built in 1888, the building has an interesting architecture. The sausage kitchen was on the second floor and it had a cement floor. Cork-lined coolers sat in the basement. Pictured here in 1907 are employees Stan Truzinski, Matt Bauler, George Spaniol, Ben H., Joe Guifkowski, Catherine Donally, Iceman Murphy, Joe Hunstiger, and Frank Hunstiger. (Courtesy of the Hunstiger family.)

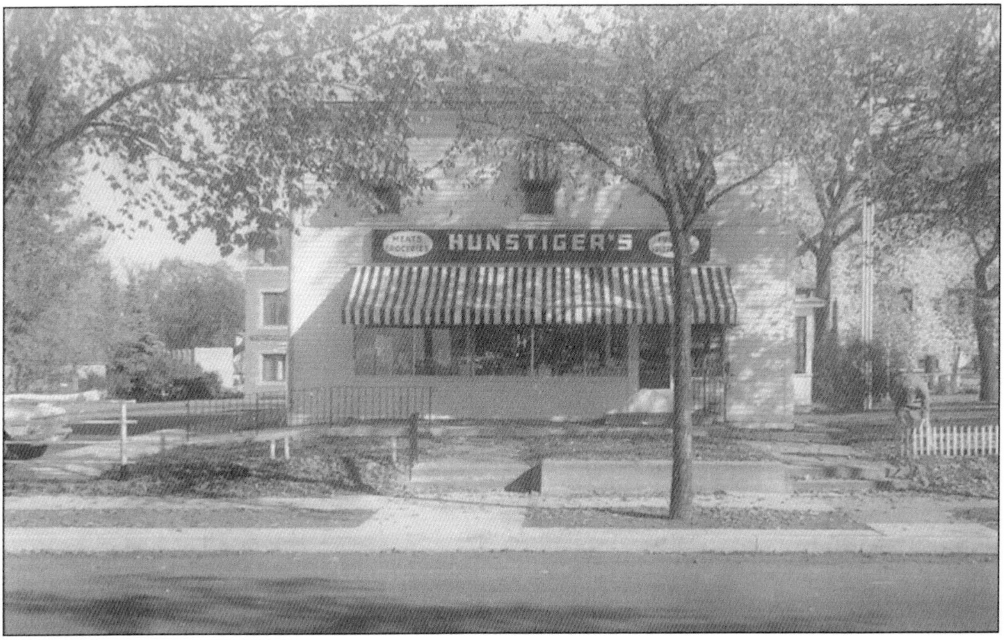


Joseph's son Anthony opened The Hunstiger Meat Market on Fifth Avenue South in 1938. This picture shows the building in 1964, two years after sons Paul and Tom took over the business. The building closed in 1987. (Courtesy of the Hunstiger family.)

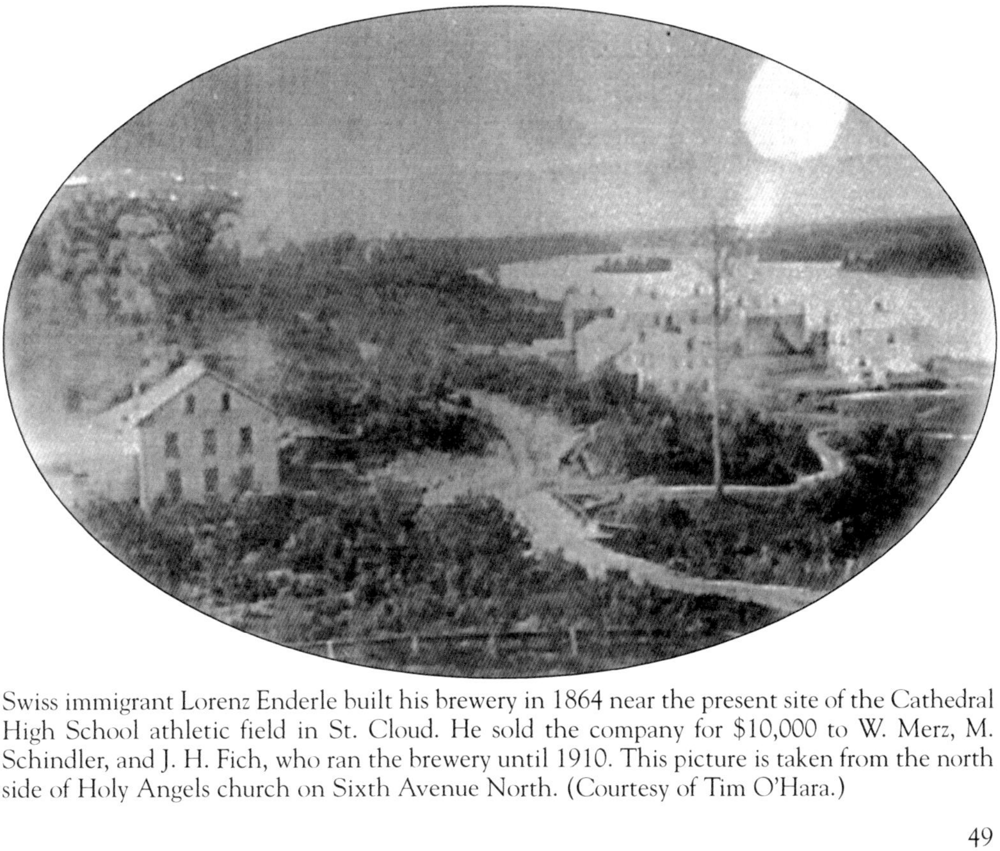

Swiss immigrant Lorenz Enderle built his brewery in 1864 near the present site of the Cathedral High School athletic field in St. Cloud. He sold the company for $10,000 to W. Merz, M. Schindler, and J. H. Fich, who ran the brewery until 1910. This picture is taken from the north side of Holy Angels church on Sixth Avenue North. (Courtesy of Tim O'Hara.)

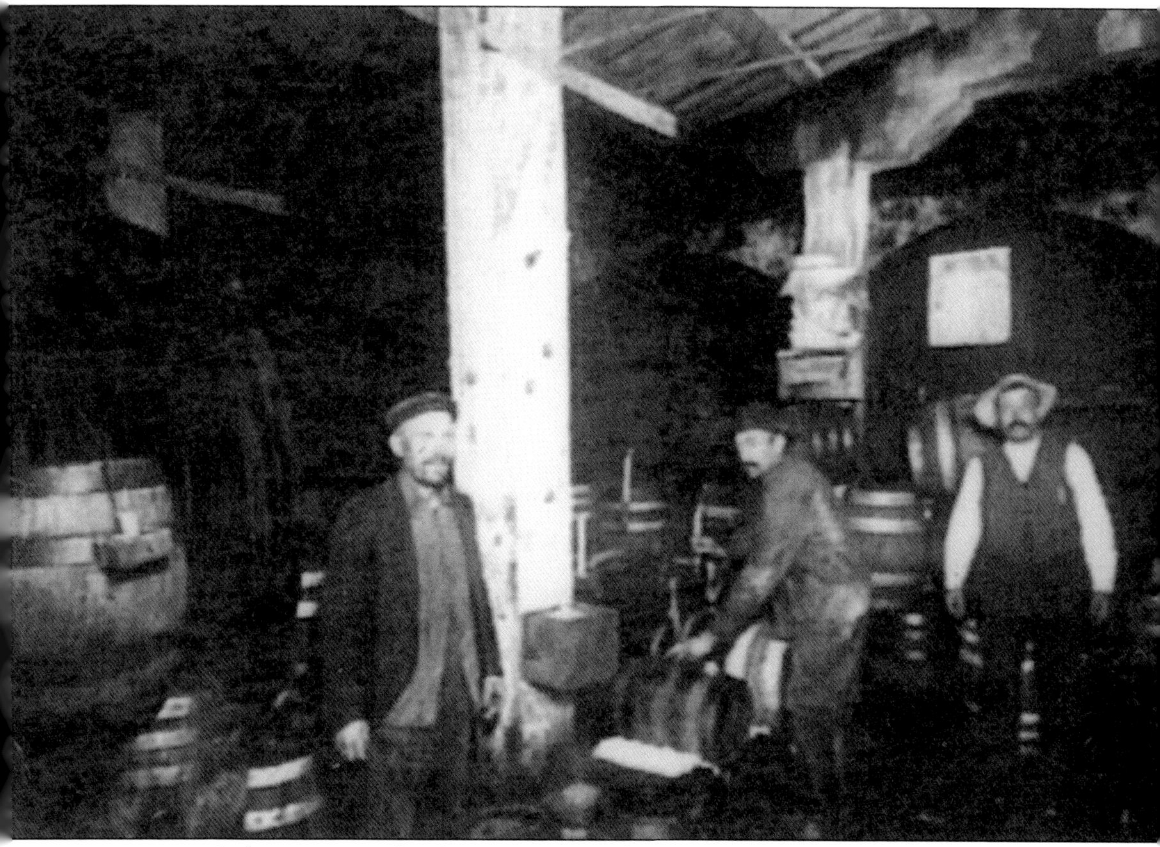

Men worked an average of 15 hours a day, 365 days a year to brew beer for local consumption. These men worked for the Cellar, Preiss, and Wimmer Brewing Company, 1918. (Courtesy of Tim O'Hara.)

# *Four*

# Getting From Here To There

By 1900 American cities no longer looked like their 18th and 19th century counterparts. The compact walking city slowly disappeared as technological innovations in transportation paved the way for the modern sprawling metropolis. For cities seeking to grow, taking advantage of new transportation methods was crucial. City and county governments took an active role in promoting and paying for new streets, bridges, streetcar lines, and even railroads. Most of the cities of Stearns County were too small to take advantage of streetcars, but all built roads and bridges to accommodate the coming of the automobile, and pursued a relationship with the railroads. The City of St. Cloud was one of the most aggressive cities in the county in pursuing transportation routes; it built a railroad bridge for the Great Northern Railroad across the Mississippi in the 1870s.

The river has been both a blessing and a curse to the county. St. Cloud marks the northern terminus for river transportation since the Sauk rapids block further barge traffic. The river provided the major transportation artery for the county for logging, mill products, and even the granite industry until the railroads expanded services after 1880. Steamboats also provided regular passenger service between St. Cloud and St. Anthony Falls beginning in 1874.

Horse and buggy and pedestrian traffic limited the geographic size of most Stearns County communities. All businesses and homes needed to be within easy walking distance. This situation changed in 1887 with the building of the first horse-drawn streetcar line in St. Cloud. The Waite Park and St. Cloud and the Sauk Rapids and St. Cloud lines primarily serviced the businesses on St. Germain Street. Routes traveled up Fifth Avenue South to Germain Street then up Ninth Avenue North, eventually reaching Second Street and Eighth Avenue North. In 1892 the line was electrified. The last run took place on April 29, 1936, when private cars and buses replaced the trolleys.

Perhaps the most significant economic and social development of the early 20th century was the automobile. The first automobile was maufactured for sale in 1895, but it was not until Henry Ford began mass-producing the inexpensive Model-T in the 1920s that the automobile became a staple of American society. Ford stated, "I am going to democratize the automobile. When I'm through everybody will be able to afford one, and about everyone will have one." He was right. The automobile revolution quickly spread to Stearns County and along with it, the "good-roads" movement. Like the railroad craze of the 19th century, the automobile revolutionized the way we get from here to there.

All Stearns County cities have been transformed from places with filthy, muddy streets and animal-powered transportation into readily accessible communities with paved, much cleaner, and more controlled surfaces. This has come about in part as a partnership of city, county, and state government, but it also reflects the pressures of modernization that have left their mark on the county. The images that follow illustrate the evolution of transportation in the county by exploring both transportation routes and the technologies we have applied to them.

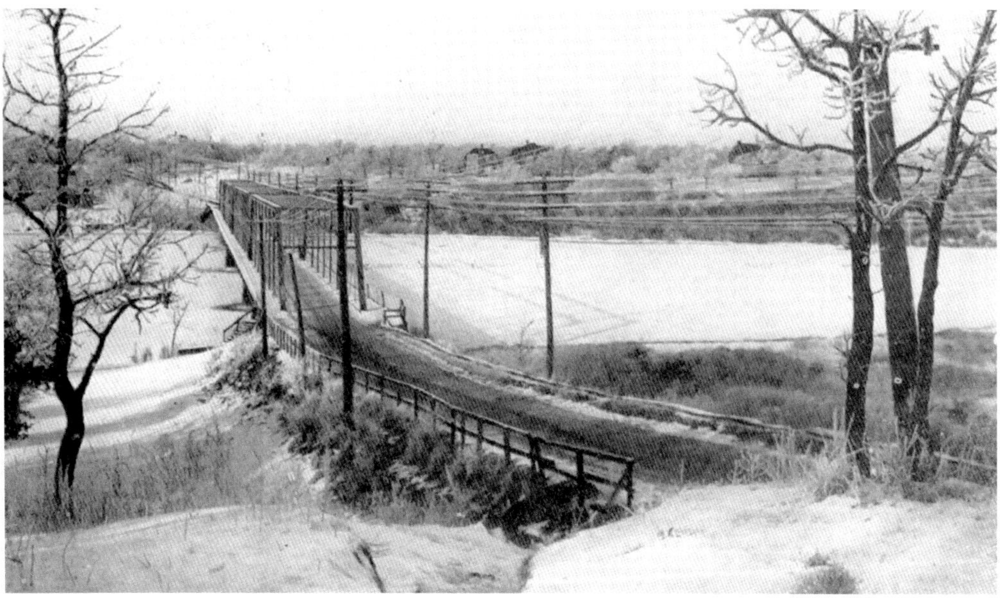

The Tenth Street Bridge stretching over the Mississippi River, St. Cloud, 1909. Horse, auto, and foot transportation have all been important to the history of St. Cloud. This bridge worked quite well for the latter two, but cars had some difficulties with the bridge in winter. As traffic increased on the bridge and stoplights were built on either side of the slope, cars in winter would often slip and slide on the incline. It was not uncommon for a car to slide off the roadway onto the pedestrian sidewalk. The bridge has been rebuilt to fix this problem. (Courtesy of Richard Kelly.)

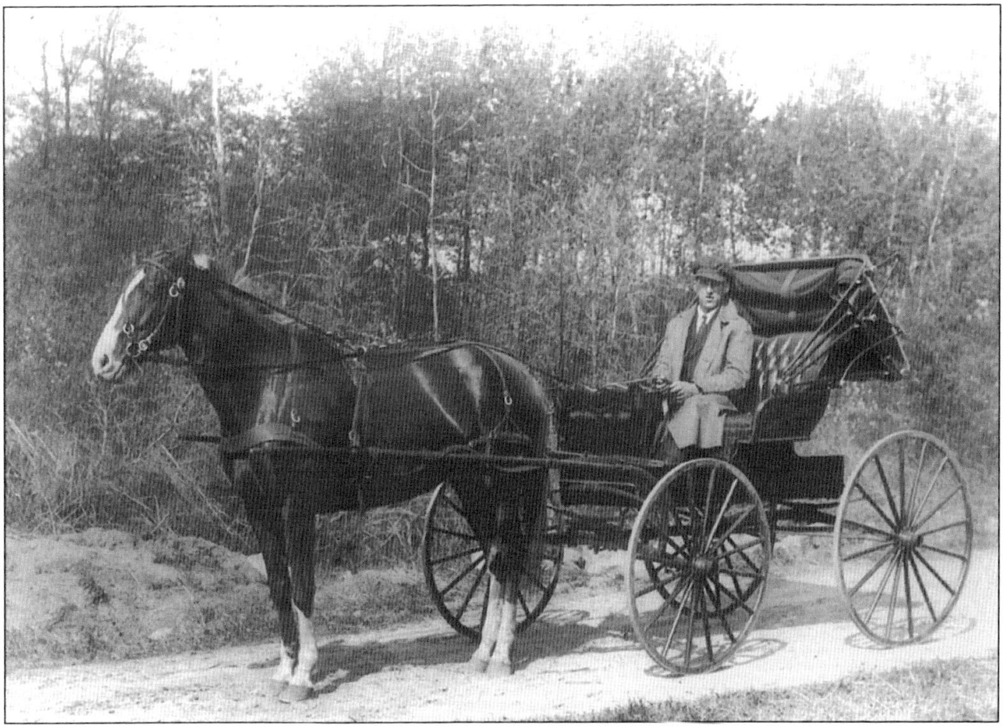

William Schultz demonstrates the most common type of conveyance in Stearns County at the turn of the 20th century—horse and buggy. (Courtesy of the Central Minnesota Historical Society.)

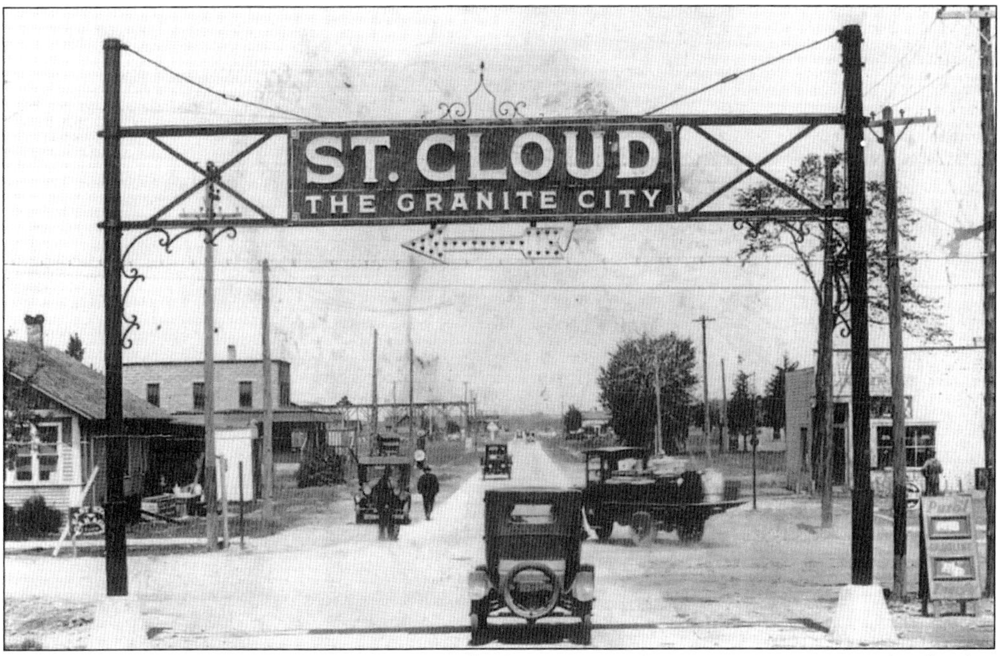


St. Cloud began to cater to automobile traffic by erecting this sign into east St. Cloud. This photo dates from 1930. (Courtesy of Roy Bernick.)

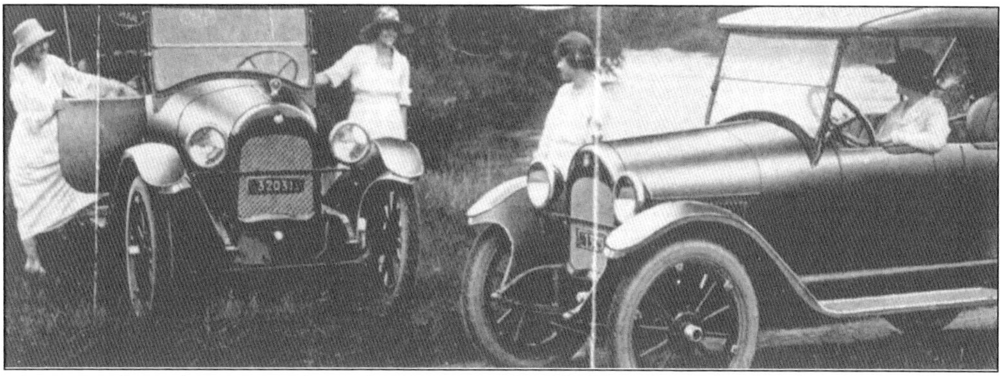

The 1920s brought women the right to vote and to drive. Here are two Pan beauties, *c.* 1920. (Courtesy of Roy Bernick.)

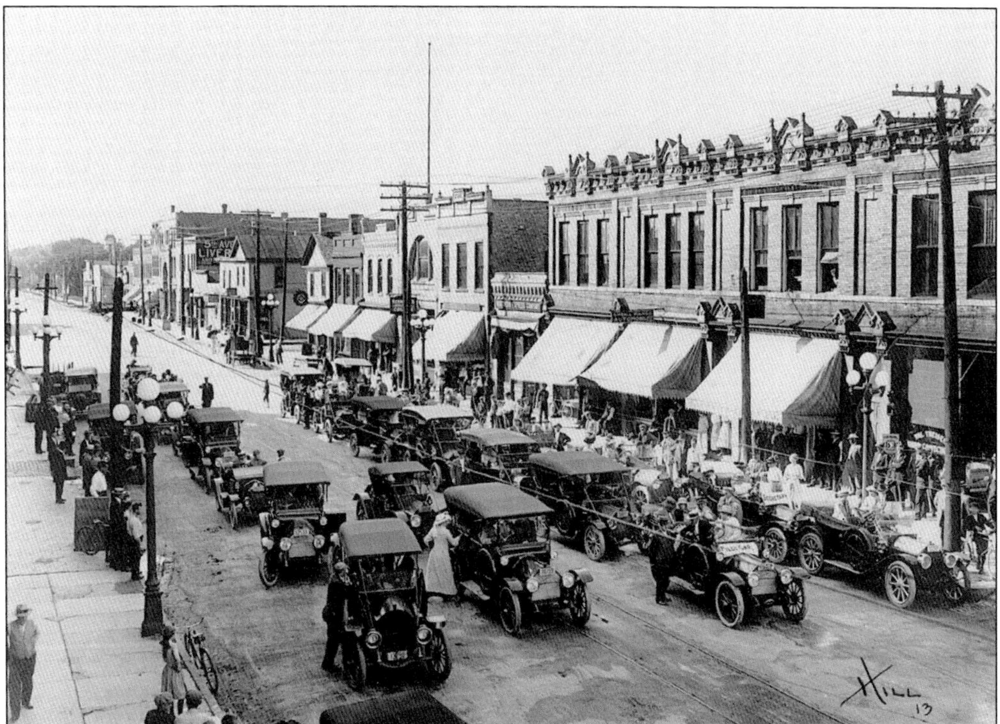

Stearns County residents expressed their love affair with the automobile in this auto tour on Fifth Avenue South in St. Cloud, July 29, 1913. (Courtesy of Roy Bernick.)

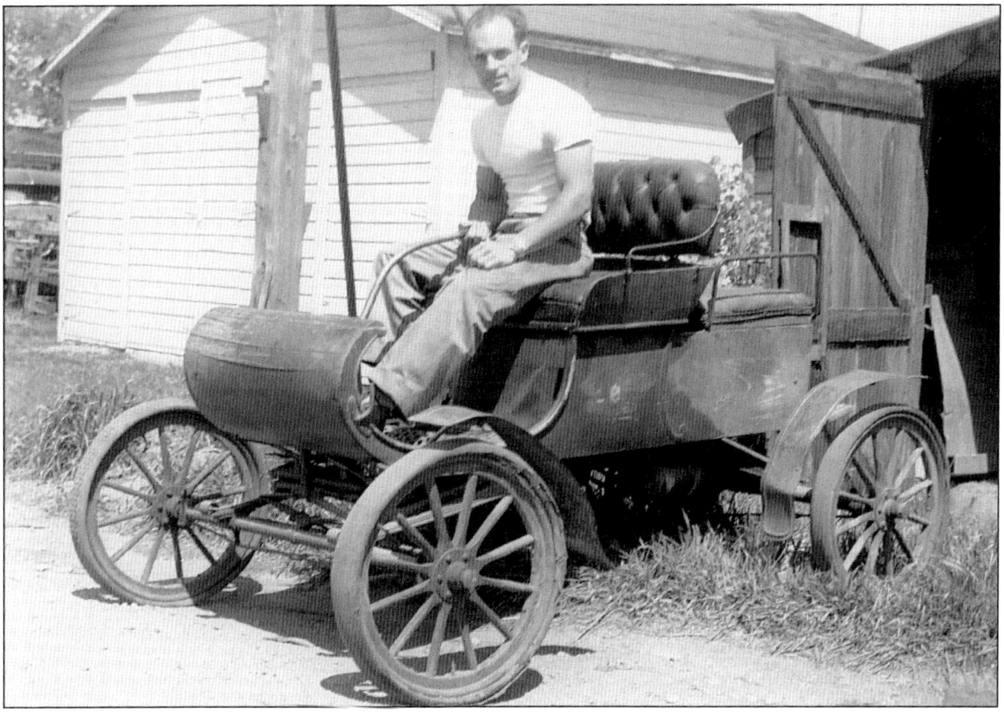

Roy Bernick became an avid collector of classic cars. He purchased his 1903, curved dash Oldsmobile in May 1955. (Courtesy of Roy Bernick.)

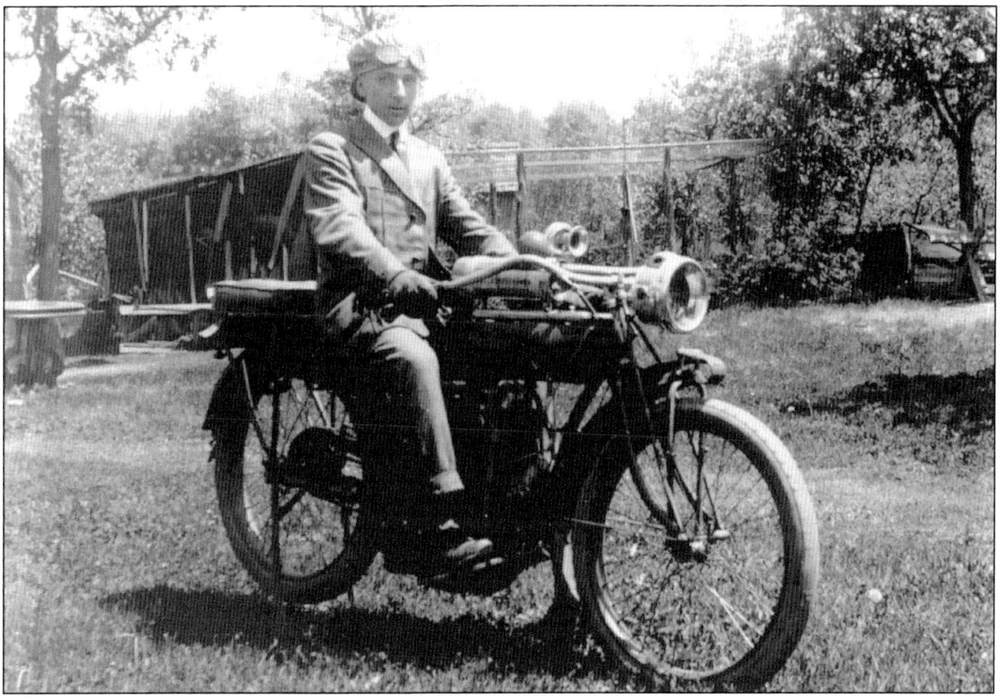

Paul Schultz is pictured on his motorcycle in Rockville, c. 1912. (Courtesy of the Central Minnesota Historical Center.)

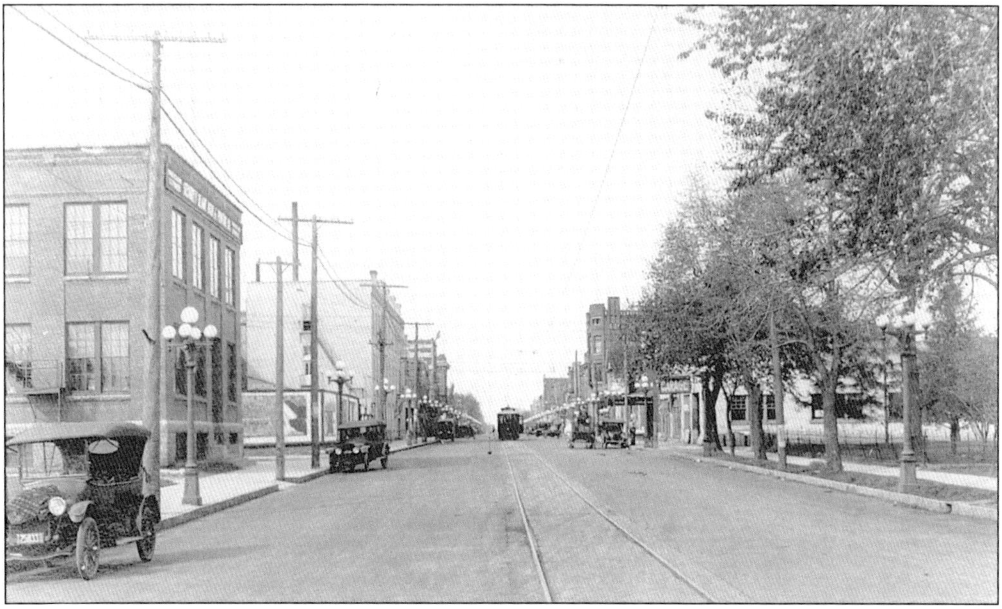

Trolleys, cars, and horse-drawn conveyances all shared the road on St. Germain Street, St. Cloud c. 1910. Note the horse drawn cart on the right, the trolley in the center, and the automobiles parked on the side of the street. The car in the foreground is a Model-T. (Courtesy of Richard Kelly.)

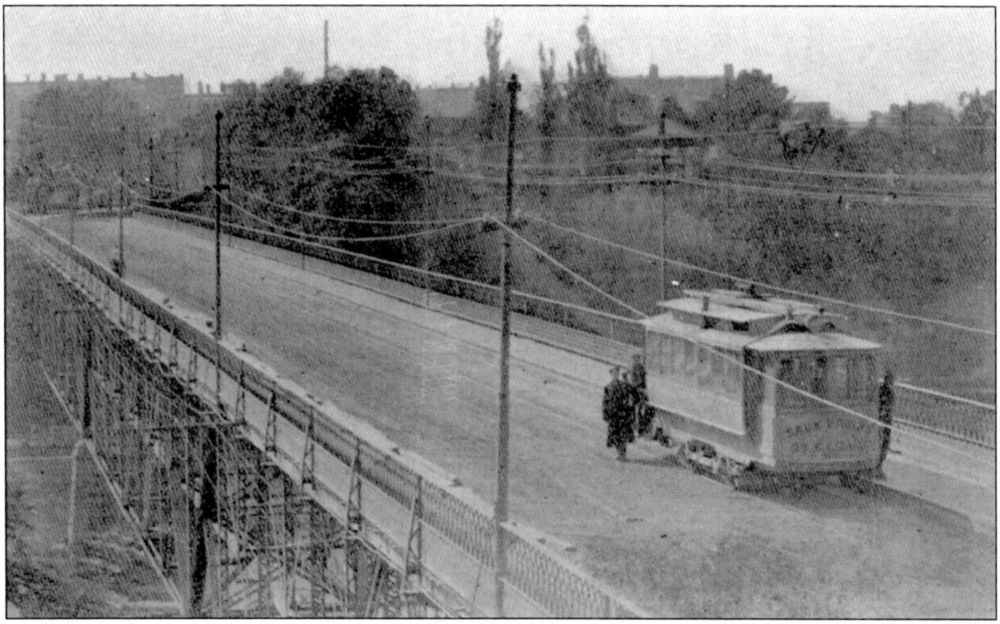

The Sauk Rapids and St. Cloud Trolley can be seen crossing the St. Germain Street Bridge in St. Cloud, 1913. Trolleys ran from six in the morning to ten at night with service every 45 minutes. (Courtesy of Richard Kelly.)

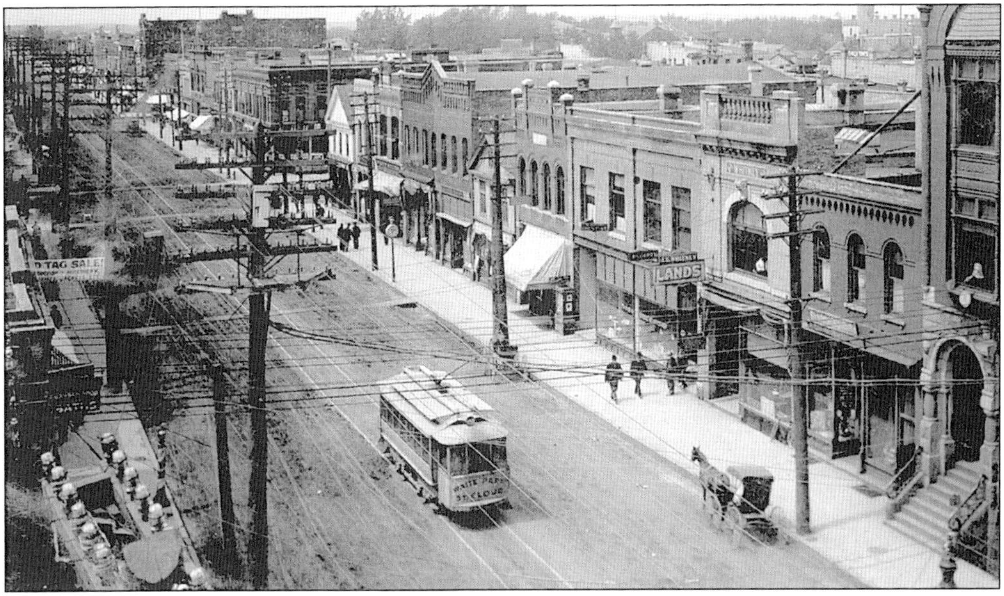

Pictured above are the Waite Park and St. Cloud Trolley on St. Germain Street, St. Cloud, 1908. Trolleys gained the local nickname "Toonervilles" because of the noise they made. (Courtesy of Richard Kelly.)

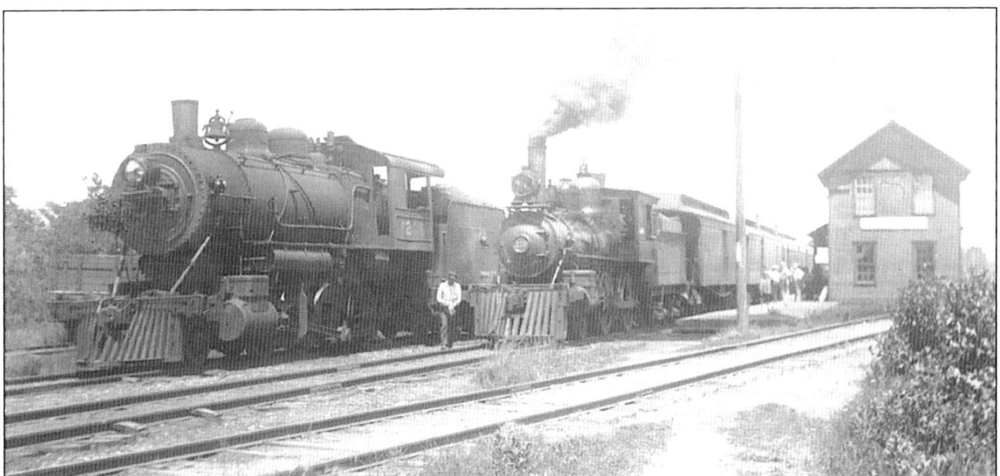

The Great Northern Railroad brought passenger and freight service to Rockville Station c. 1910. The depot closed in August 1952, when passenger service was discontinued. (Courtesy of the Central Minnesota Historical Center.)

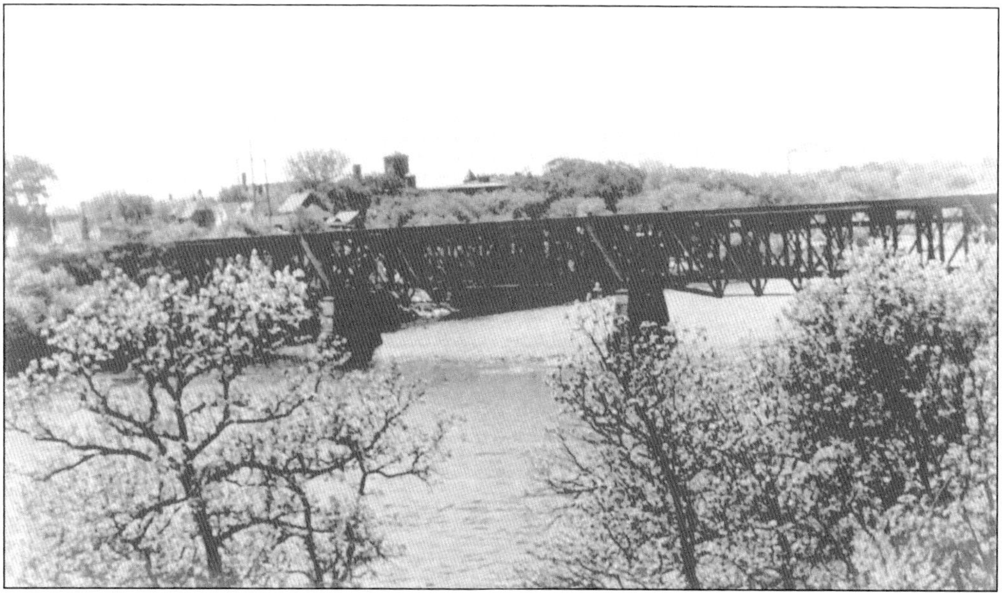

The Great Northern Railroad Bridge over the Mississippi River, St. Cloud, is pictured above c. 1945. The bridge was built in 1872 by the City of St. Cloud in order to attract the railroad to the town. The bridge continues to be used today by the Burlington, Northern, and Santa Fe Railroad. It is used exclusively for freight traffic. (Courtesy of the Central Minnesota Historical Center.)

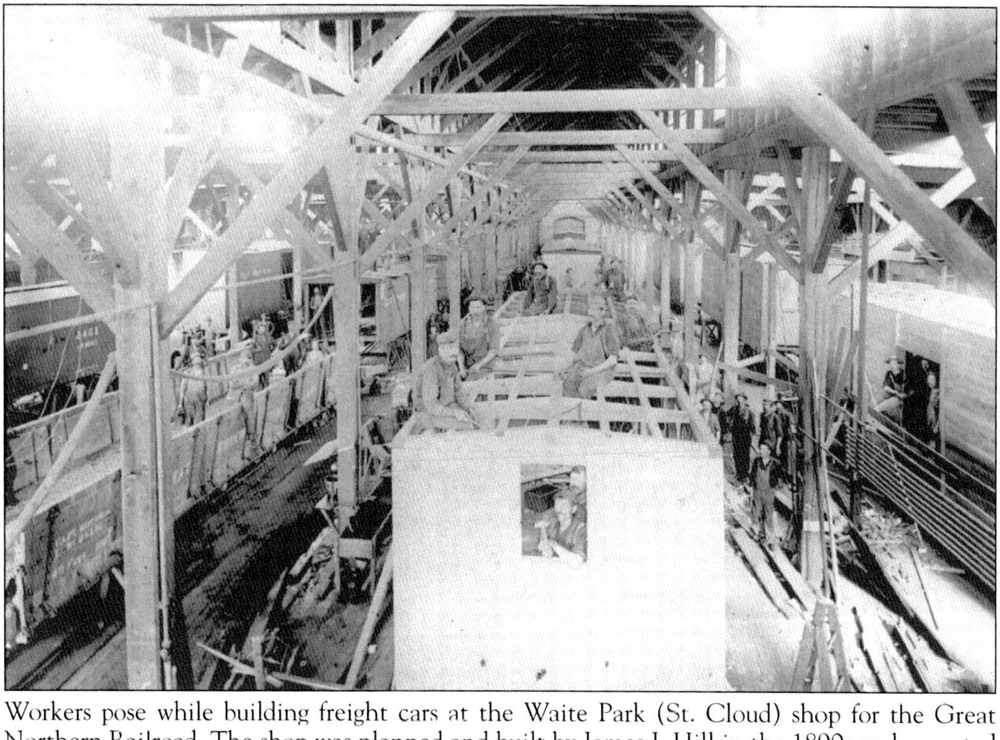

Workers pose while building freight cars at the Waite Park (St. Cloud) shop for the Great Northern Railroad. The shop was planned and built by James J. Hill in the 1890s and operated until the late 1980s when a railroad merger forced its closure. The shop built freight cars, mail cars, and cabooses. (Courtesy of Charlie Grafft.)

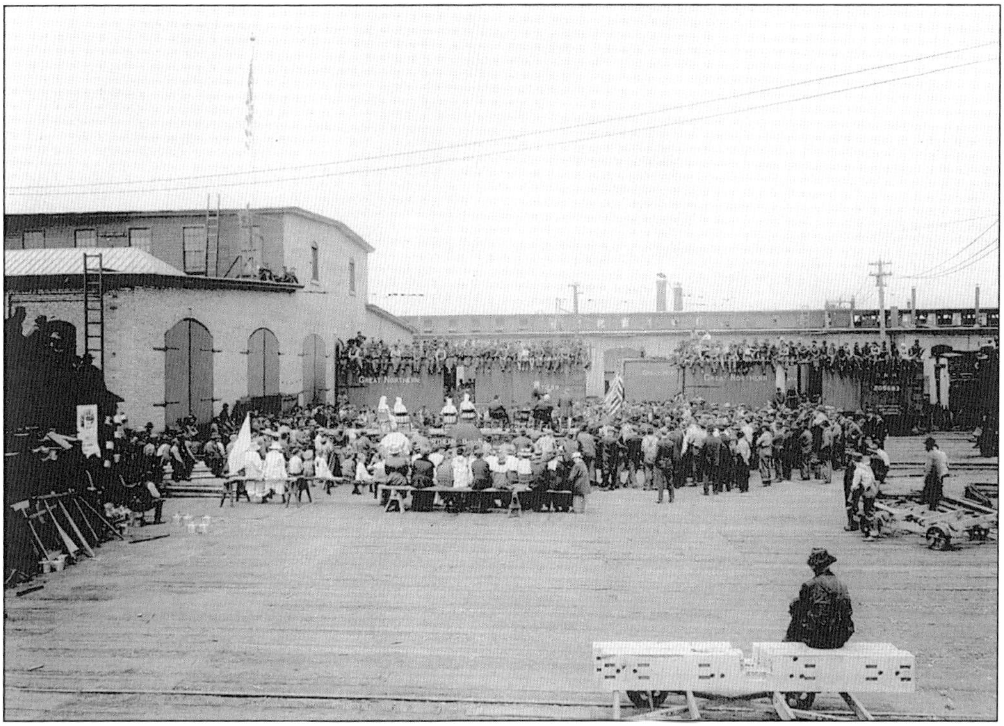

The Red Cross holds a wartime rally for war bonds at the St. Cloud shop, c. 1942. Men, women, and children, both employees and community members, were invited to support the war effort. (Courtesy of Charlie Grafft.)

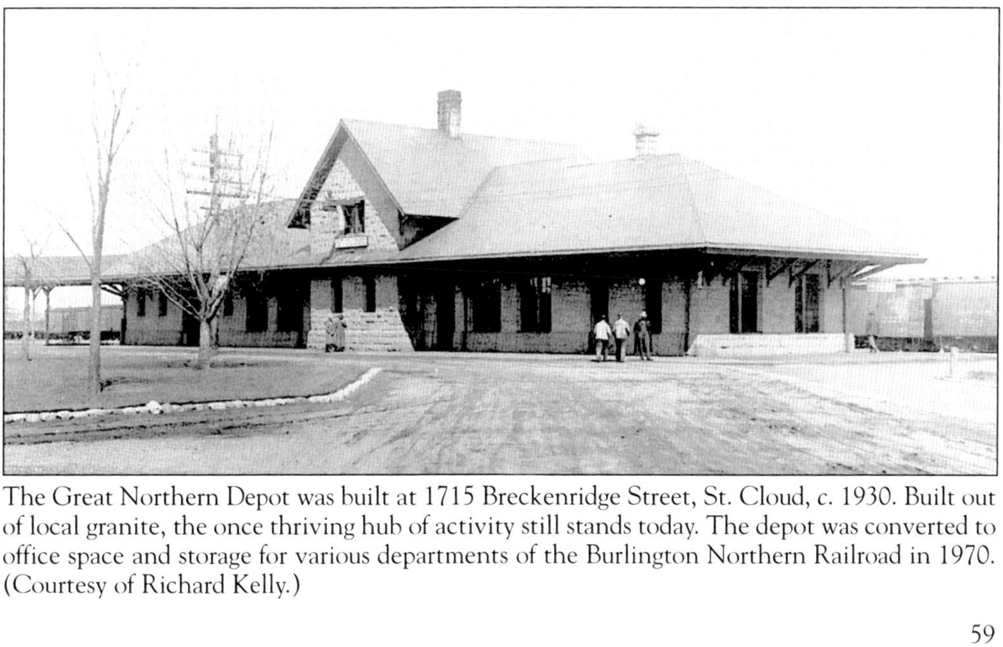

The Great Northern Depot was built at 1715 Breckenridge Street, St. Cloud, c. 1930. Built out of local granite, the once thriving hub of activity still stands today. The depot was converted to office space and storage for various departments of the Burlington Northern Railroad in 1970. (Courtesy of Richard Kelly.)

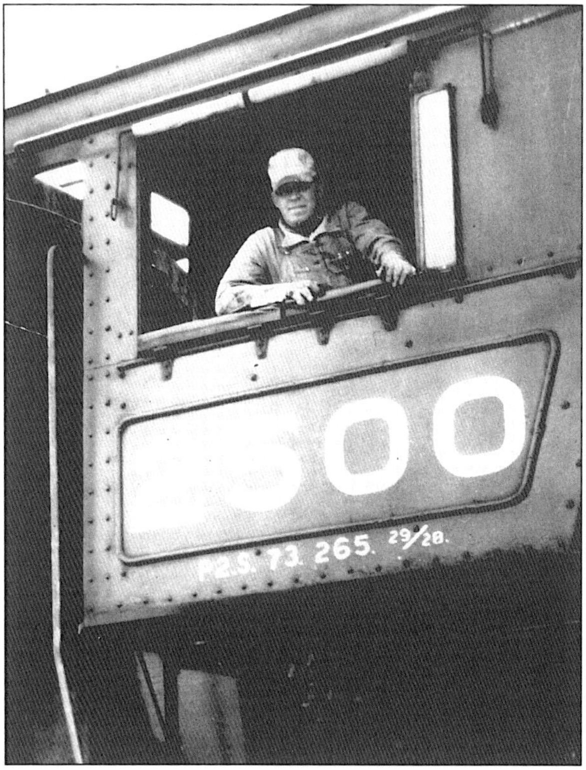

Guy Grafft, an engineer for the Great Northern Railroad, poses in his steam locomotive c. 1941. Grafft ran freight between St. Cloud and Fargo. (Courtesy of Charlie Grafft.)

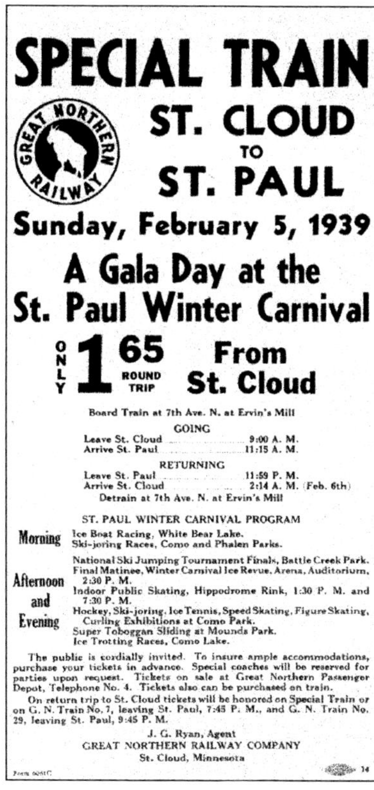


The Great Northern Railway advertised a special train from St. Cloud to St. Paul to attend the St. Paul Winter Carnival in 1936. For $1.65 round trip, Stearns County residents could escape the Depression for a day. (Courtesy of Charlie Grafft.)

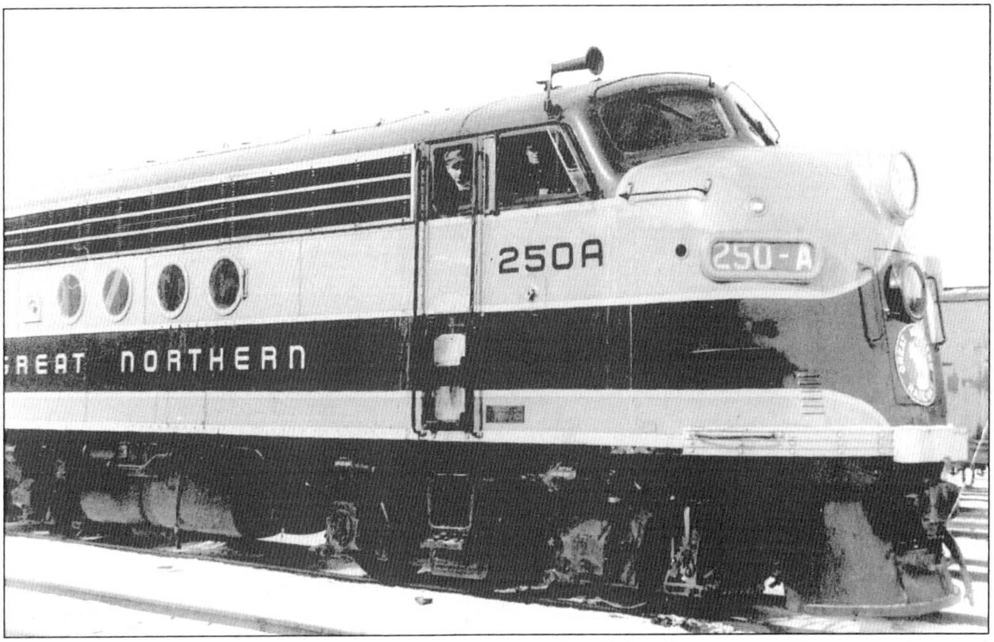

Guy Grafft and Roland Hunter pose in their new diesel freight engine. Hunter had served as Grafft's fireman on the steam engine and was learning how to operate a diesel engine. Diesel had less power than steam so two or three engines were required to haul a freight train. (Courtesy of Charlie Grafft.)

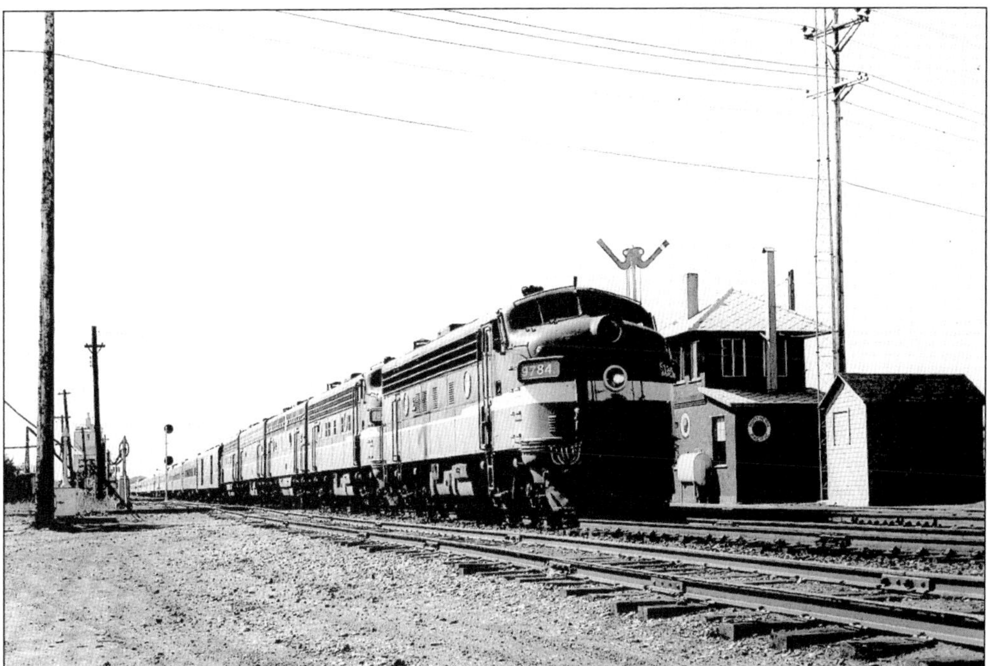

The Great Northern "Main Streeter" is shown crossing at St. Cloud, on June 3, 1971. The normal 6-car configuration of the train has been swollen to 20 cars due to a special sleeper-lounge-diner movement. (Courtesy of Don Hofsommer.)

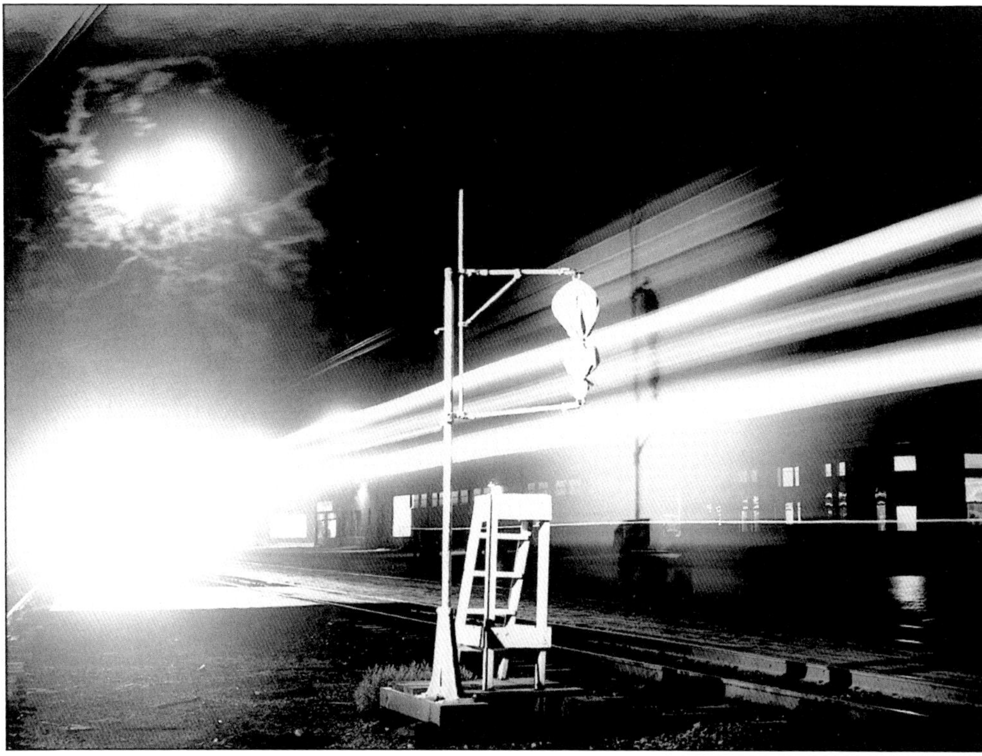

The last operating mail "catch" left in Minnesota is made by the St. Paul and Miles City R.P.O. on the Burlington Northern North Coast Limited, July 1970. This is train #25 at St. Cloud. As the train passed through town at 45 mph, the handler would grab the waiting mailbag a few minutes after 10:00 nightly. (Courtesy of Don Hofsommer.)

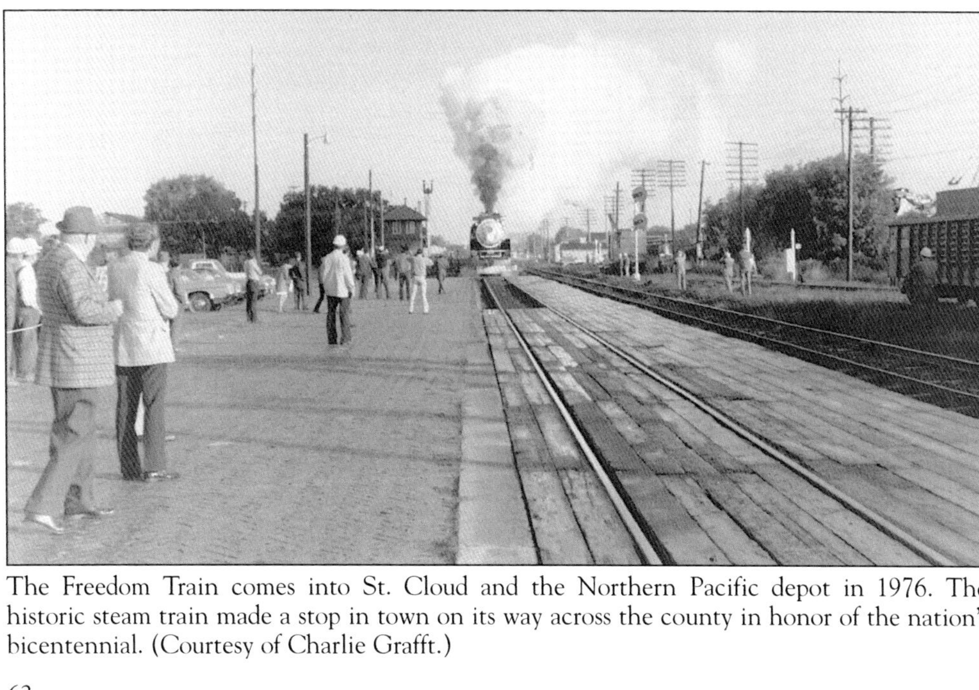

The Freedom Train comes into St. Cloud and the Northern Pacific depot in 1976. The historic steam train made a stop in town on its way across the county in honor of the nation's bicentennial. (Courtesy of Charlie Grafft.)

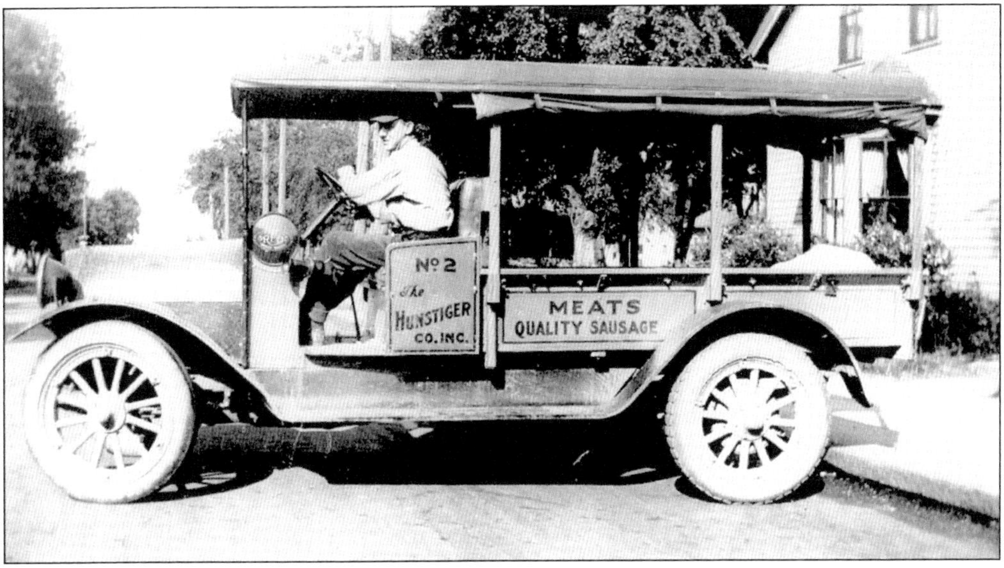


Trucking facilitated the delivery of products to stores and homes. The Hunstiger Company used these trucks to deliver to private homes and businesses. The top photo is dated about 1917 and the bottom photo from 1964. (Courtesy of the Hunstiger family.)

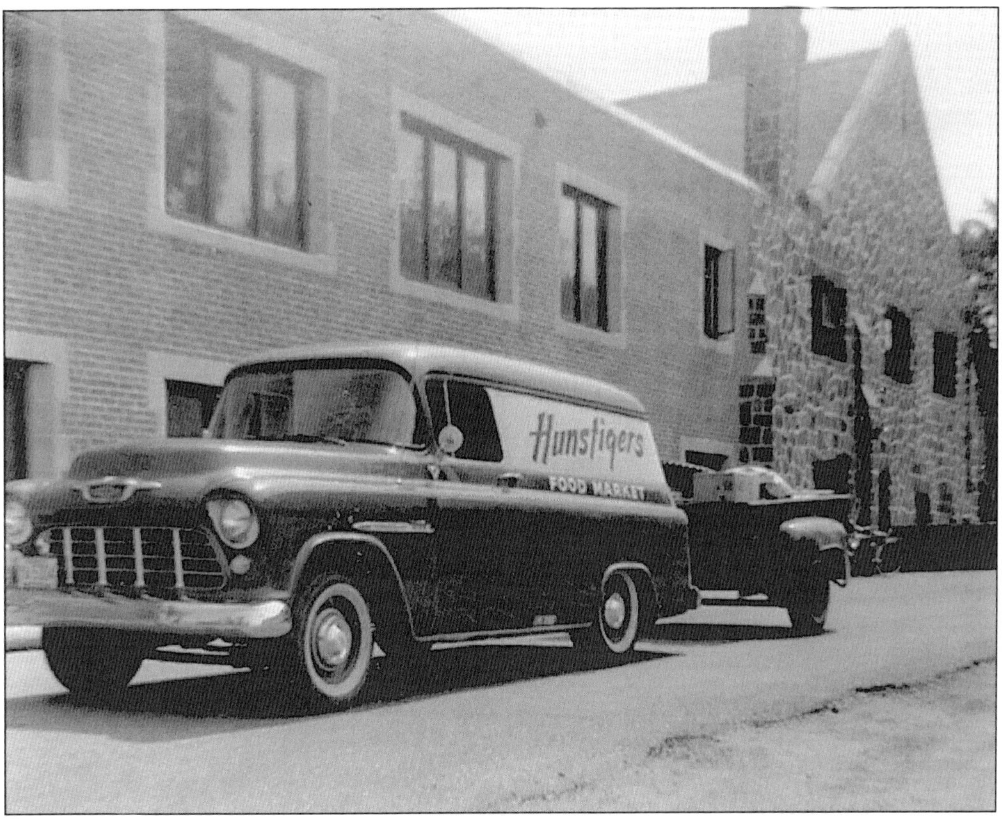

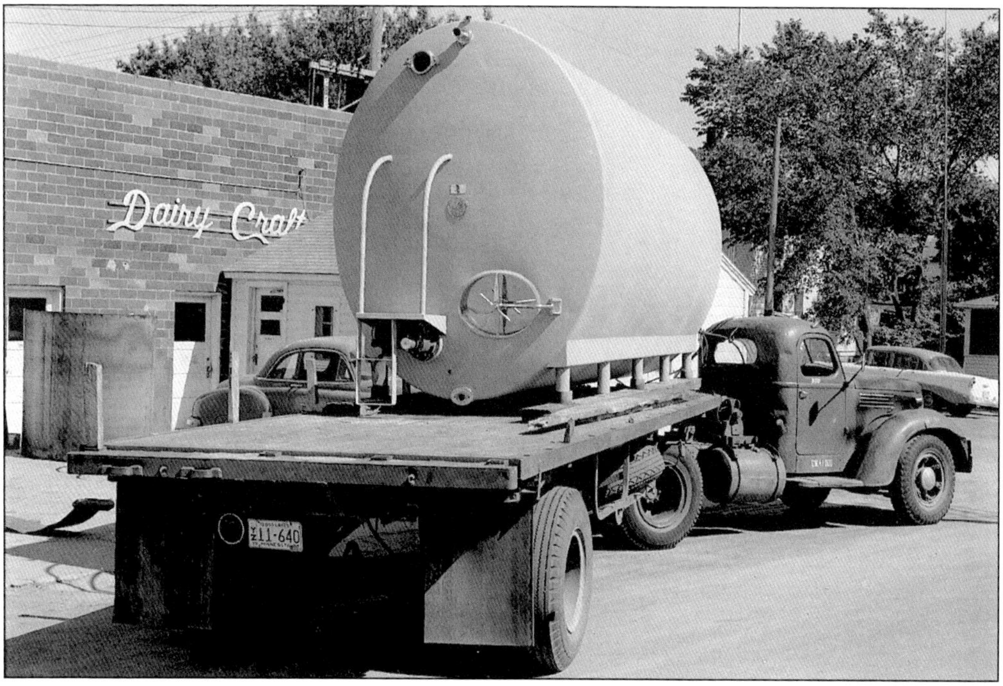


Dairy Craft Industries used large flatbed trucks to haul equipment used in the dairy industry, c. 1955. (Courtesy of the Central Minnesota Historical Center.)

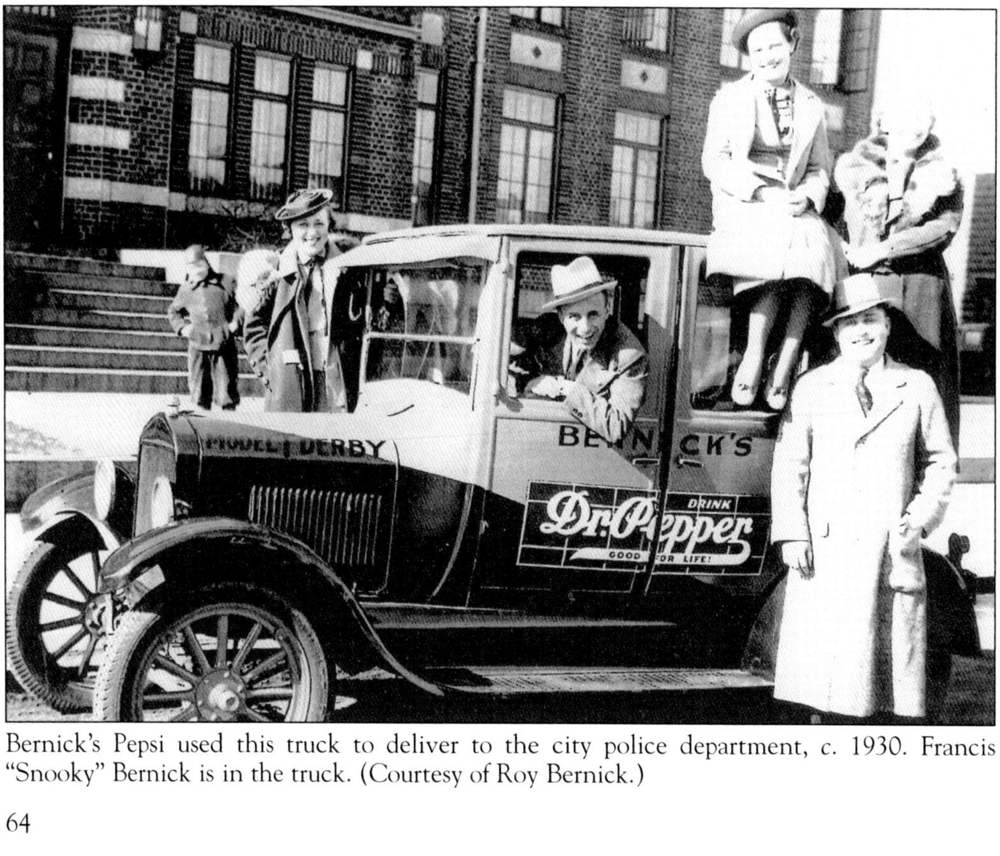


Bernick's Pepsi used this truck to deliver to the city police department, c. 1930. Francis "Snooky" Bernick is in the truck. (Courtesy of Roy Bernick.)

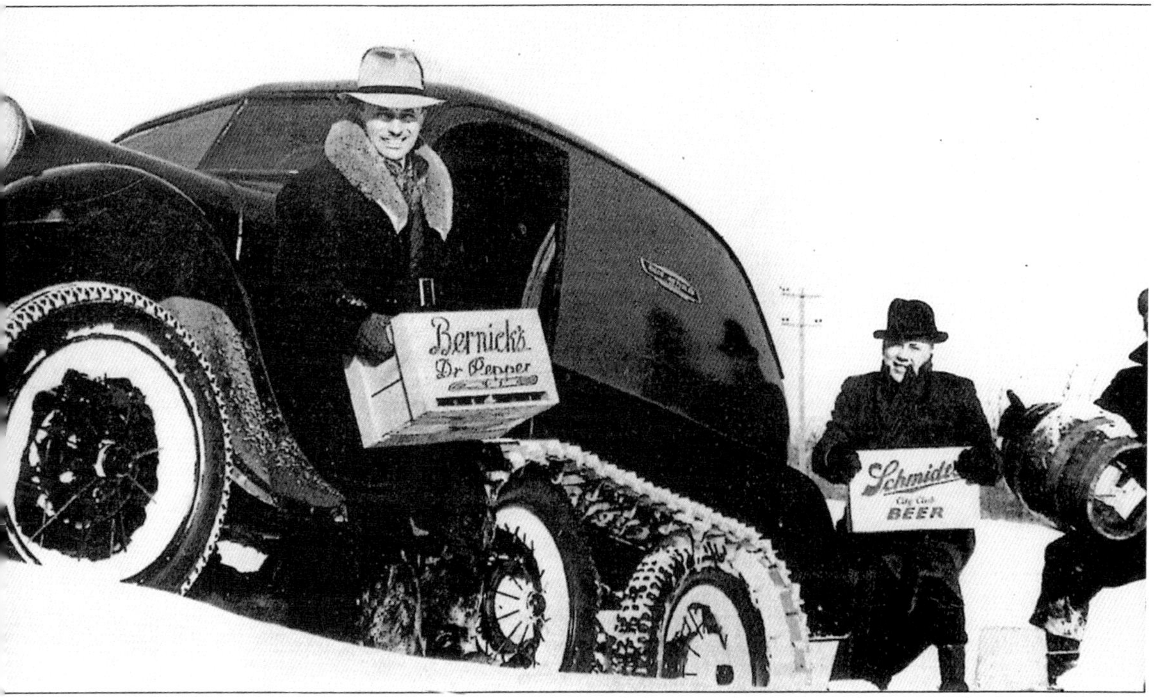


Snooky Bernick carries a case of Dr. Pepper in front of the St. Cloud Bernick's Pepsi plant, c. 1940. Note the special snow treads on the rear of the truck. (Courtesy of Roy Bernick.)

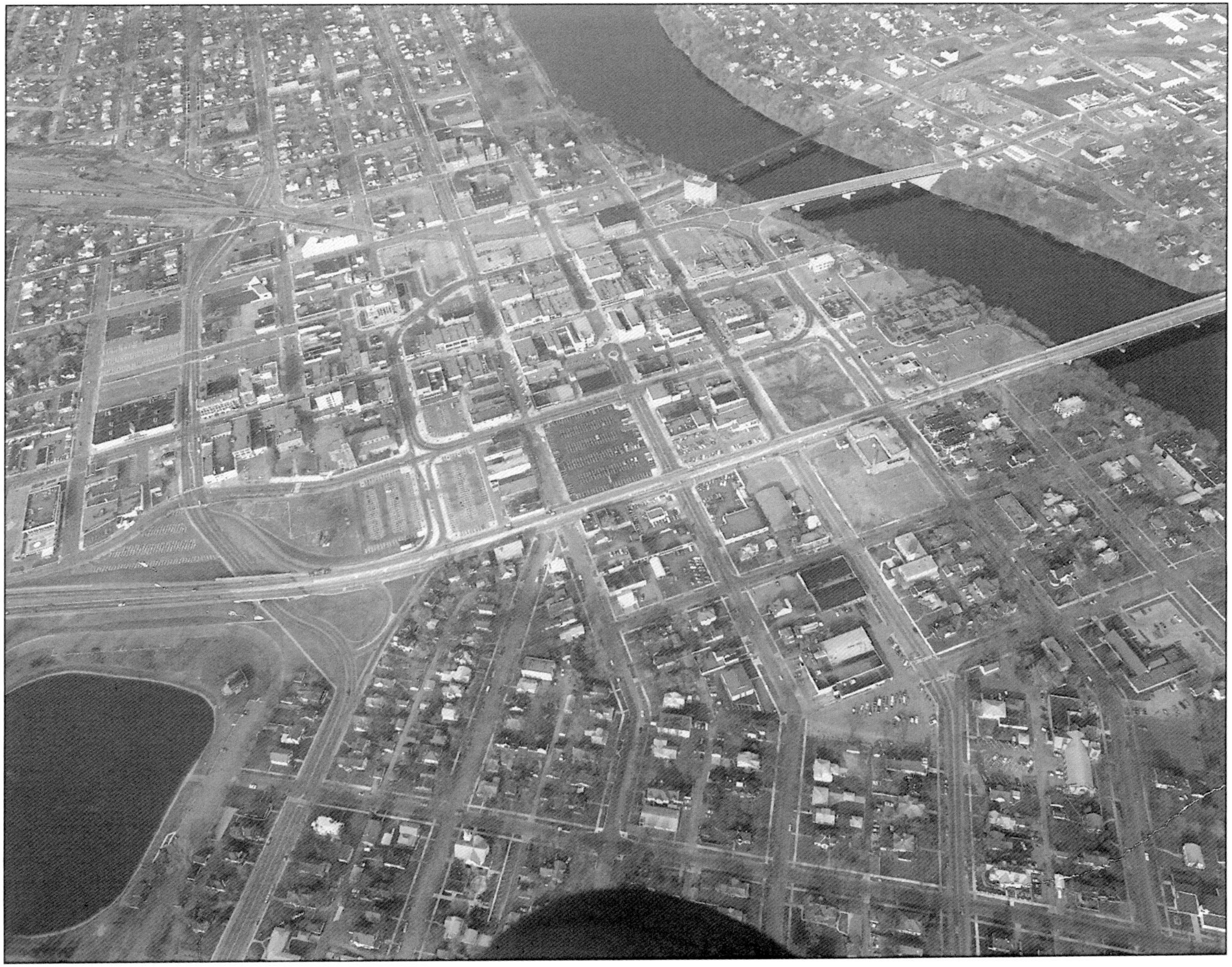

This aerial photo shows the main transportation corridors of St. Cloud in the 1970s. At the top right, the Great Northern Railroad Bridge crosses the Mississippi. Below that are the First Street Bridge and the Division Street Bridge. Division Street (Highway 23) is the main east/west corridor through town. Ninth Avenue on the left provides the main north/south access. The "Ring Road" around downtown, built as part of the 1968 plan, has been removed. (Courtesy of the Hunstiger family.)

# *Five*

# Rest and Relaxation

Many of the smaller cities in Stearns County grew from a new industry in America in the late 19th and early 20th centuries—the leisure industry. Beginning in the 1890s, mechanization and assembly-line production helped reduce the average workweek for manufacturing workers from 66 hours in 1860 to 60 in 1890 and 47 in 1920. These reductions meant not only shorter workdays but also freer weekends. Middle-class, white-collar workers in the cities spent eight to ten hours a day on the job and often worked only half a day or not at all on weekends. Even on farms, mechanization helped to expand free time. To be sure, many had no time for leisure; thousands still spent 12 or 14-hour shifts in steel mills and sweatshops. Nevertheless, more Americans began to have time for a variety of diversions, and for the first time a substantial segment of the economy began providing for—and profiting from—leisure. By the early 1900s, many Americans were enmeshed in the business of play.

Stearns County benefited immensely from this revolution. Stearns County could offer the best of both worlds to American travelers. In St. Cloud they could find a growing urban center, and just miles away in Avon they could find a peaceful rural getaway. For those seeking nature, Stearns County had it all—rolling, wooded hills, tranquil lakes, awe-inspiring plains, granite outcroppings, and the mighty Mississippi River. Resorts could be found throughout the county, at Fairhaven, Avon, Cold Spring, and Collegeville. Today there are over 90 parks in the county covering 1,200 acres, more than 500 lakes and protected wetlands that sport some of the best fishing in the Upper Midwest, 8,000 acres of waterfowl production and hunting areas, more than 40 resorts and campgrounds, more than 10 golf courses, and 2 downhill ski areas.

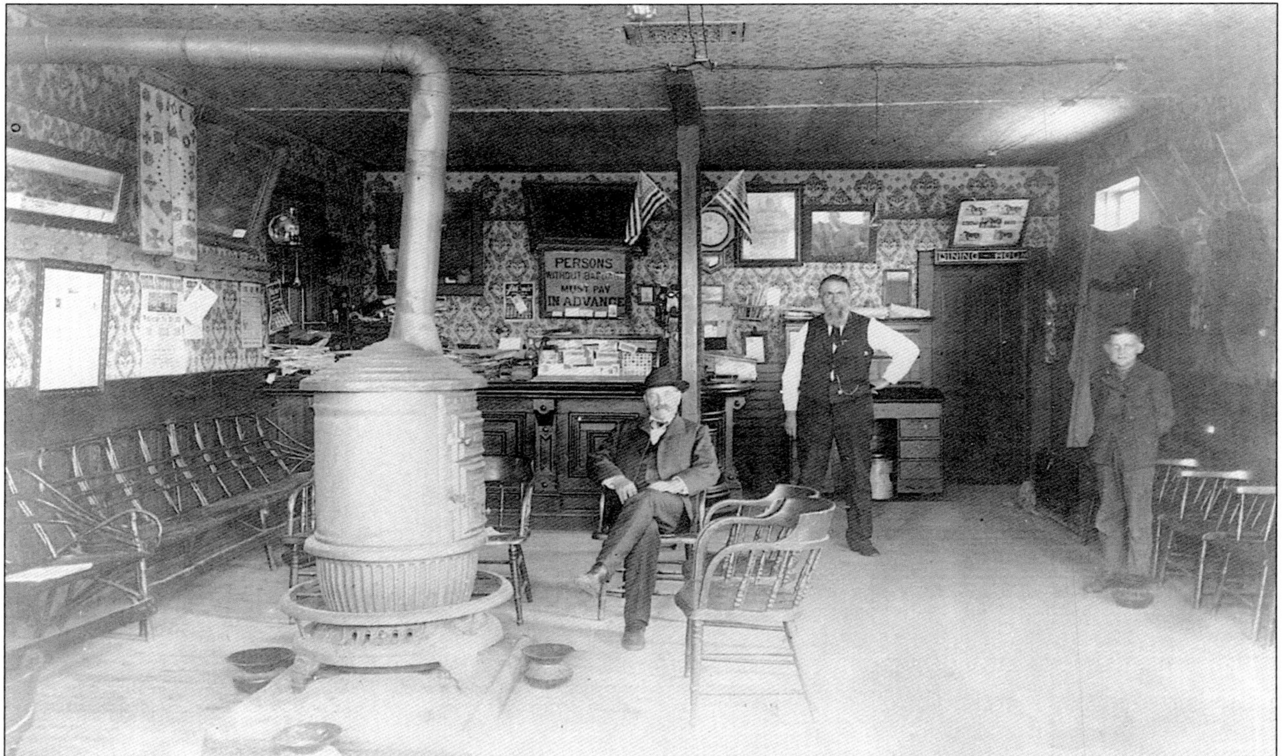


One of the many popular relaxation activities at the turn of the 20th century was a game of checkers around the stove in a hotel lobby. This is the Minnesota House Hotel in St. Cloud, *c.* 1910. (Courtesy of the Central Minnesota Historical Center.)

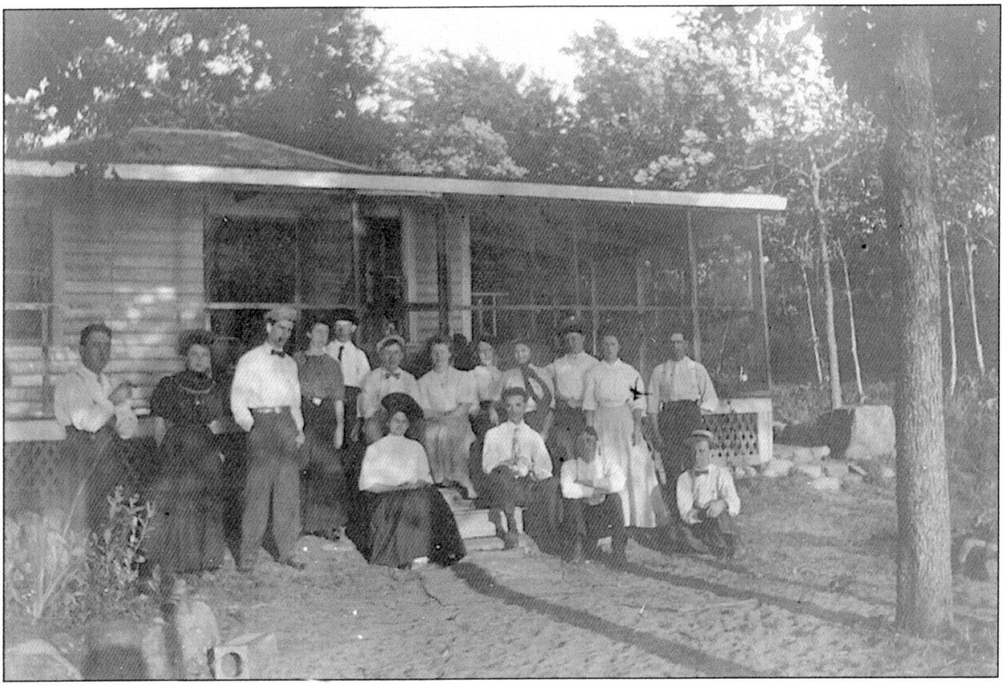

Above is a postcard image of Shady Nook Cottage at Avon on the shores of Upper Spunk Lake, 1907. The woman in the back row marked with the X is named Carolyn. She sent this postcard to her friend Helen McPhail in Everett, Washington. (Courtesy of Richard Kelly.)

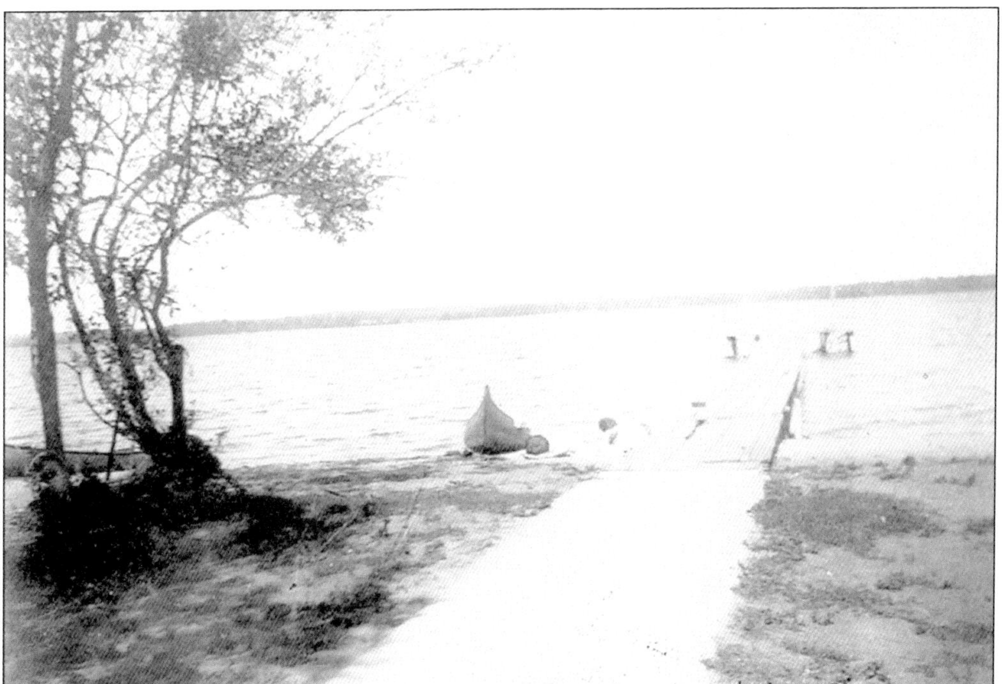

A perfect summer day at Fair Haven, c. 1907. A snooze on the beach finished off a day of canoeing and swimming in the lake. (Courtesy of Richard Kelly.)

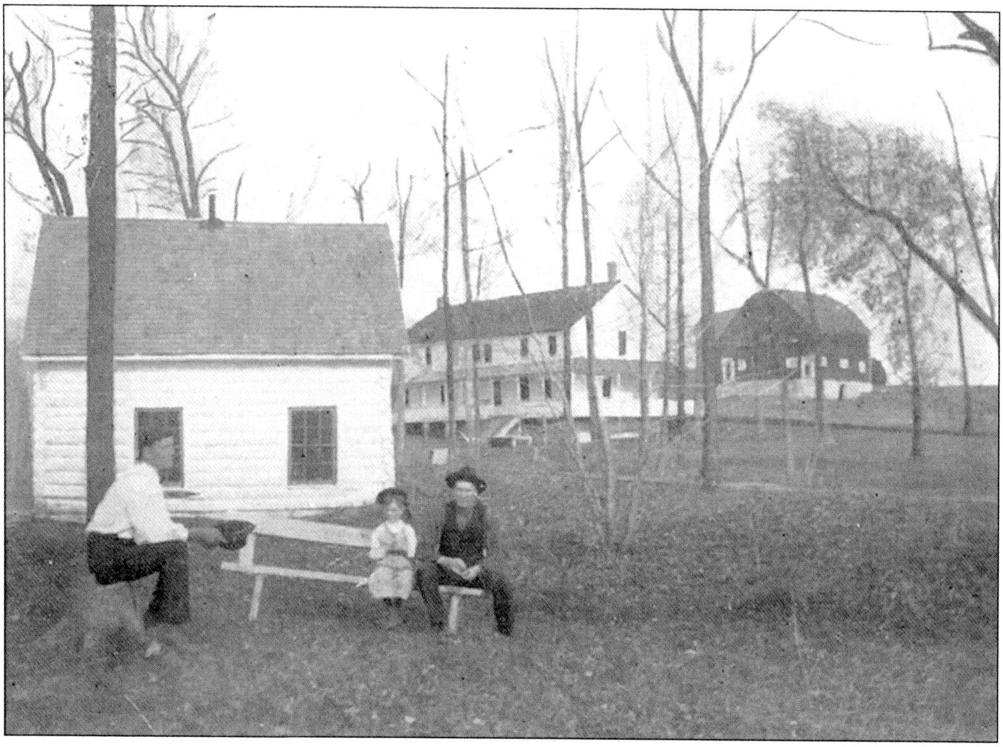

Here are two images of the resort at Fair Haven, 1907. Families could stay in the cottages or in the larger hotel. The family in the top photo had traveled from Valley City, North Dakota, to enjoy the lake. (Courtesy of Richard Kelly.)

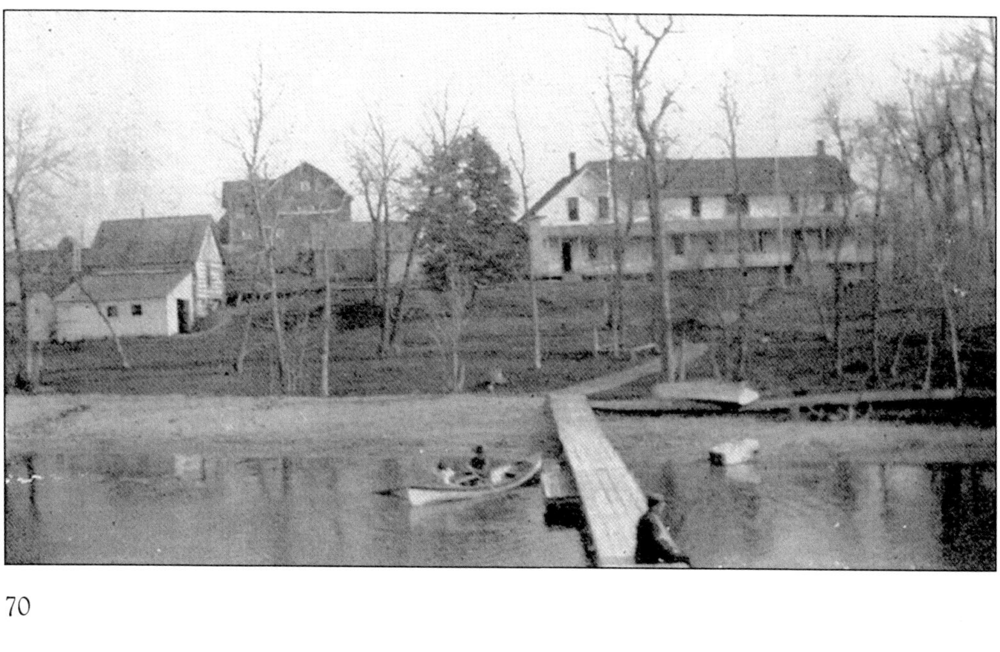

Mathilda and Harry Burns of St. Cloud enjoyed boating on Pearl Lake in 1940. (Courtesy of Jenny Giambruno.)

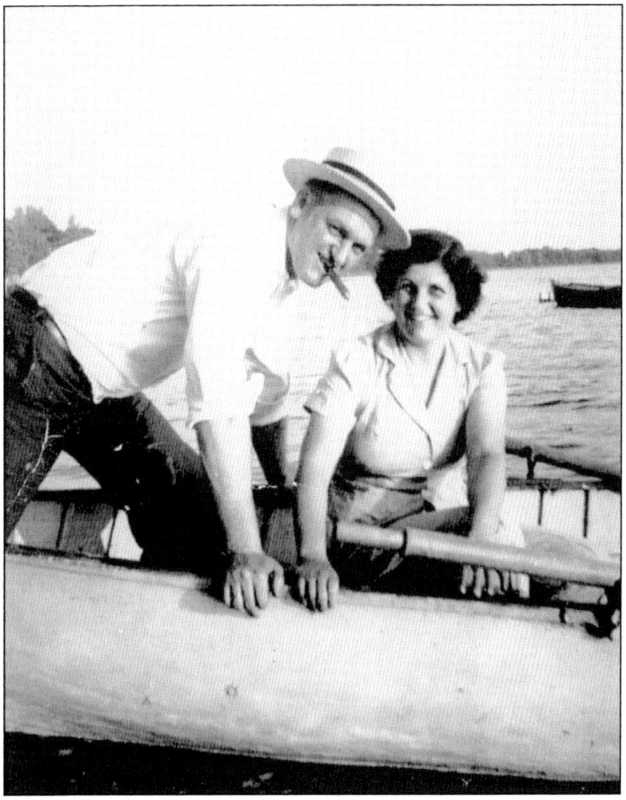

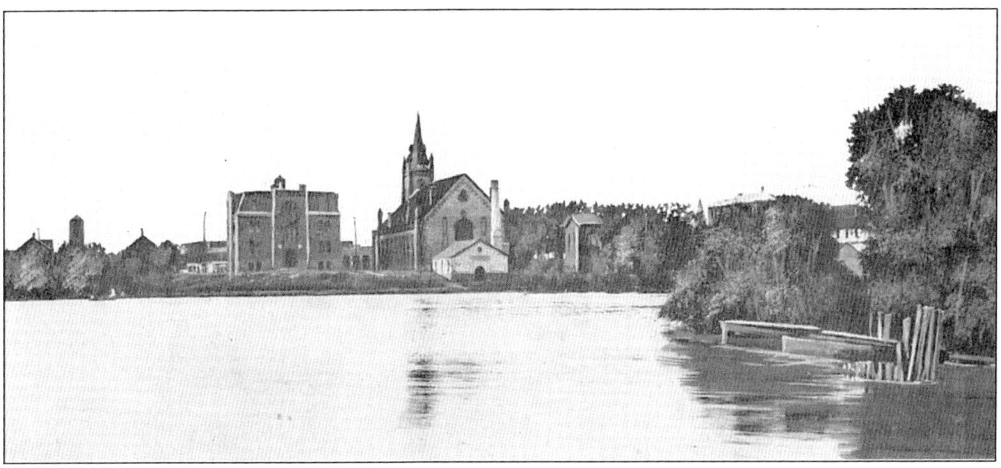

For those unable to leave the city in the summer, a boat ride on Lake George in St. Cloud could help one find some rest and relaxation, c. 1911. The lake continues to be an important recreational asset to St. Cloud. It is open for paddleboats in the summer and ice-skating in the winter. Immaculate Conception Church and St. Mary's School are in the background. (Courtesy of Richard Kelly.)

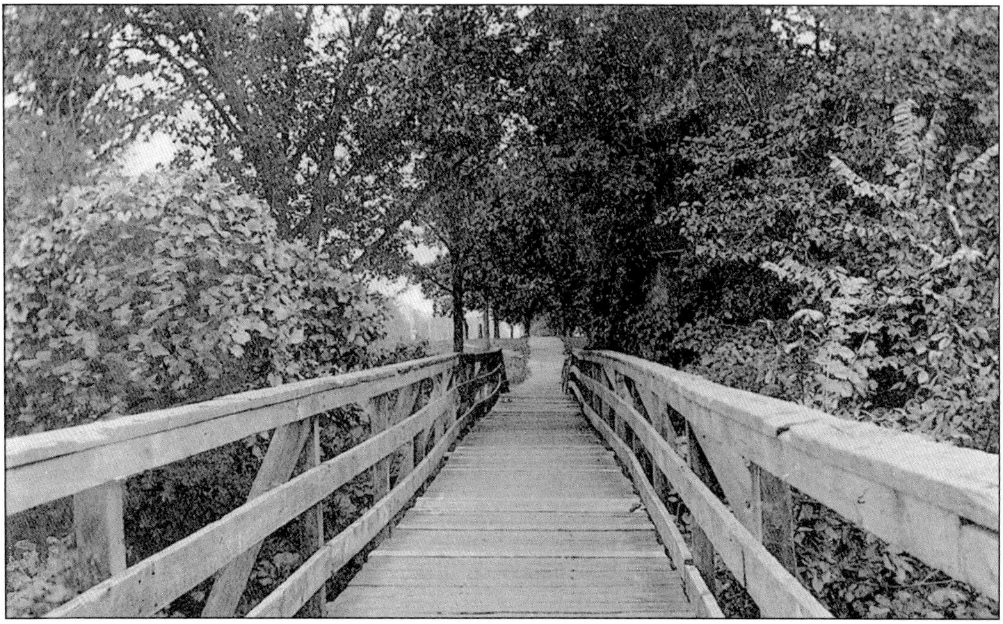

For some Stearns County residents, a stroll across the footbridge "Lover's Lane" in St. Cloud, was recreation enough, *c.* 1910. The bridge crossed a ravine that connected Lake George to the Mississippi River. (Courtesy of Richard Kelly.)

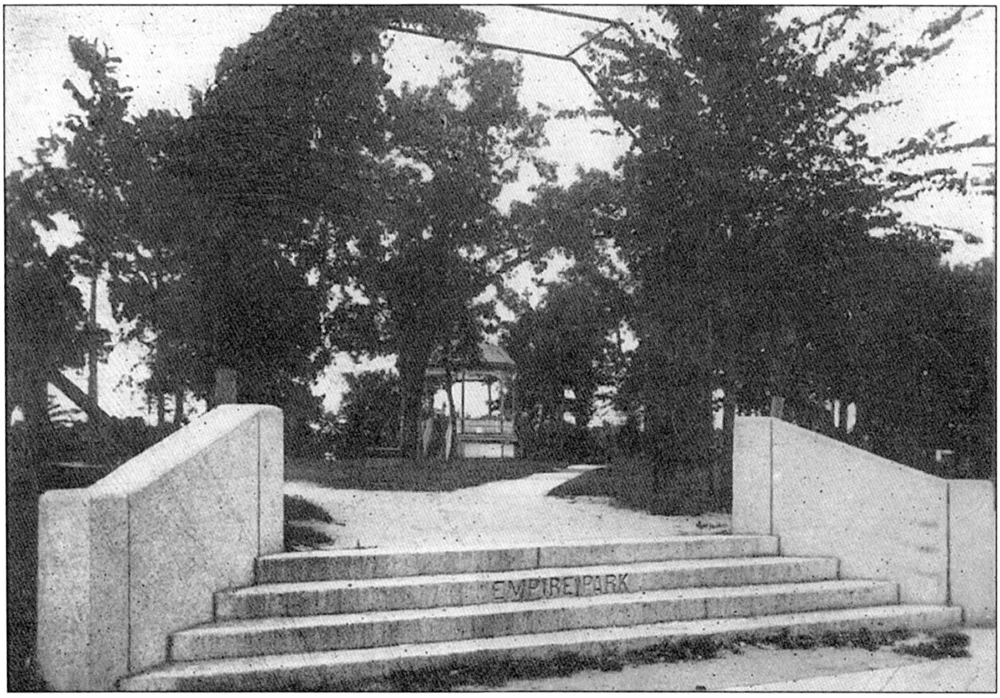


Pictured above are the stairs and bandstand at Empire Park, St. Cloud, 1909. This beautiful park on the shores of the Mississippi has been destroyed and a power substation put in its place. The park provided a lunchtime haven for downtown employees, particularly those working in the Carter building, across the street. (Courtesy of Richard Kelly.)

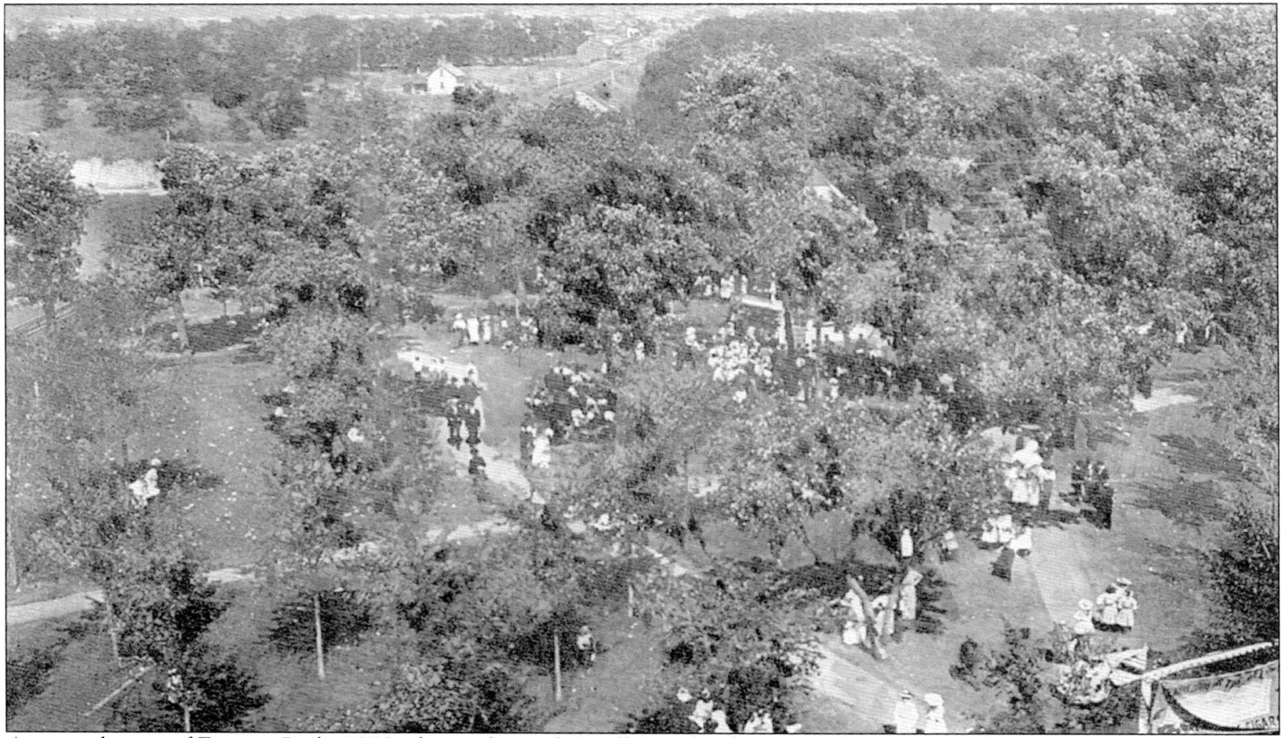

An aerial view of Empire Park, 1908, shows the park in all its splendor as a gathering place for festivals and community picnics. (Courtesy of the Central Minnesota Historical Center.)

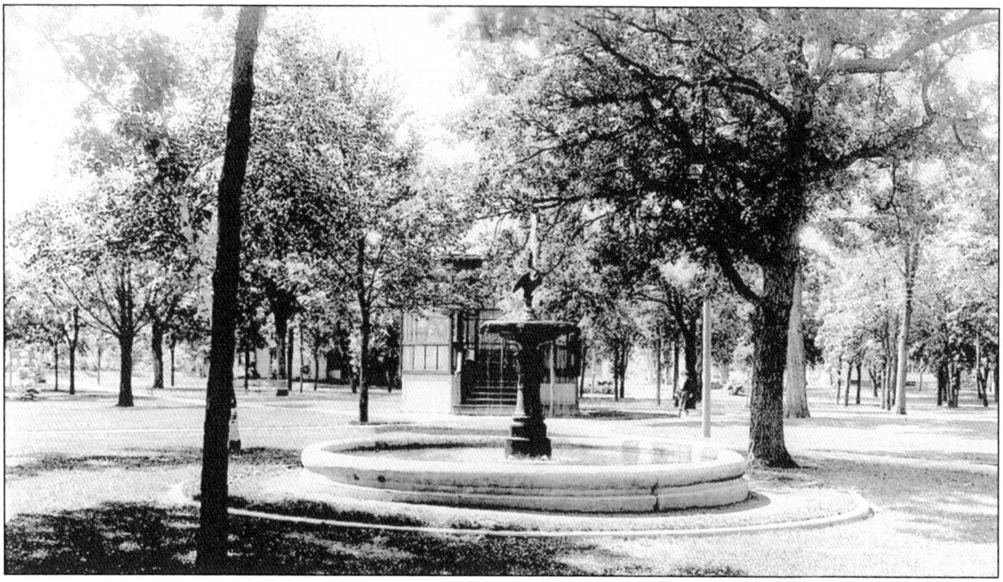

Here are two views of Barden Park, or "Central Park," in St. Cloud. The park was created in 1855 and the city incorporated in 1856. The park was the focal point for gatherings of the Southside neighborhood. (Courtesy of Richard Kelly.)

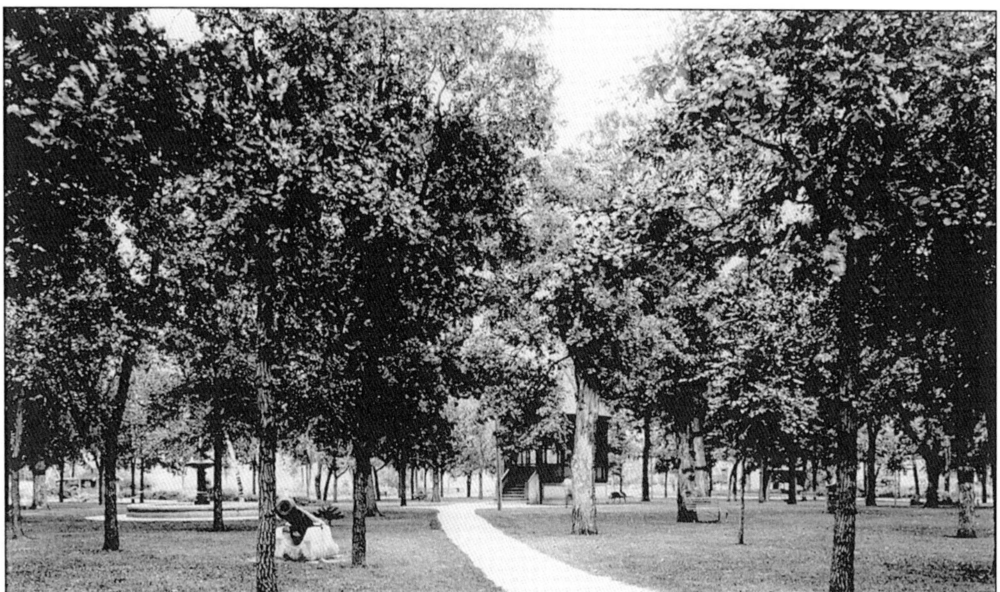

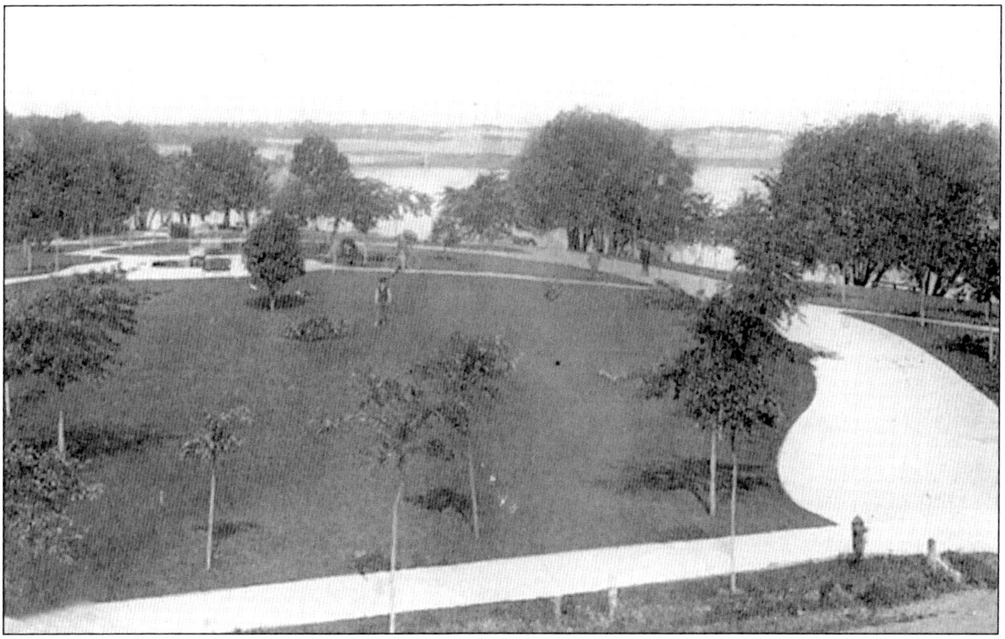

A local dime store paid for this promotional postcard of the city park in Sauk Centre, 1906. (Courtesy of Richard Kelly.)

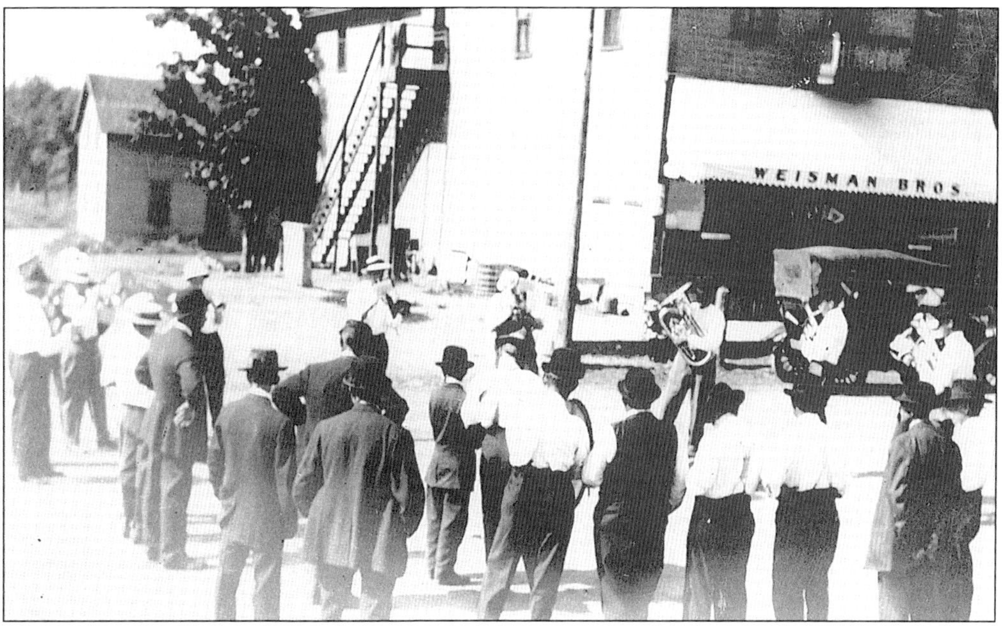


Musicians stop for a musical interlude in front of the Weisman Brothers General Store in Rockville, *c.* 1920. (Courtesy of the Central Minnesota Historical Center.)

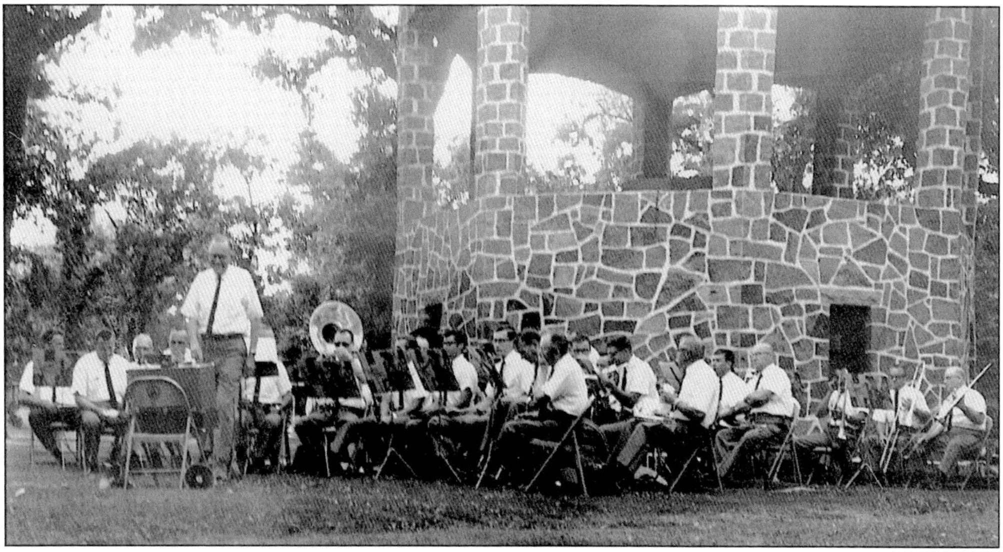

The St. Cloud Area Musicians Union prepares for a concert in Barden Park in 1966. The band made its headquarters in the old Unity Church on Division Street until the building was torn down in 1980. (Courtesy of the Central Minnesota Historical Center.)

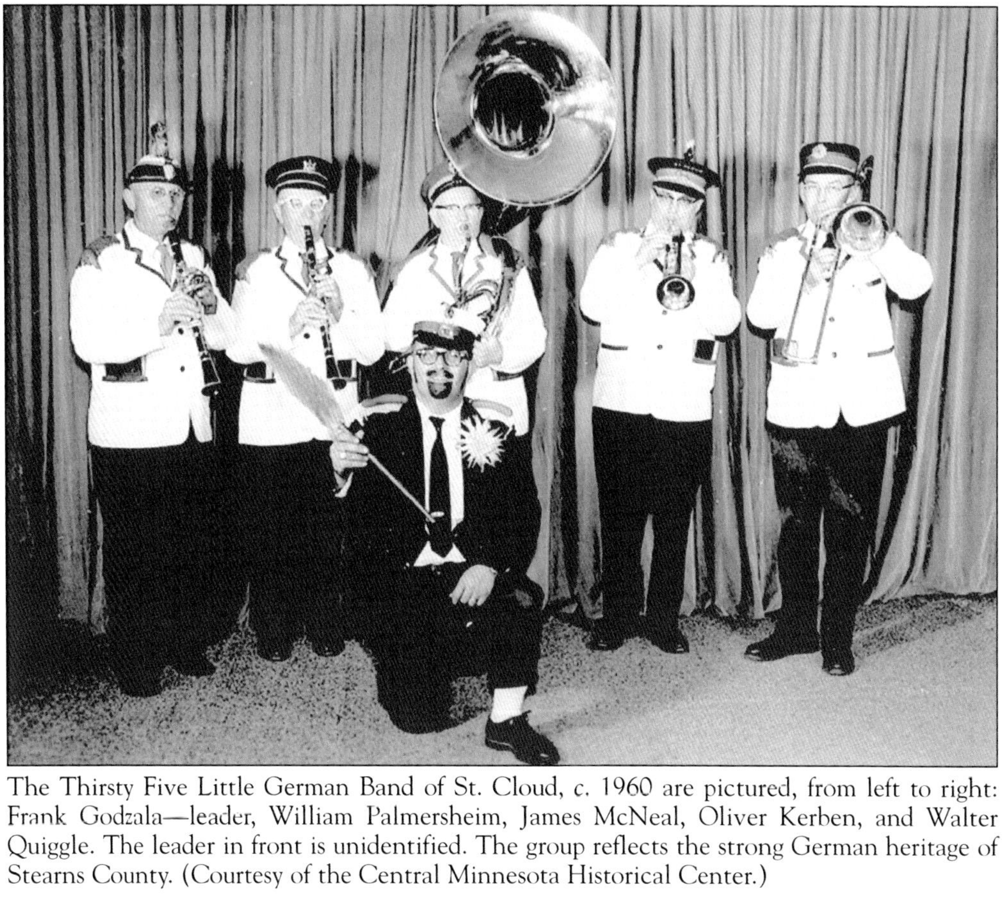

The Thirsty Five Little German Band of St. Cloud, c. 1960 are pictured, from left to right: Frank Godzala—leader, William Palmersheim, James McNeal, Oliver Kerben, and Walter Quiggle. The leader in front is unidentified. The group reflects the strong German heritage of Stearns County. (Courtesy of the Central Minnesota Historical Center.)

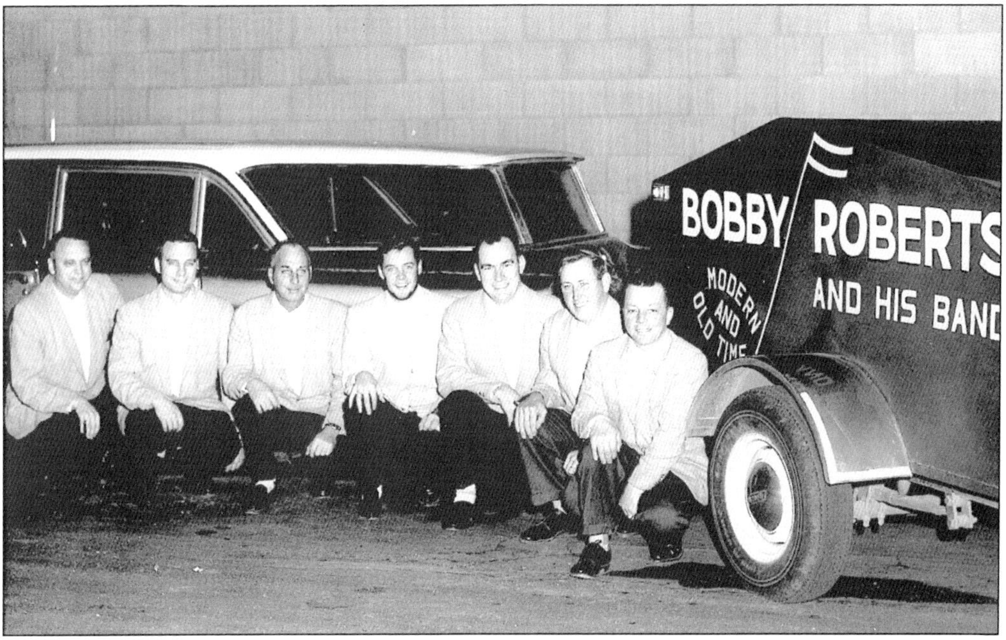


Bobby Roberts and his band performed modern and old time music, c. 1961. They are Don Hall, Gilbert Hall, Percy Parsons, Louis Dinndorf, John Hoffmann, and Robert (Bobby Roberts) Lauer. (Courtesy of the Central Minnesota Historical Center.)

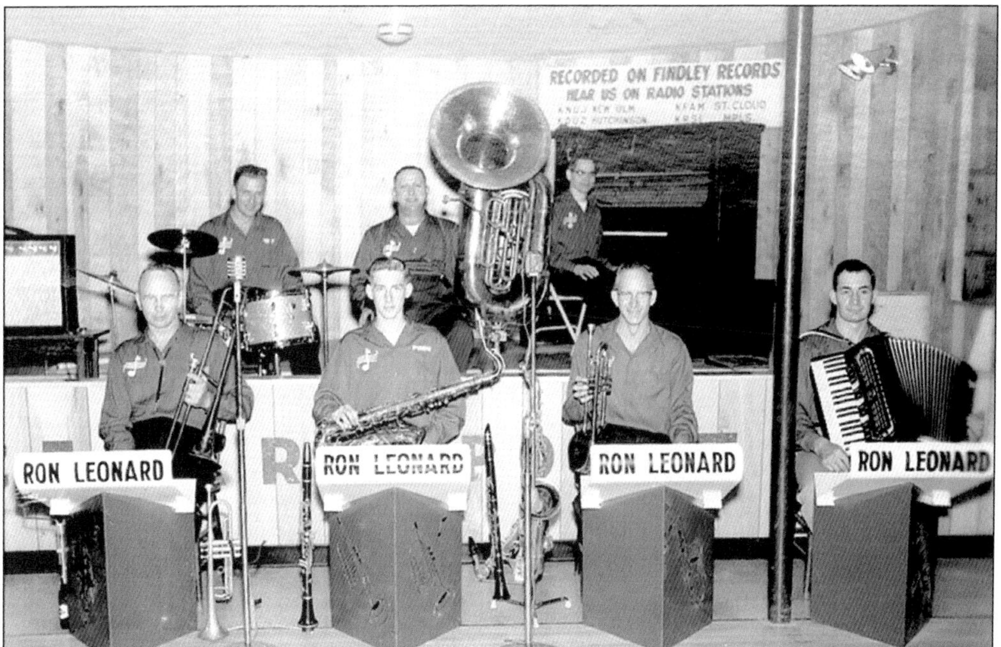


The Ron Leonard Band are pictured above, performing in the early 1960s. (Courtesy of the Central Minnesota Historical Center.)

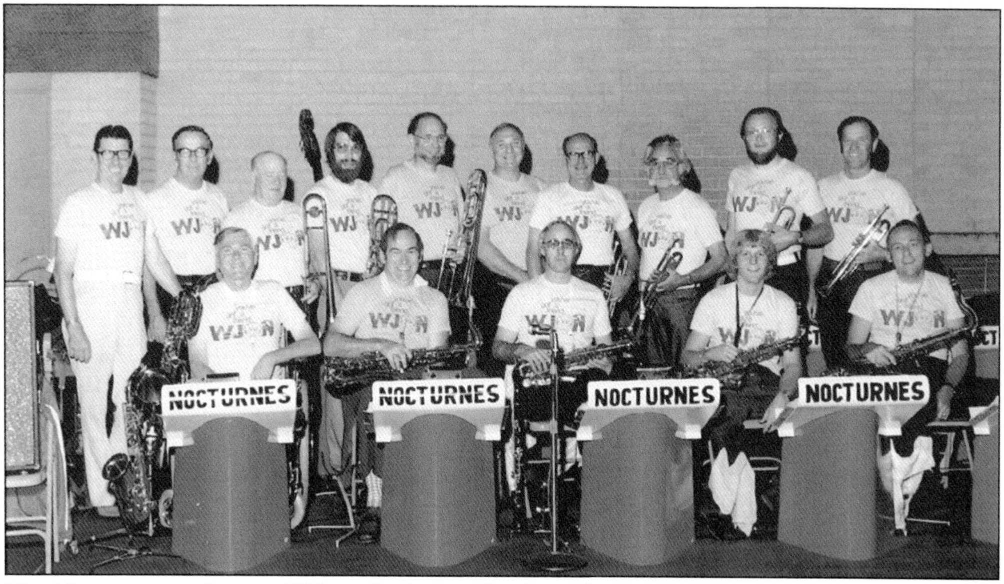


The Nocturnes perform at Wilson Park, St. Cloud, in this 1975 image. Members included Jess Skelton, Walter Quiggle, Archie Seguin, John Froelich, Kenton Frohrip, Harold Bach, Tom Meyer, Andy Vavricka, Allen Bachelder, Math Mimbach, William Bach, Louie Dinndorf, Donald Anderson, Robert Bach, and Harold Dinndorf. (Courtesy of the Central Minnesota Historical Center.)

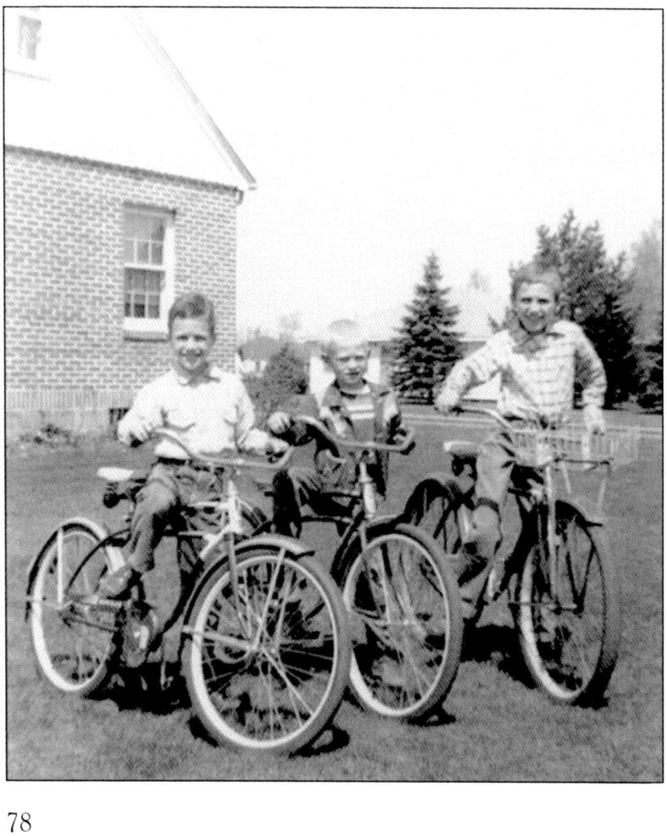

Summertime brought the Brixius children and their friends out for bicycle rides in St. Cloud. From left to right: Andrew, Phillip Gardner, and Albert A., c. 1957. (Courtesy of Kari Brixius.)

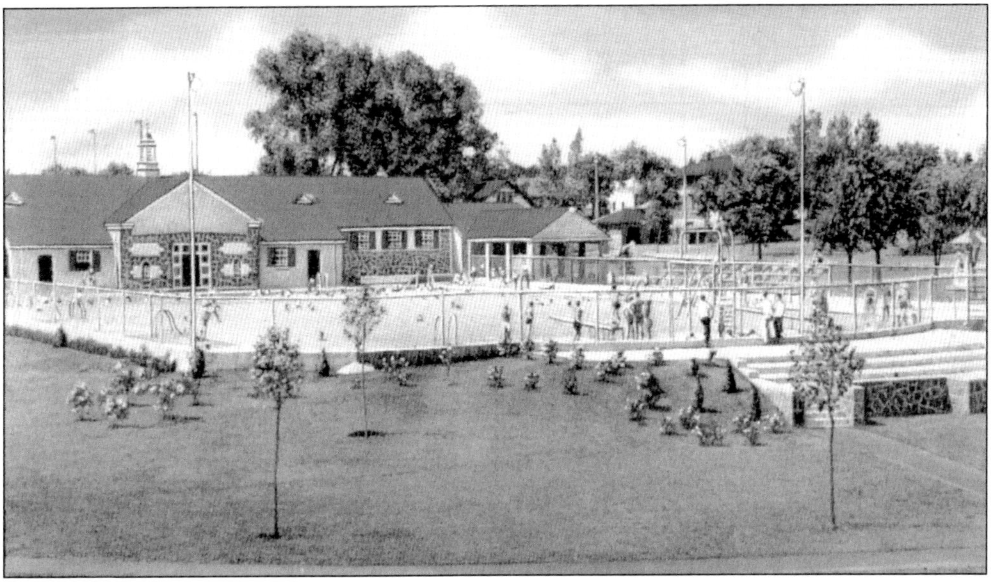

Summertime also marked the opening of the municipal swimming pool at St. Cloud, built in 1945 on the shores of Lake George. (Courtesy of the Central Minnesota Historical Center.)

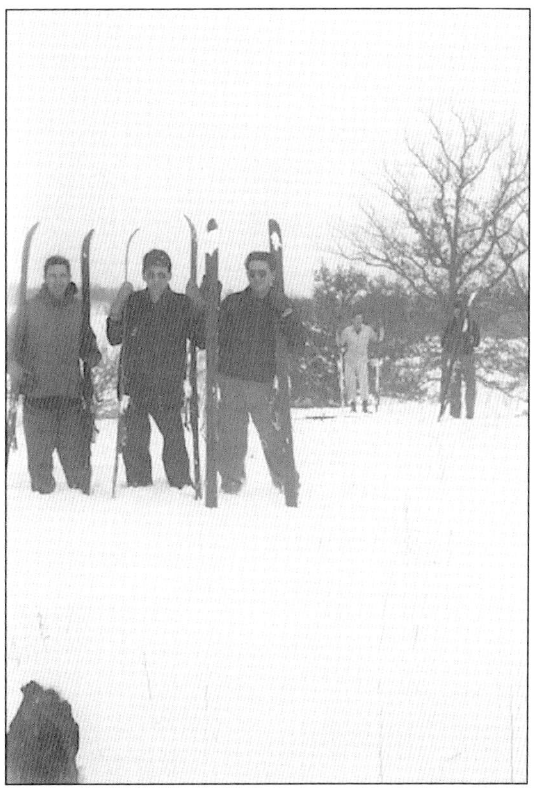

Stearns County residents are not deterred by the weather from enjoying the outdoors. Bruts Welsch, Tom Hunstiger, and Juan Gonzalez, St. John's University classmates, enjoy cross-country skiing in 1945. (Courtesy of the Hunstiger family.)

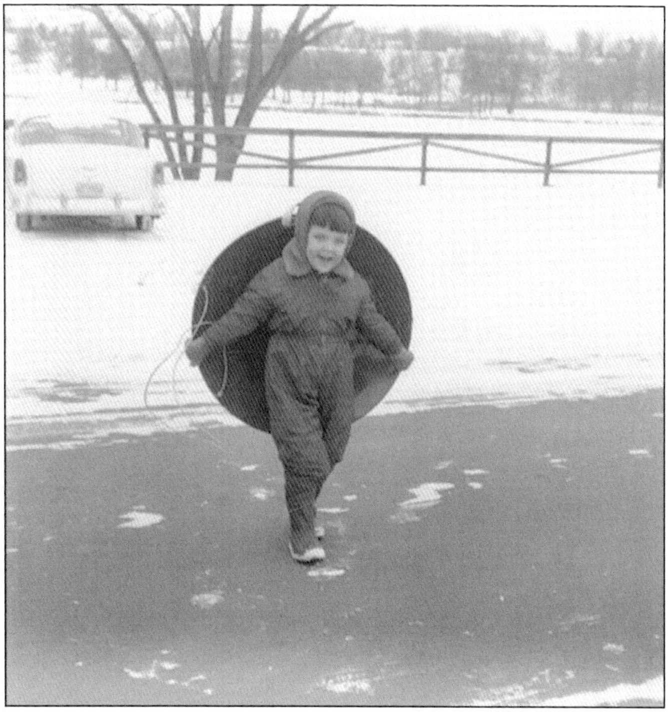

Little ones could also enjoy winter recreation. Terry Rawlings carries her sliding saucer in 1957. (Courtesy of Jenny Giambruno.)

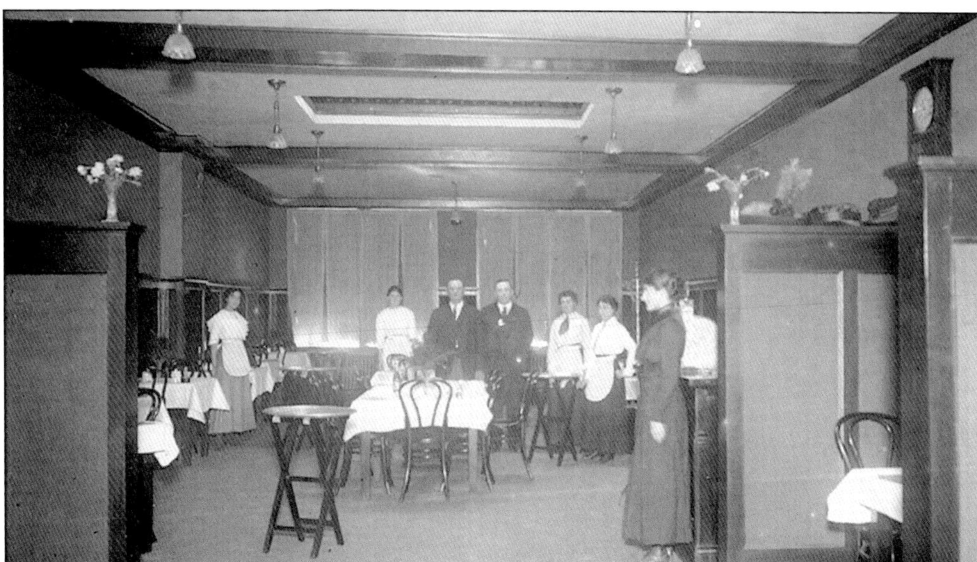

J.P. Wagner ran a second-floor eatery out of his building at 715 St. Germain Street. According to city directories, it was only in business in 1914. The building now houses McRudy's Pub. (Courtesy of Richard Kelly.)

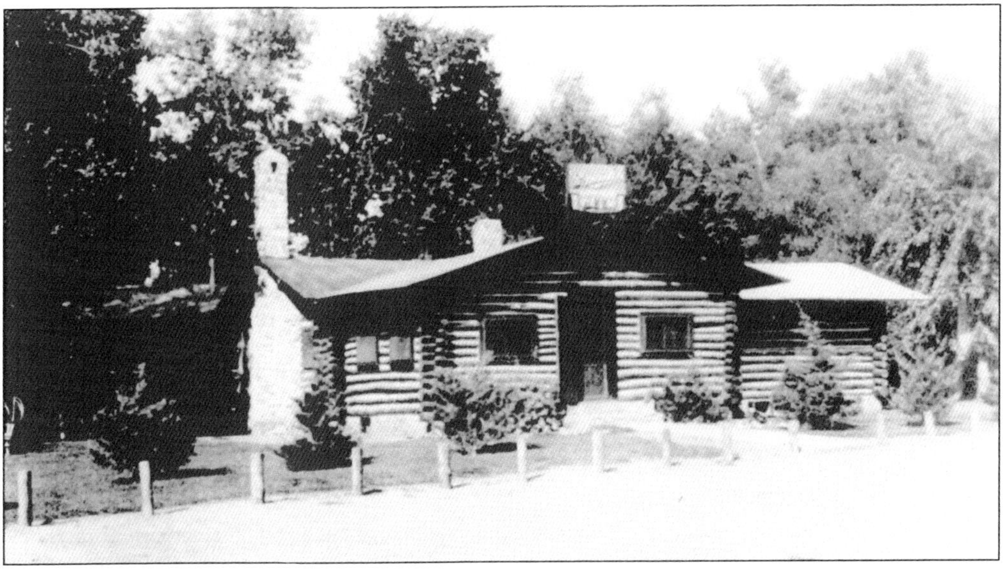

Prohibition did not deter Stearns County residents from the occasional nip. In the 1920s, Brickey's, a speakeasy on the Sauk River in Waite Park, openly flaunted the law. The facility housed both a restaurant and cabins. It was purchased in 1974 by Anton and Lorraine Gaetz who continue to operate Anton's Restaurant with their children. (Courtesy of the Gaetz family.)

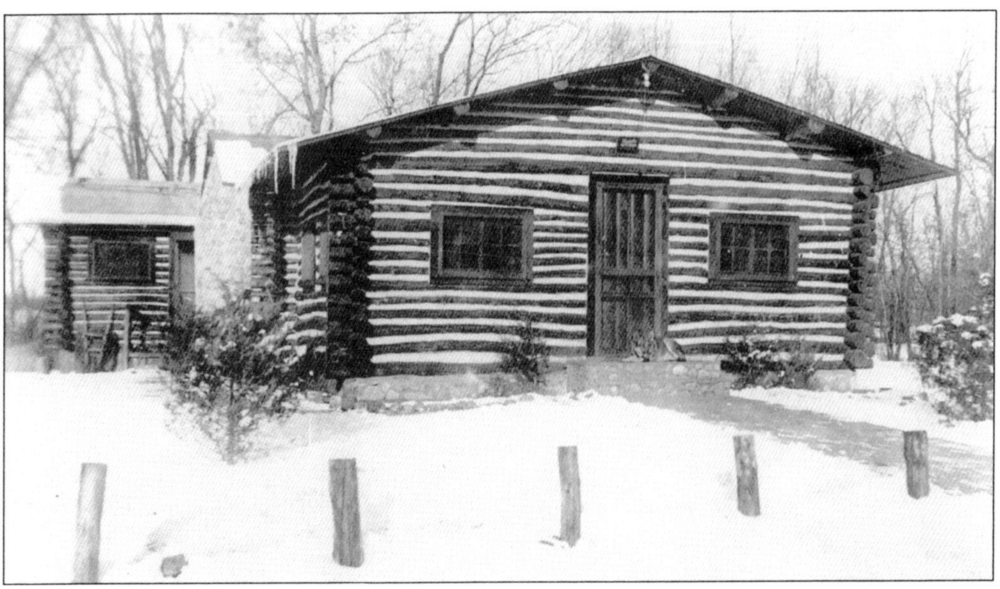

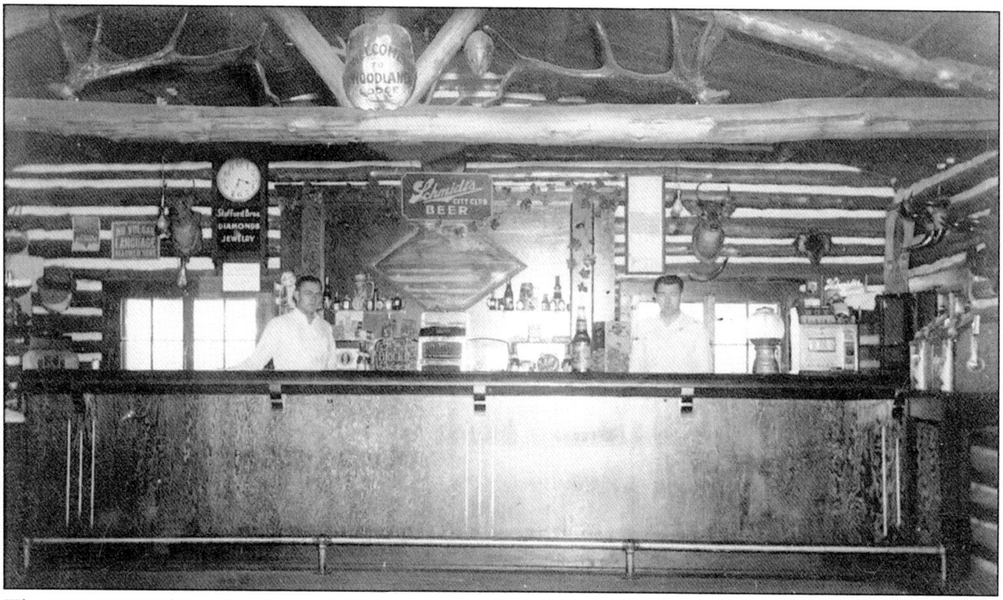


The interior of Brickey's shows the bar and the strong western motif. (Courtesy of the Gaetz family.)

O'Hara Brothers' Brew Pub and Restaurant on Third Street North, St. Cloud looked very different in 1958 when it was known as Sid and Cecil's Little City. Sid and Cecil O'Hara set up shop in 1945 selling groceries, 3.2% beer, hot beef sandwiches, and Polish sausage. Sid's sons, Tim and Mick, bought the business in 1978 and opened the O'Hara Brothers' Pub and Restaurant. They added a brewery in 1996. (Courtesy of Tim O'Hara.)

The Wagon Wheel Nite Club on Highway 52, 3 miles west of St. Cloud, c. 1950, offered "fine liquors, sizzling steaks, chicken dinners and an orchestra every night." (Courtesy of the Central Minnesota Historical Center.)

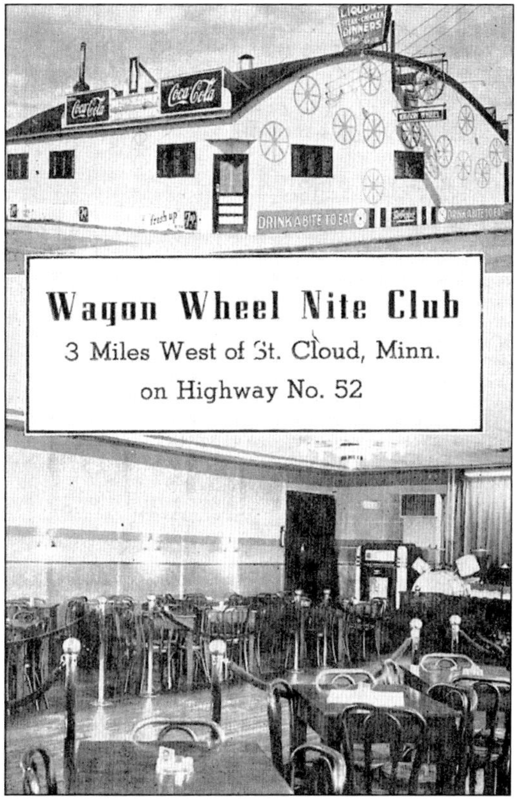


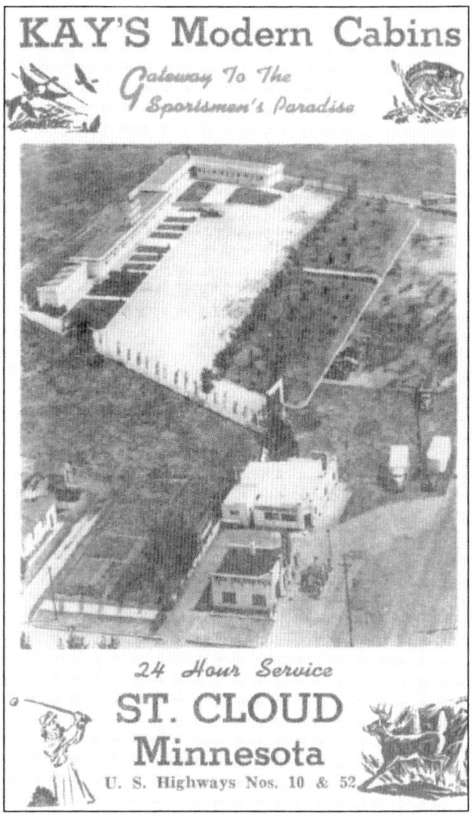


Kay's Modern Cabins located on Lincoln Avenue Southeast at the junction of Highways 10 and 52 in 1950, sold itself as the "Gateway to the Sportsmen's Paradise." The facilities included a 23-room, air-conditioned and heated auto court with private rest rooms and showers. A trailer camp, Skelly Service and Restaurant were also connected to the court. It clearly catered to the post-war auto age. (Courtesy of Richard Kelly.)

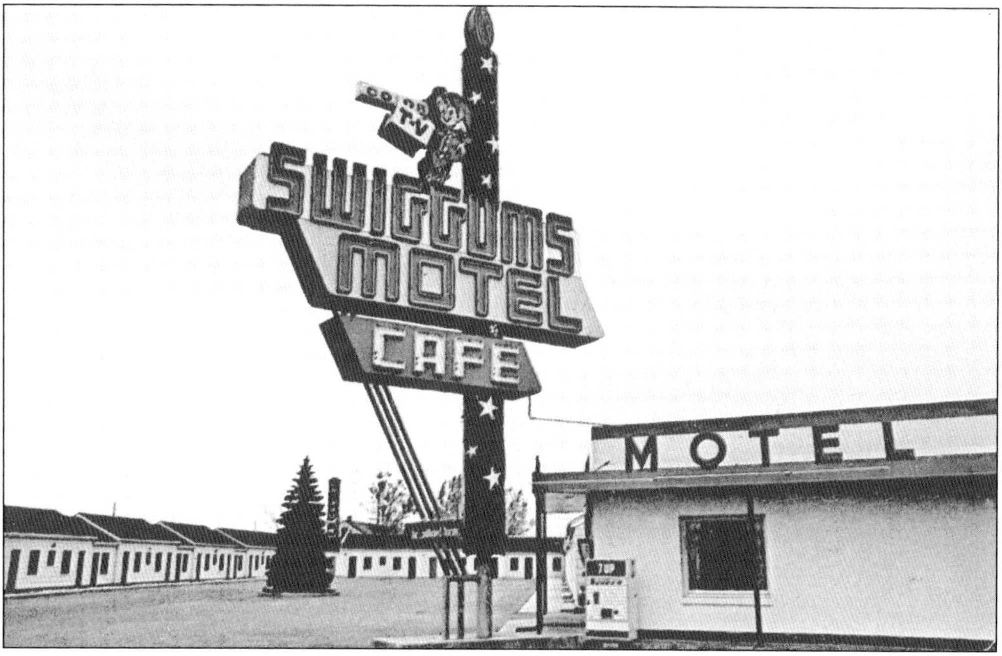


In 1950, Justin, Bernard, and Palmer Swiggum of Madison, MN, purchased the Fred May Be Inn property on Division Street, St. Cloud, and opened Swiggums Motel and Café. The motel offered hot water heat in a tub and shower, carpeted rooms, and color T.V. Charles Kirby bought the property in 1966 and it was torn down in 1989. (Courtesy of Richard Kelly.)

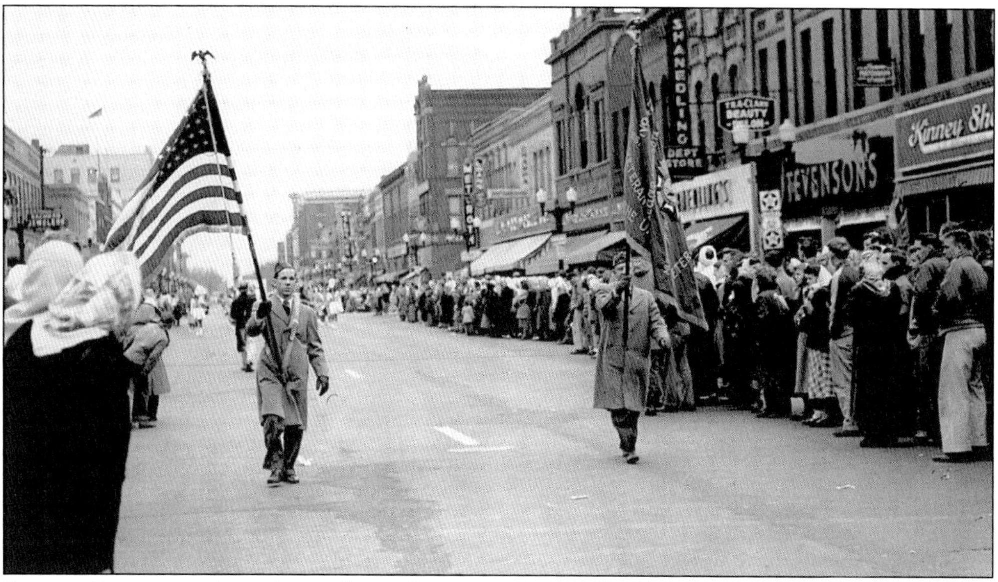


Stearns County residents have always been patriotic and willing to serve their country. They were among the first volunteers to fight in both the Civil War and the Spanish-American War. Residents honor veterans in this Veterans Day parade in St. Cloud, c. 1945. This picture shows the parade headed east down St. Germain Street. (Courtesy of Richard Kelly.)

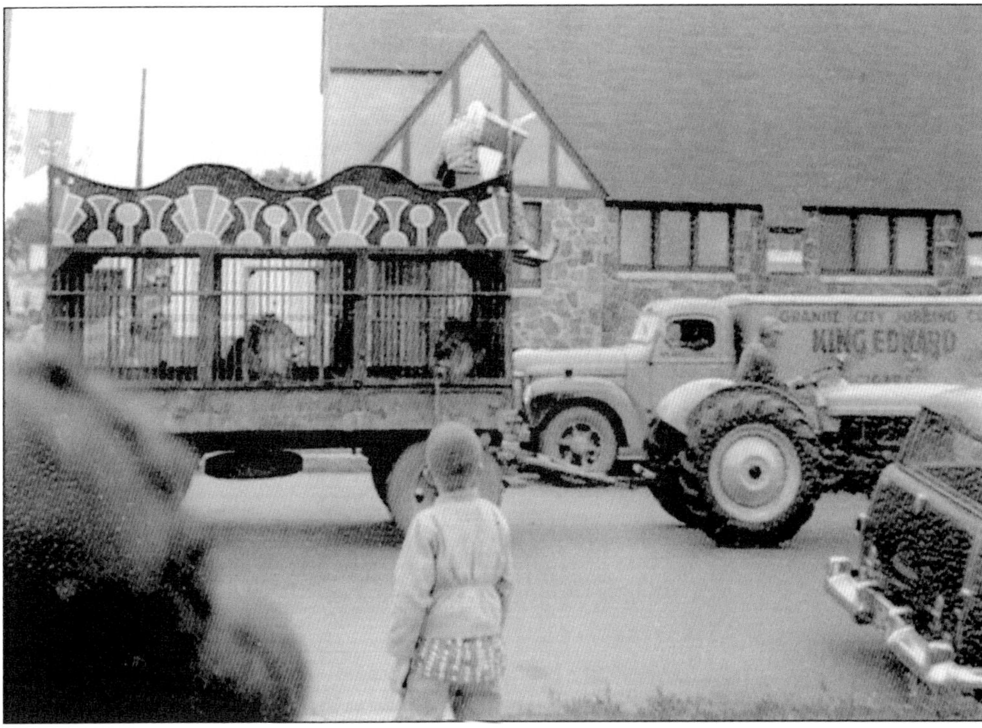


These images show the circus in St. Cloud, 1954. The parade marched down Third Street with the elephants marching tail to trunk and the lions in their cage. (Courtesy of Kari Brixius.)

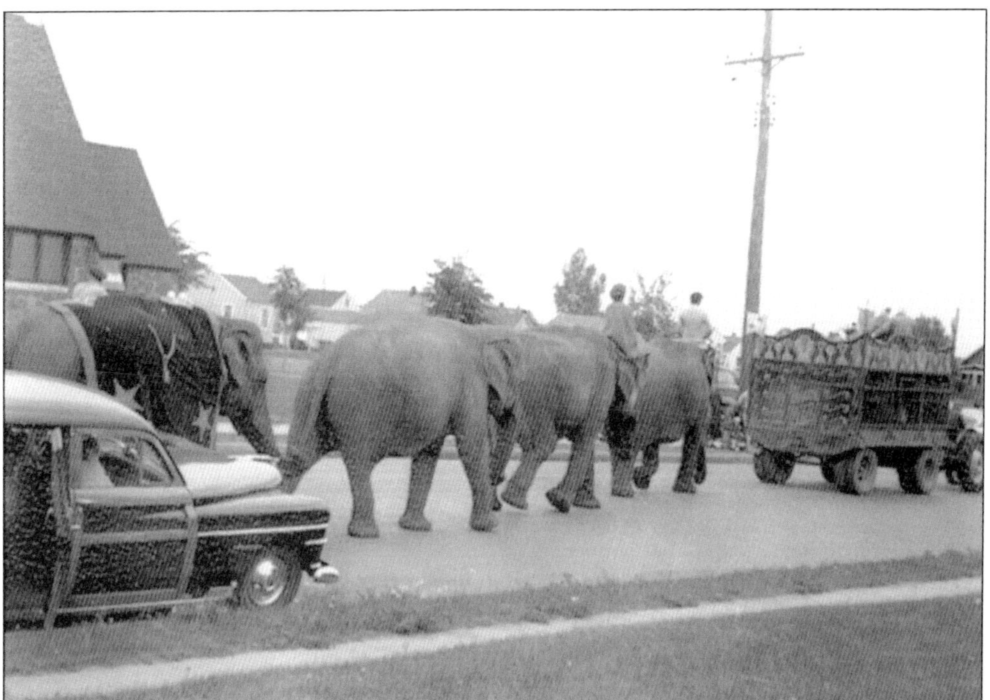

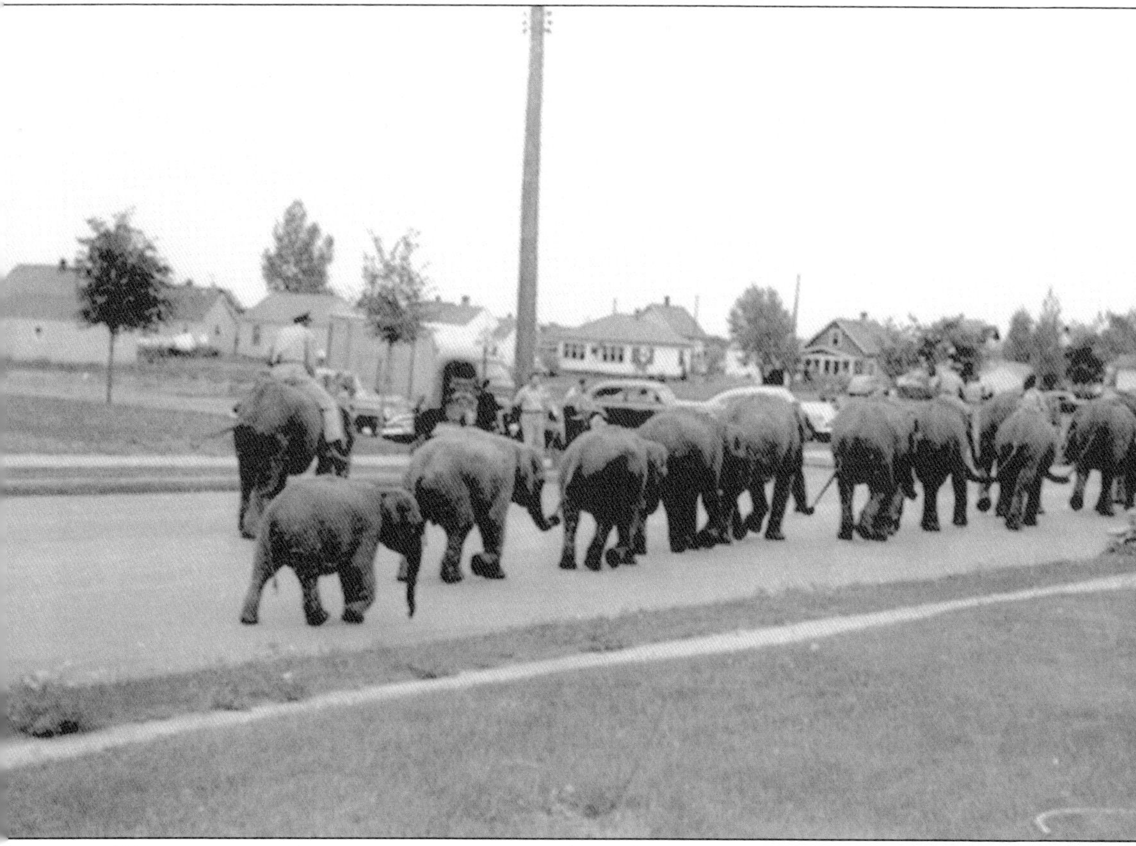

The circus parade comes to an end and residents return to their homes. (Courtesy of Kari Brixius.)

# *Six*

# SCHOOLS AND SCHOLARS

Free public education could be found in Stearns County as early as 1856 when the Reverend Father Cornelius Wittmann opened the first school in the home of Joseph Edelbrock in St. Cloud. This school was soon followed by the building of an official schoolhouse in Lower Town in 1858. By 1860 there were ten schools in operation in the county in St. Cloud, St. Joseph, Clearwater, Brockway, Richmond, Paynesville, Fair Haven, and Maine Prairie.

Stearns County schools paralleled the changes in public education experienced across the nation. As late as the 1870s, rural society relied on children to do farm work and schools were located far apart, thus Americans attended school for an average of only four years. By 1900, as we became an urban nation and more children were removed from farm work, pressures on school space soared. Boosted by compulsory-attendance laws, public school enrollments rose from 6.9 million in 1870 to 17.8 million in 1910. During the same period the number of public high schools grew from 500 to over 10,000. Stearns County schools also experienced a jump in school attendance and new graded schools, high schools, and junior high schools were built throughout the county.

In the 1910s, the progressive impulse of the nation also affected Stearns County schools. Schools became not just places where children learned "the facts," but places where children learned to lead productive and fulfilling lives. This emphasis on personal growth also lay behind the growth of college education for Americans. Between 1870 and 1910, the number of colleges and universities in the nation grew from 563 to nearly 1,000. Stearns County hosted three such institutions: St. John's University, the College of St. Benedict, and St. Cloud State University. The images in this section show the variety of school buildings in the county and some of the many scholars who passed through them.

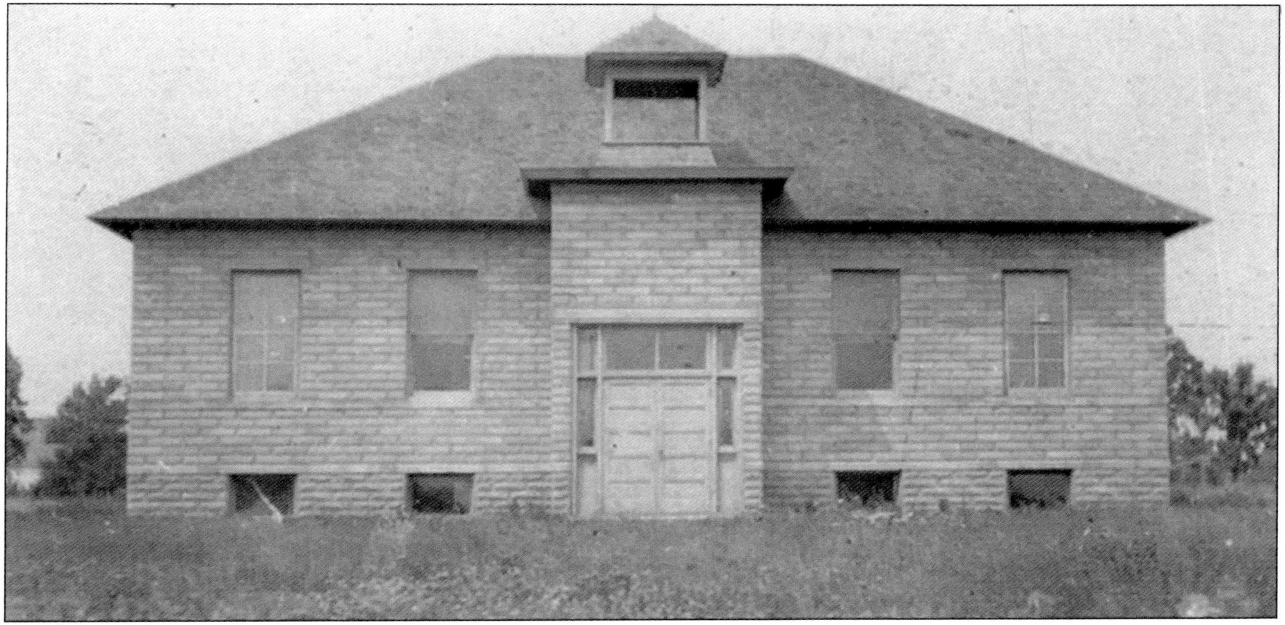

Pictured above is the schoolhouse at Fair Haven, the Ruehle School, *c.* 1910. District 79 was organized in 1870. An original one-room log structure was replaced in 1900 by the brick building shown here. It is named after Peter Ruehle, a neighboring landowner. (Courtesy of Richard Kelly.)

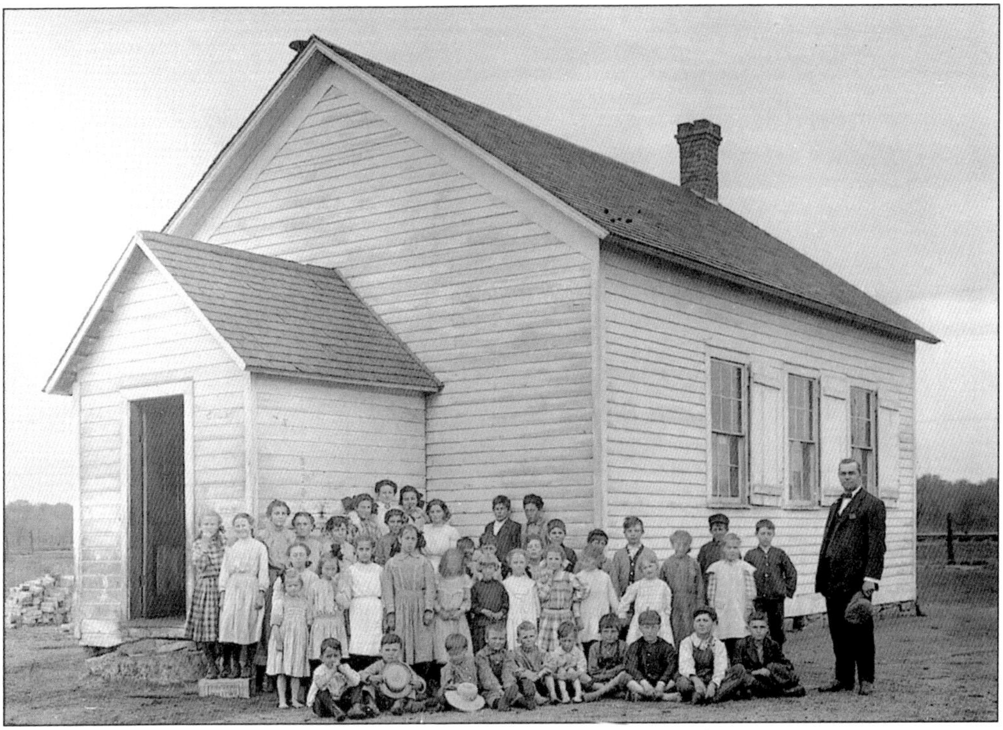

Students pose with their teacher in front of the one-room schoolhouse at Rockville, *c.* 1910. This school building was moved twice in one night as village residents and outlying farmers fought over its location. (Courtesy of the Central Minnesota Historical Center.)

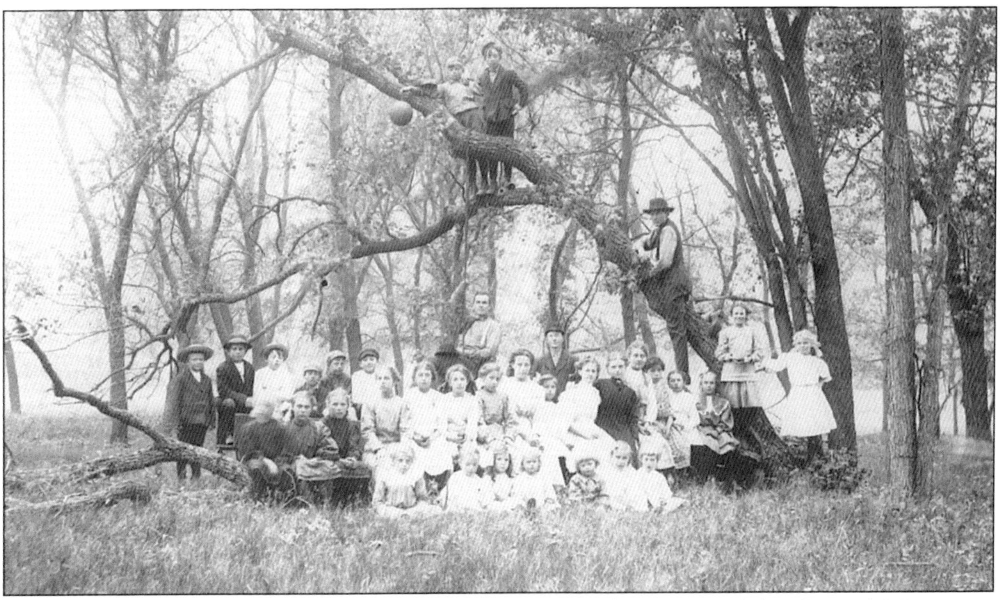

Rockville students enjoy a rural school picnic, *c.* 1910. (Courtesy of the Central Minnesota Historical Center.)

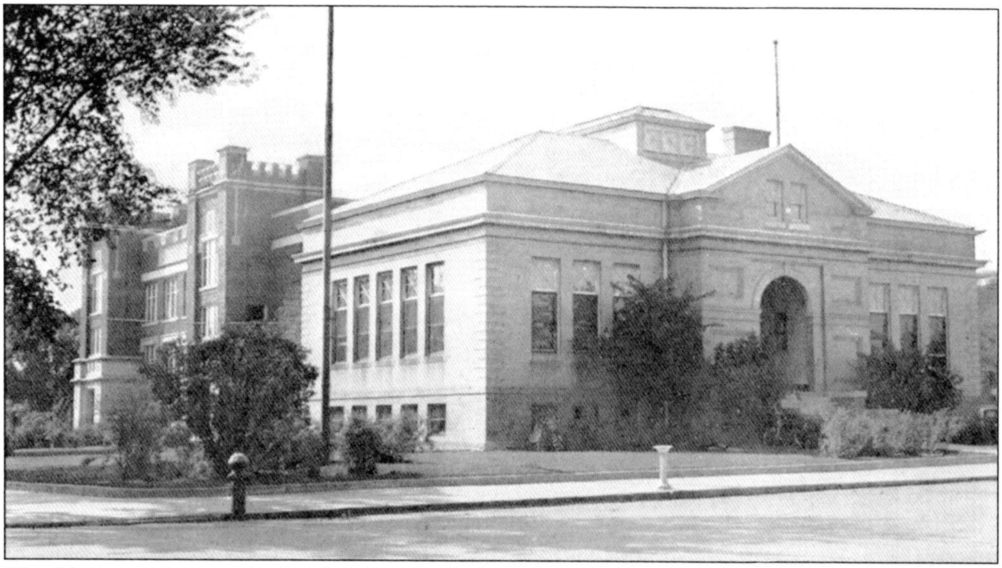

The library and junior high school in Sauk Centre was where Sinclair Lewis learned to read. This postcard dates from 1940. (Courtesy of the Central Minnesota Historical Center.)

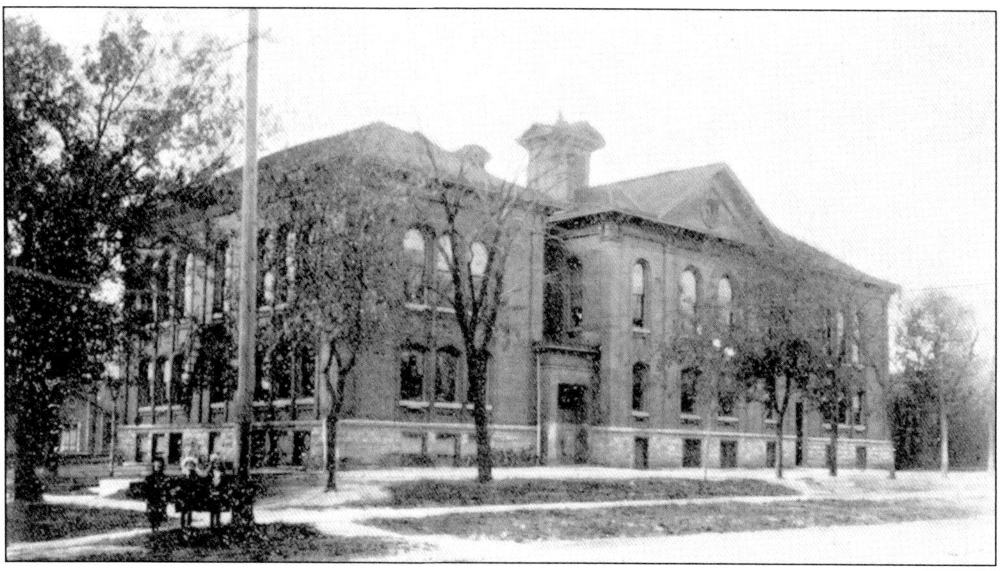

Union School opened in 1870 and served as the high school at St. Cloud. This photo dates from 1910. The building was the first substantial public school building in the city. Later additions were added over time. It also served as central junior high and central elementary before the city bought the location for a new city hall. (Courtesy of Richard Kelly.)

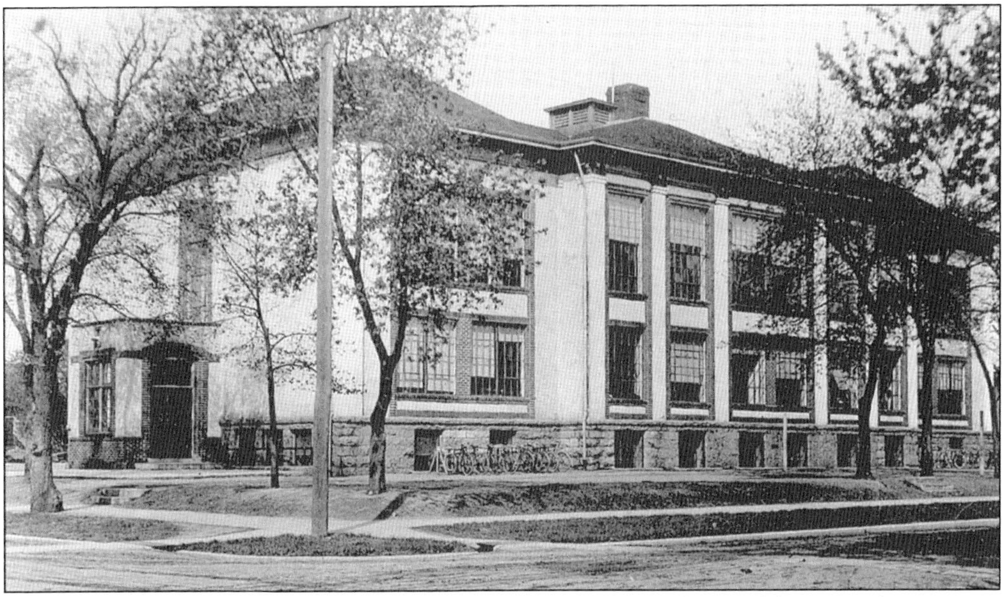

This postcard is identified as Union School, yet it bears no real resemblance to the previous picture of the high school. This is most likely the junior high addition, c. 1930. (Courtesy of Richard Kelly.)

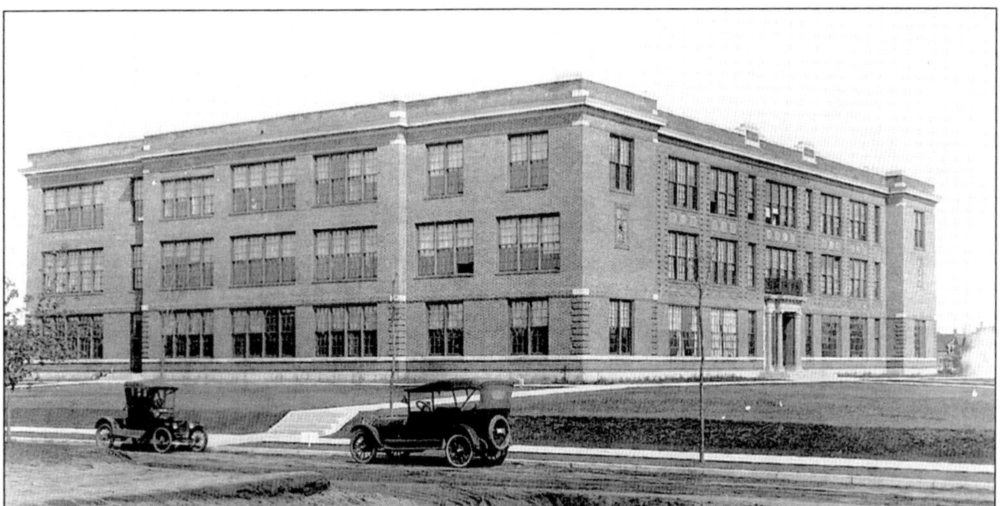

Technical High School in St. Cloud opened in 1917 and continues to serve residents in the southern half of the city. Students in the north and from St. Joseph attend Apollo High School. This photo dates from about 1920. (Courtesy of Richard Kelly.)

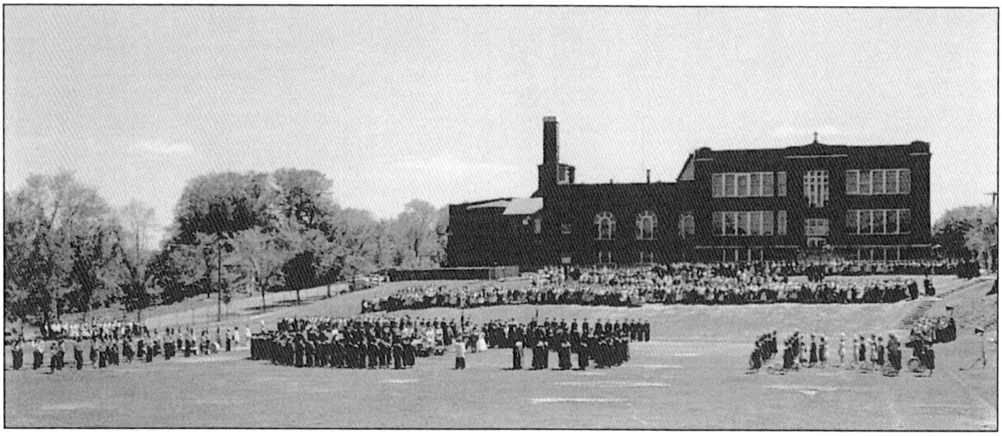

Cathedral High School opened in St. Cloud in 1902 by having the ninth grade take classes on the third floor of Holy Angels Catholic Grade School. In 1915 a separate building was opened and an addition was built in 1958. Here students participate in living rosary exercises on the athletic field in 1950. (Courtesy of the Central Minnesota Historical Center.)

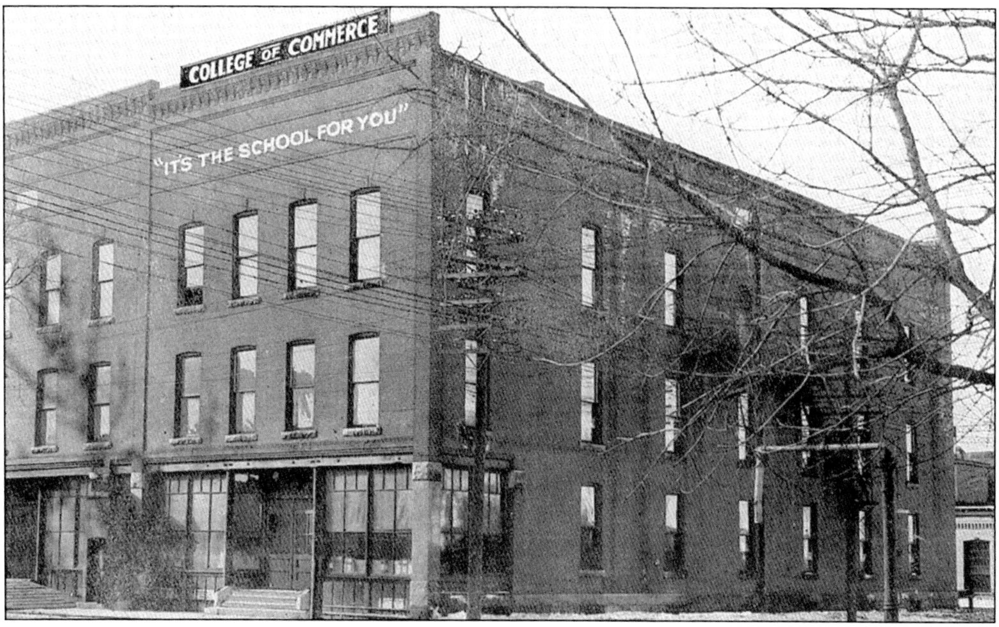


The College of Commerce was located in the Carter Building, St. Cloud, c. 1910. Business schools were started in most American cities at this time to train clerical staff. (Courtesy of Richard Kelly.)

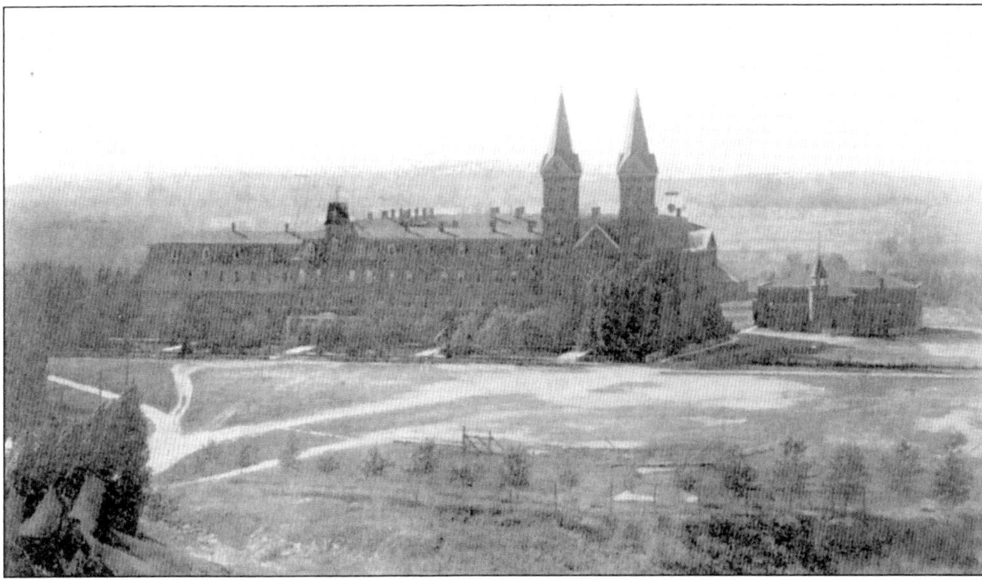

St. John's University sold itself as the "largest Catholic institution in the West" in Collegeville, c. 1900. St. John's also houses a monastery, prep school, and the Hill Monastic Manuscript Collection. (Courtesy of Richard Kelly.)

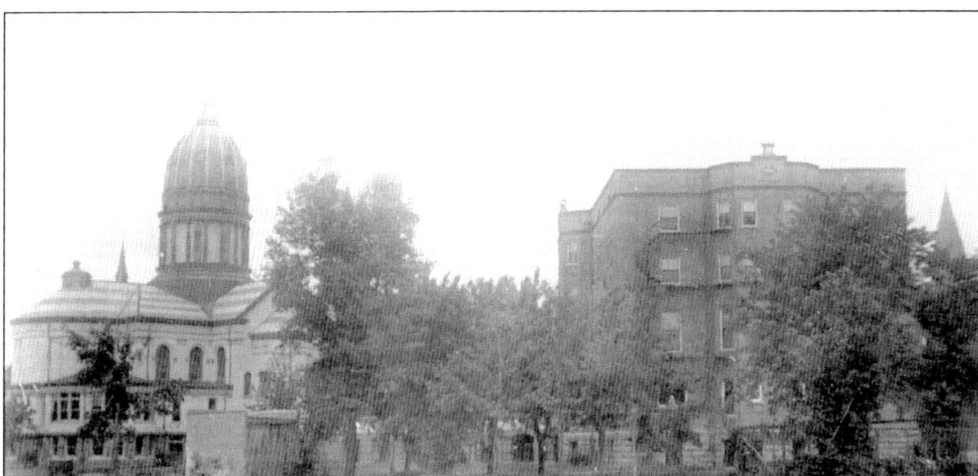

St. Benedict Chapel and Academy in St. Joseph are pictured above in this 1916 image. The academy eventually became the College of St. Benedict, a sister institution to St. John's University. The two became co-educational in 1967. (Courtesy of Richard Kelly.)

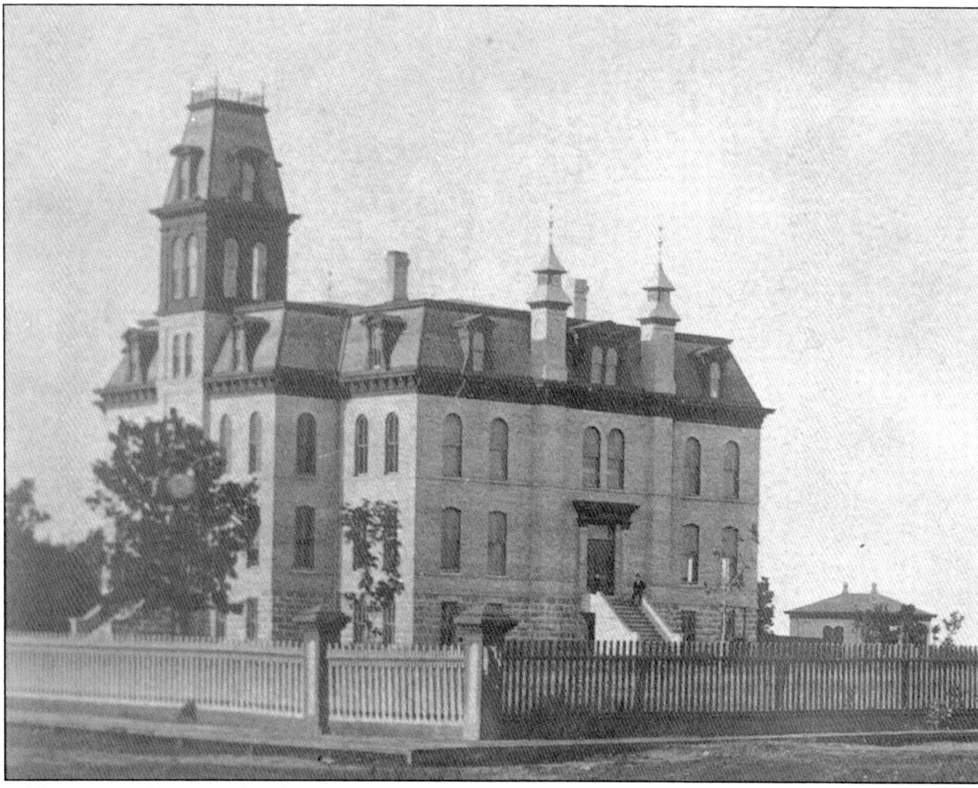

Old Main at the St. Cloud Normal School (St. Cloud State University) in 1877 is one of the many architectural beauties of the county that has been a victim of modernization. (Courtesy of the Central Minnesota Historical Center.)

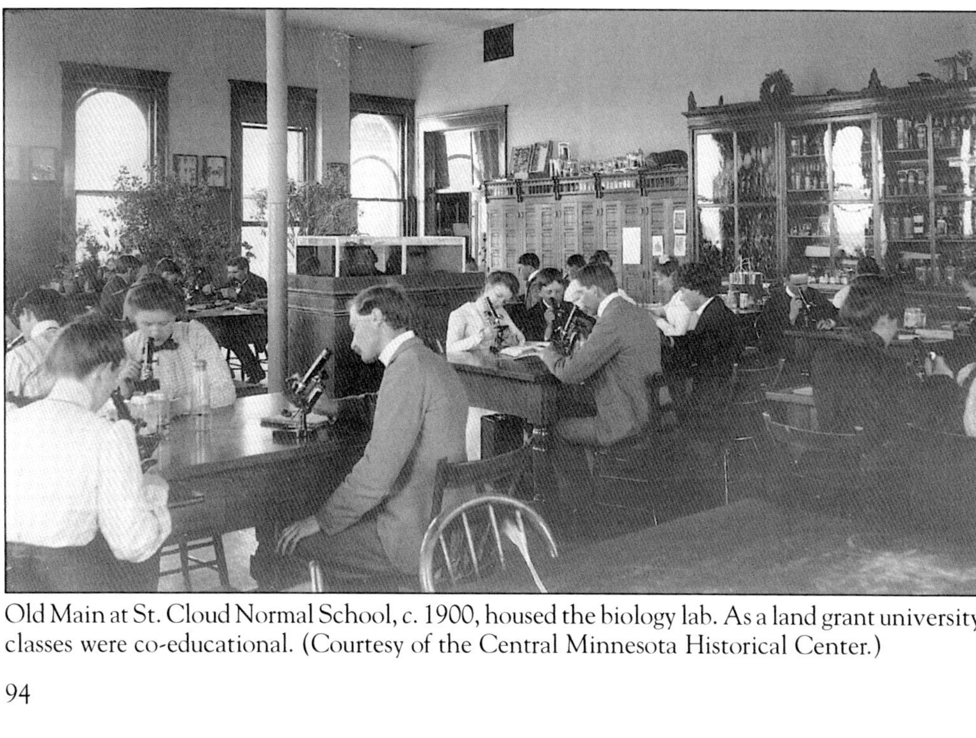

Old Main at St. Cloud Normal School, c. 1900, housed the biology lab. As a land grant university, classes were co-educational. (Courtesy of the Central Minnesota Historical Center.)

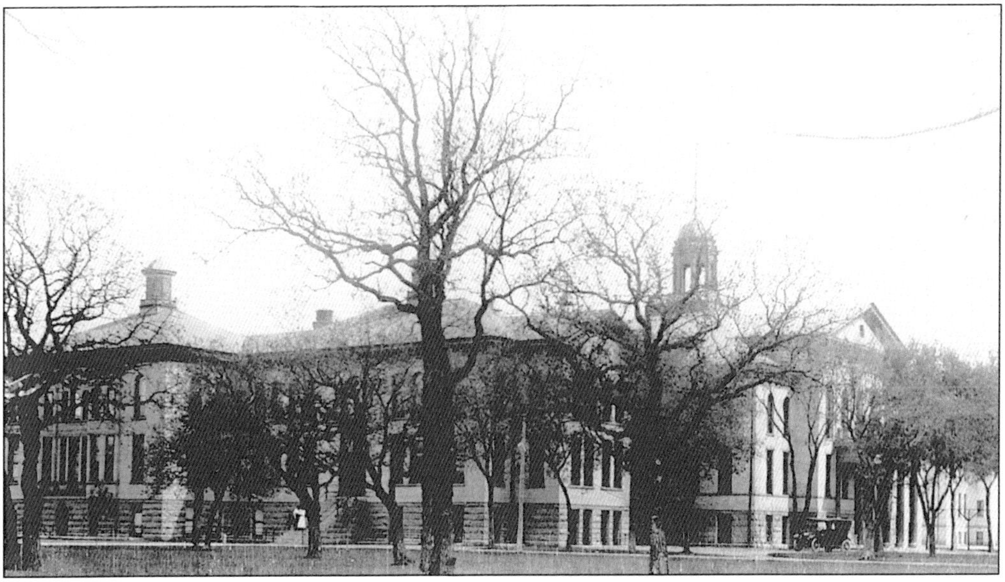

Pictured is the main building at the St. Cloud Normal School, 1913. (Courtesy of Richard Kelly.)

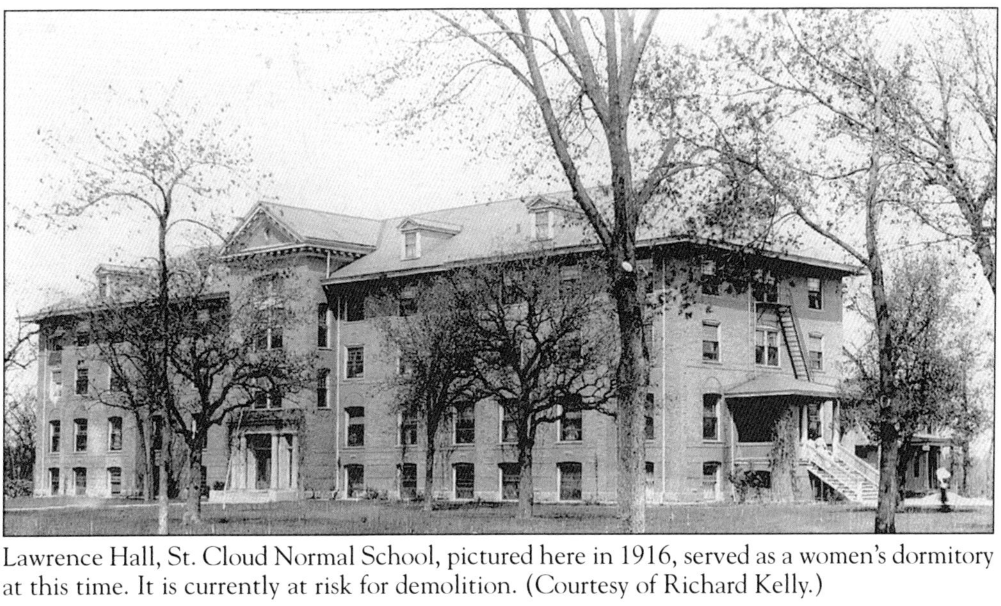

Lawrence Hall, St. Cloud Normal School, pictured here in 1916, served as a women's dormitory at this time. It is currently at risk for demolition. (Courtesy of Richard Kelly.)

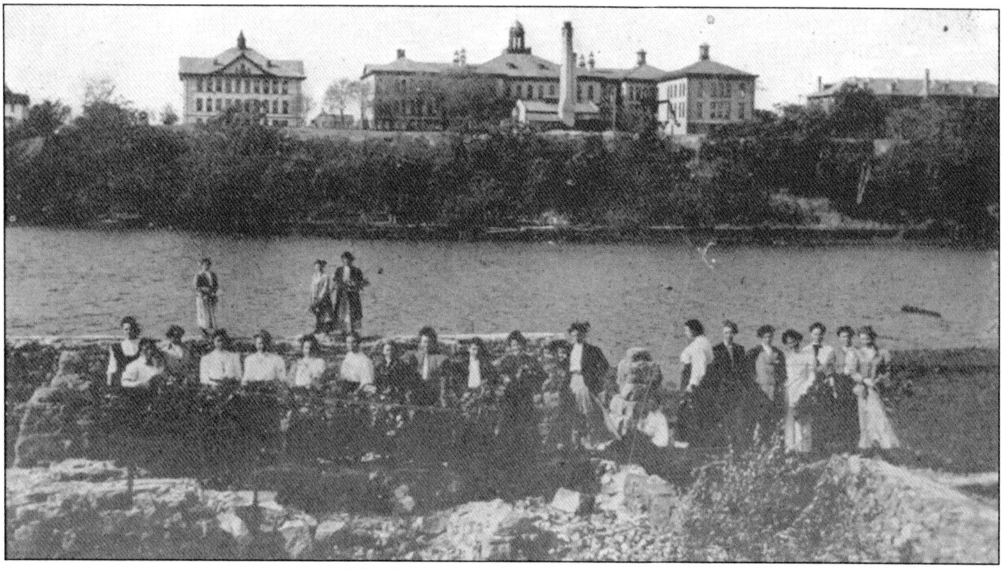

Students pose on the east side of the Mississippi River across from the St. Cloud State Normal School. Riverview and Shoemaker Halls are in the background. (Courtesy of Richard Kelly.)

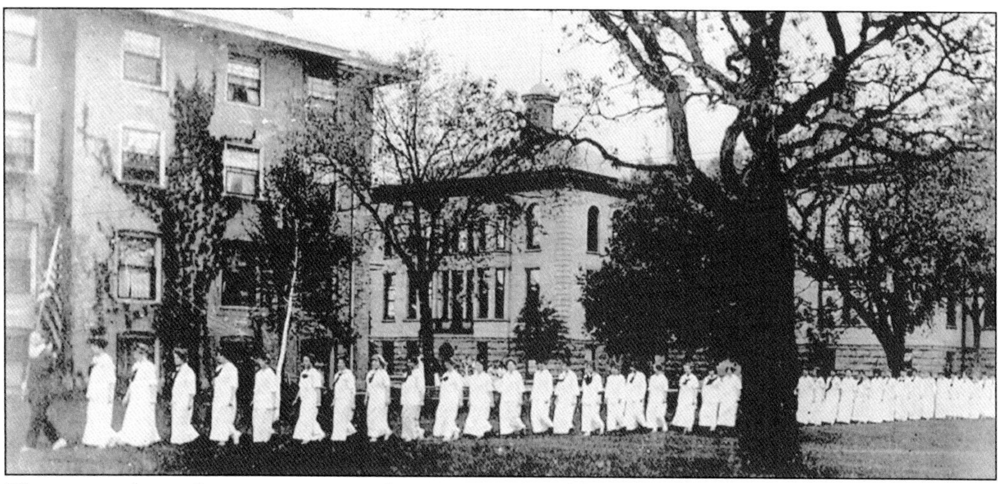

The image above shows a peace parade protesting World War I at the St. Cloud Normal School, c. 1916. (Courtesy of Richard Kelly.)

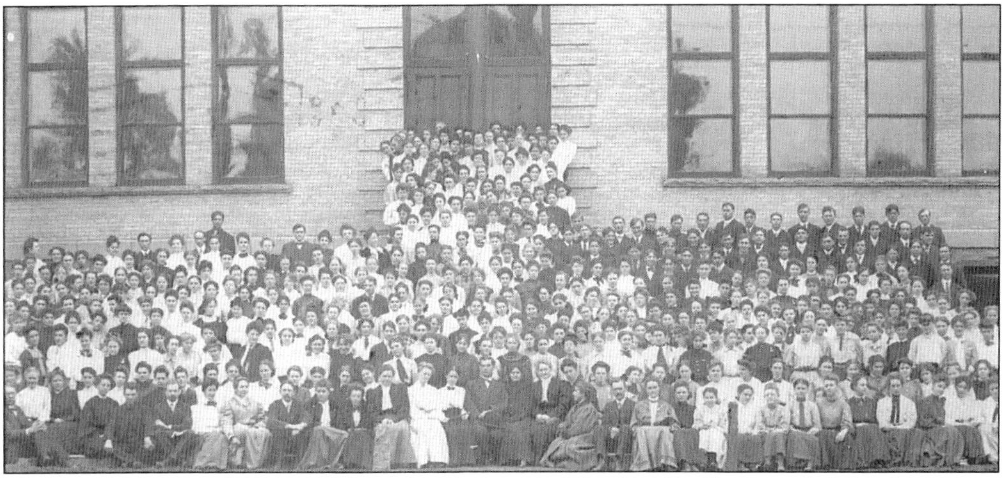

Students and faculty pose in front of Old Main at the St. Cloud Normal School, c. 1906. (Courtesy of Richard Kelly.)

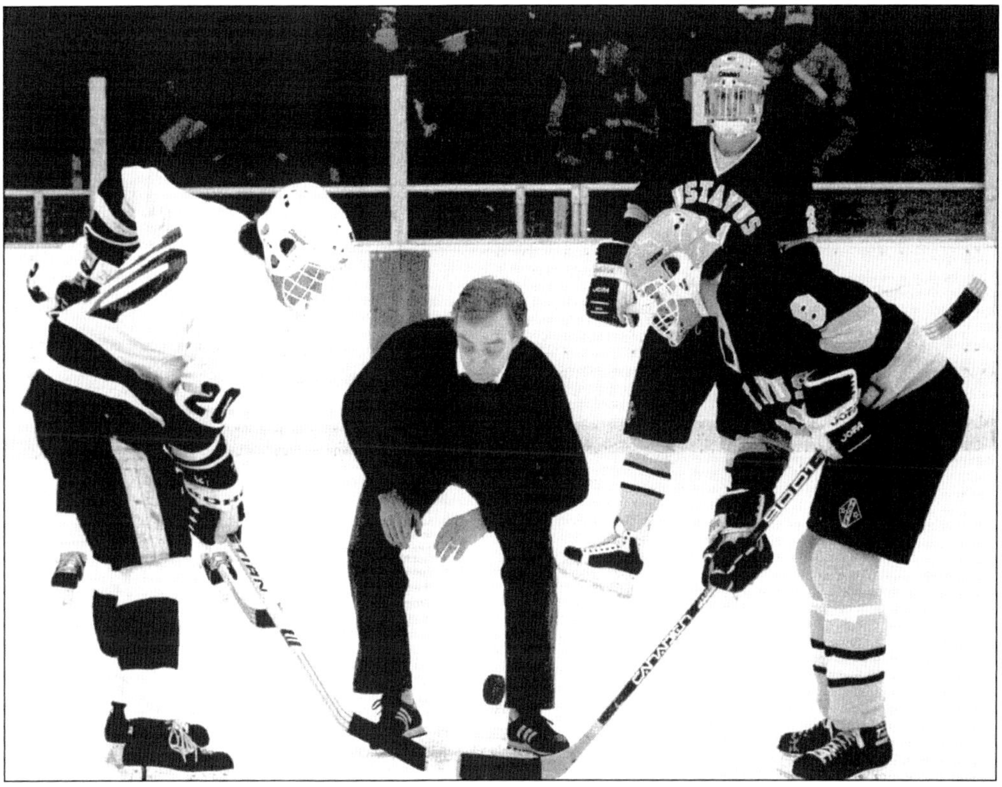

State Representative Jim Pehler drops the puck at a St. Cloud State hockey game against Gustavus Adolphus. This was opening night, November 1986. (Courtesy of the Central Minnesota Historical Center.)

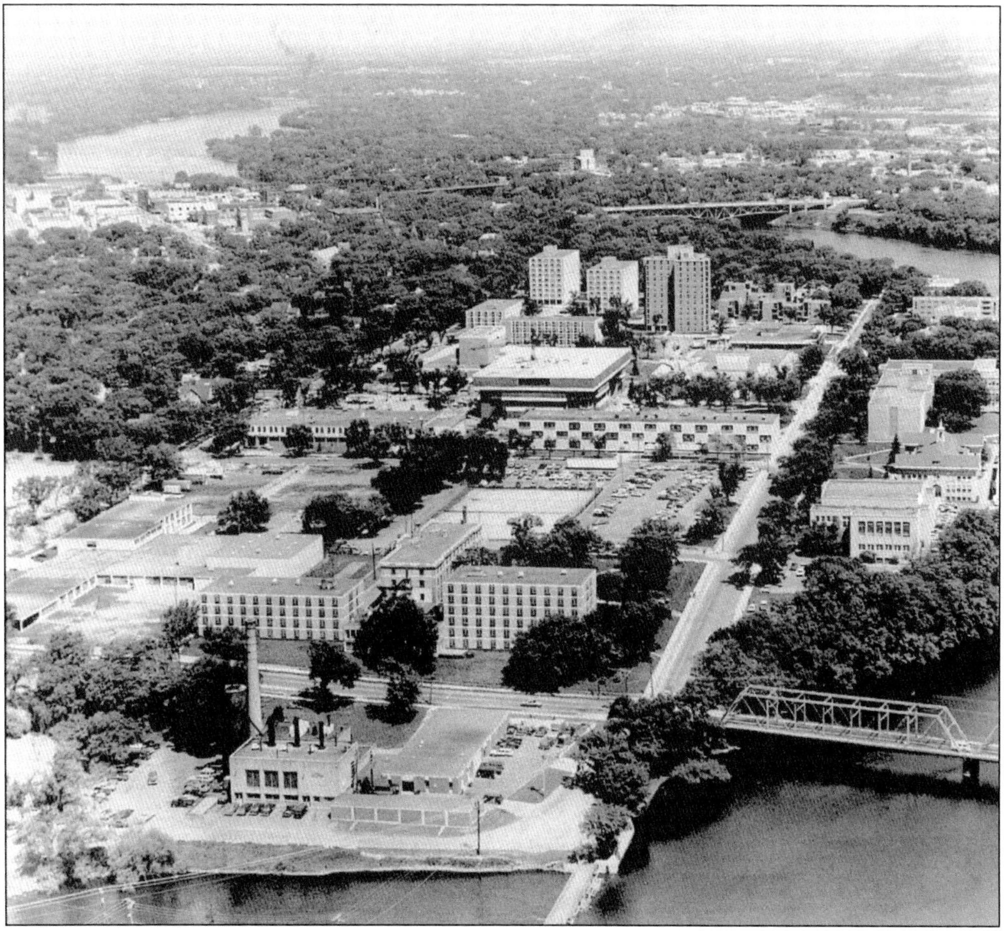

Here is an aerial view of St. Cloud State University looking north, c. 1970. The Tenth Street Bridge is in the foreground, Centennial Hall—which housed the library until 2000—is in the center of campus. (Courtesy of the Central Minnesota Historical Center.)

# *Seven*

# Saving Souls

No history of Stearns County would be complete without a look at the powerful influence of religion, particularly the Christian denominations, on the community. In a secular nation, religion has permeated almost every facet of the lives of many Stearns County residents. Churches were some of the first public buildings built in newly founded towns and cities and the influence of religion can be felt in the way residents conduct business, educate their children, and respond to natural and man-made disasters.

Although other Christian denominations are also represented in the county, it is Catholicism that primarily shapes the religious flavor. Catholics first came to the area in the early 1850s as missionaries intent on converting the local Indian population. These individual priests would not have left that indelible mark on the county had it not been for the efforts of the Rev. Francis X. Pierz who encouraged German Catholic settlers from Iowa and other states to immigrate to the area. Serving as a missionary at Crow Wing, Pierz came to believe that Stearns County was ideal country for thrifty settlers who would get along well with the Indians. As a religious booster, he solicited immigrants in a German Catholic newspaper published in Cincinnati and he also wrote a prospectus on the area, published in 1855, describing the many advantages offered by the territory. The response was a large influx of German Catholics who left a permanent mark on the county. Today, the Catholic church in Stearns County still remains a strong institution even in light of growing pressures from a secular world and a declining number of priests.

The images that follow show many important church buildings of a variety of Christian denominations in the county and several key religious events. Many of these buildings have been destroyed by fire or by the pressures of modernization and city growth and development. Several are of special note. The interior photos of Holy Angels Church, in particular, are rare and show the incredible artistry that has been lost. More and more church buildings will be at risk as the population grows and older neighborhoods fight decay. It is up to residents to fight and save these valuable historic buildings.

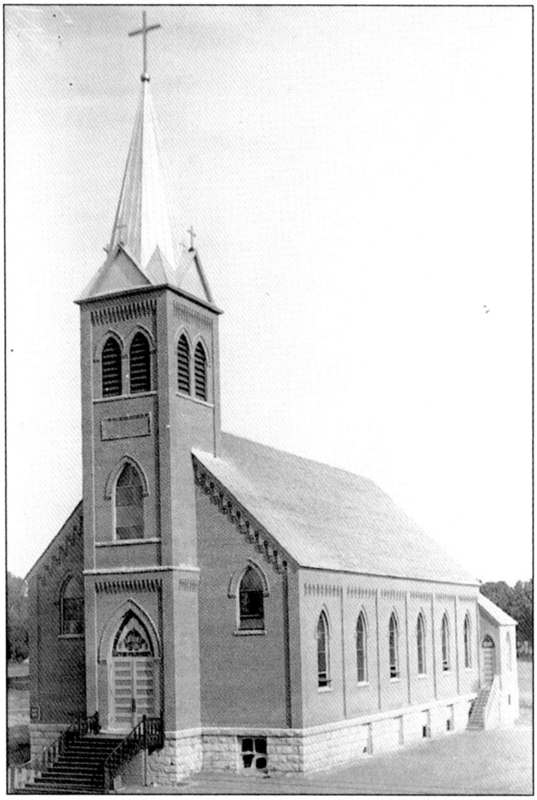

These two views show the interior and exterior of Rockville Catholic Church, c. 1912. (Courtesy of the Central Minnesota Historical Center.)

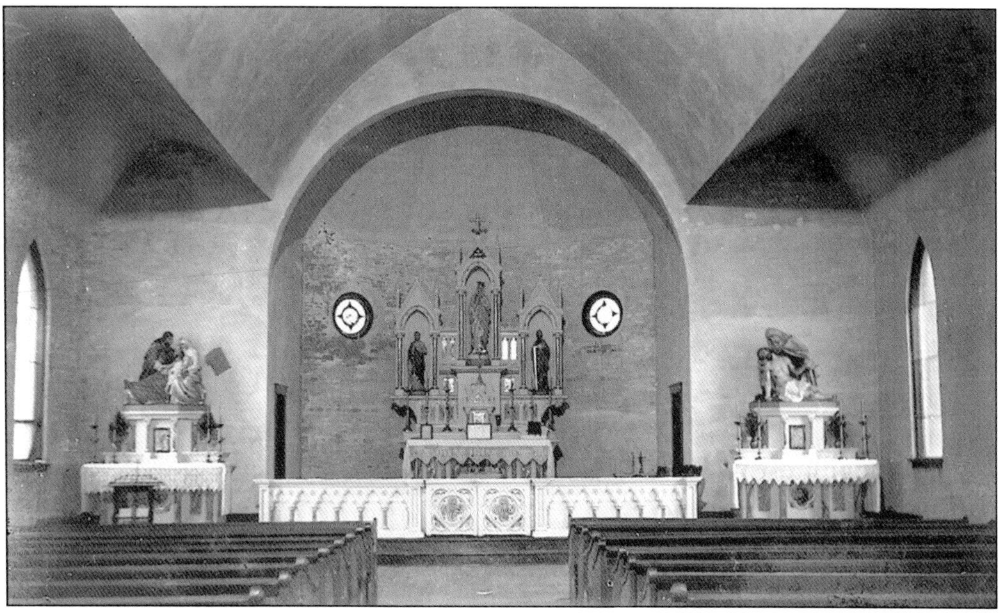

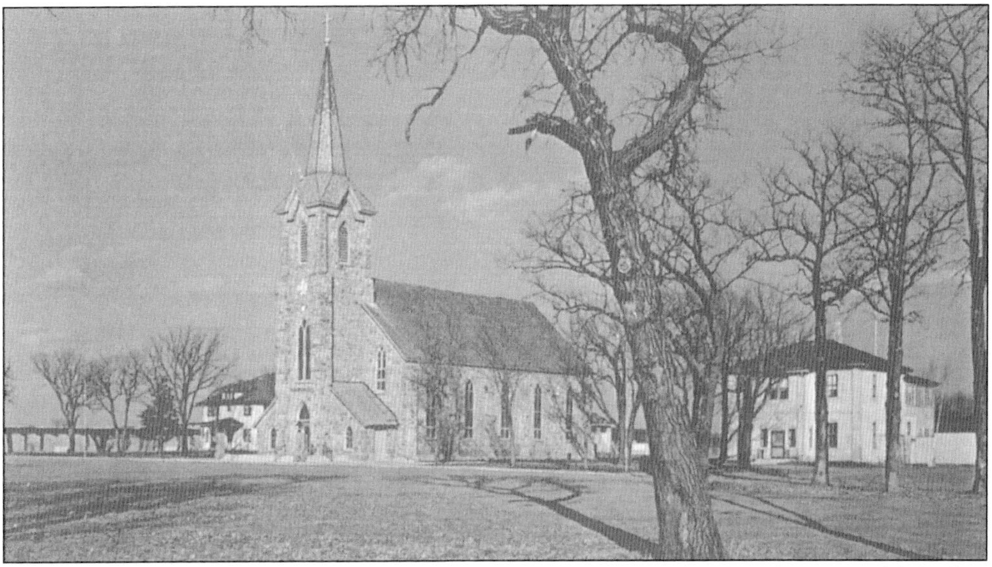

Pictured above is St. Wendelin Church, Luxemburg, *c.* 1965. The church was established in 1859, but the present church was not built until 1872 and the rectory until 1876. The church, rectory, and convent were restored and renovated between 1960 and 1963. A new school was built in 1963–64. (Courtesy of Richard Kelly.)

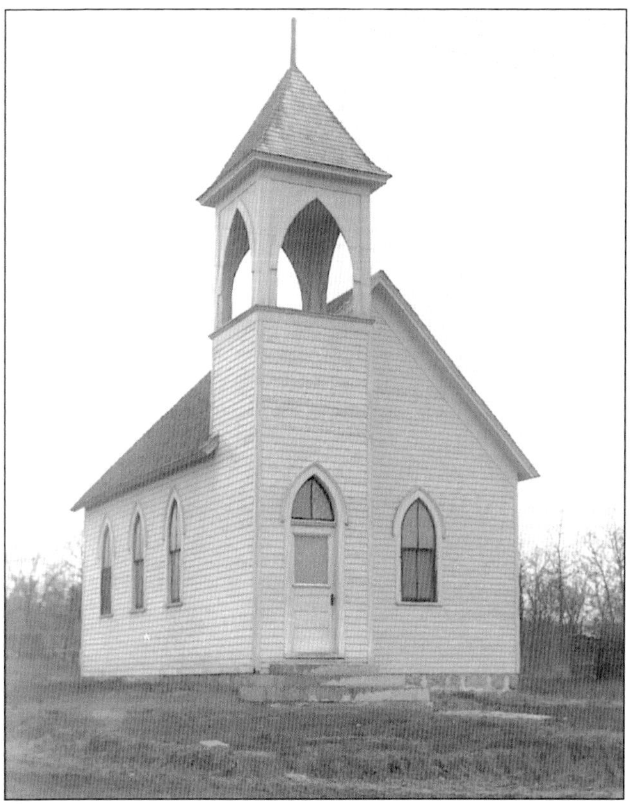

The Presbyterian Church in St. Cloud was built in 1917 and provided services for residents on the south side of town. (Courtesy of the Central Minnesota Historical Center.)

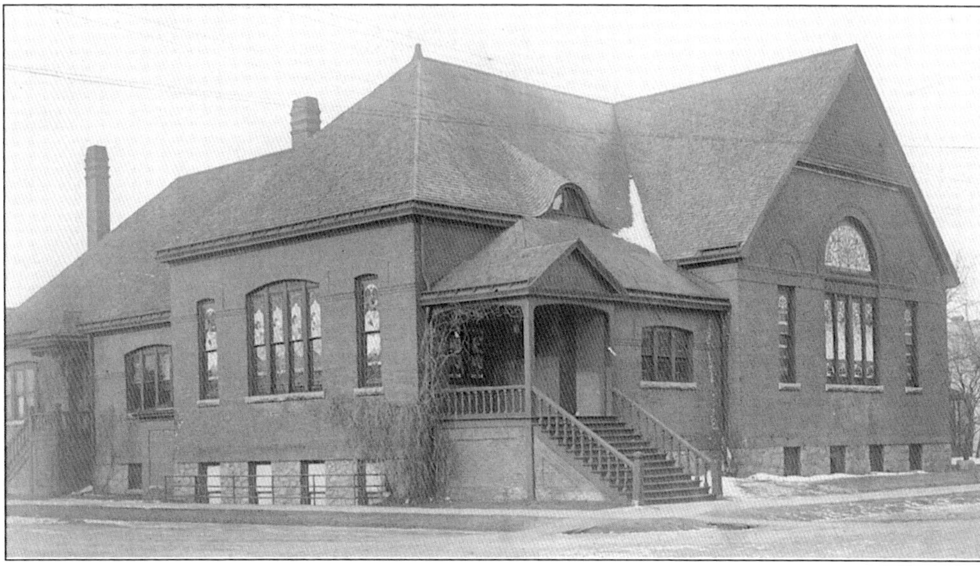

Unity Church, St. Cloud, c. 1910, an unique, shingle-style building, was located at the corner of Division Street and Fourth Avenue. The city band practiced there until it was torn down in 1980 to make room for the Norwest (Wells Fargo) Center. (Courtesy of Richard Kelly.)

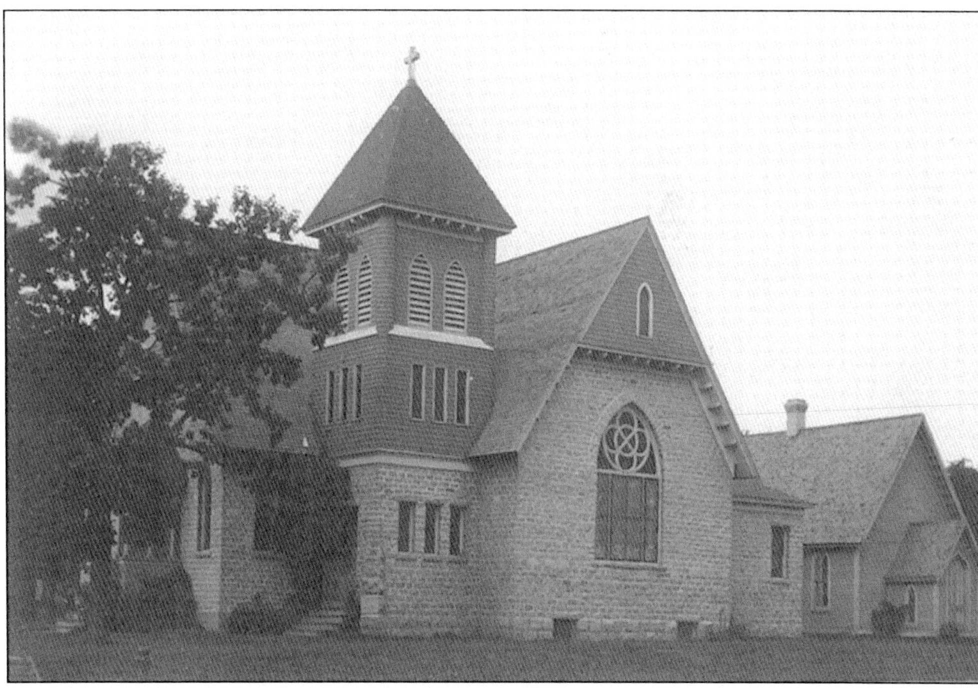

St. John's Episcopal Church in St. Cloud, pictured here c. 1910, was built in 1856. This church was one of many victims of lightning strikes and burned to the ground. (Courtesy of Richard Kelly.)

Built in 1883 and serving as the pro-cathedral for St. Cloud, Holy Angels Church was never designated by the Vatican as a cathedral. It was struck by lightning in 1933 as it celebrated its 50th anniversary and burned completely. The three steeples were not rebuilt. The church currently serves as a theater for Cathedral High School. (Courtesy of Richard Kelly.)

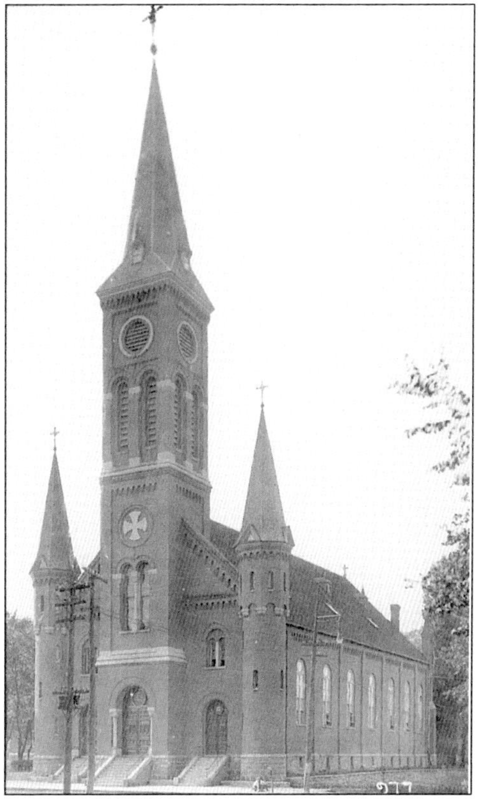

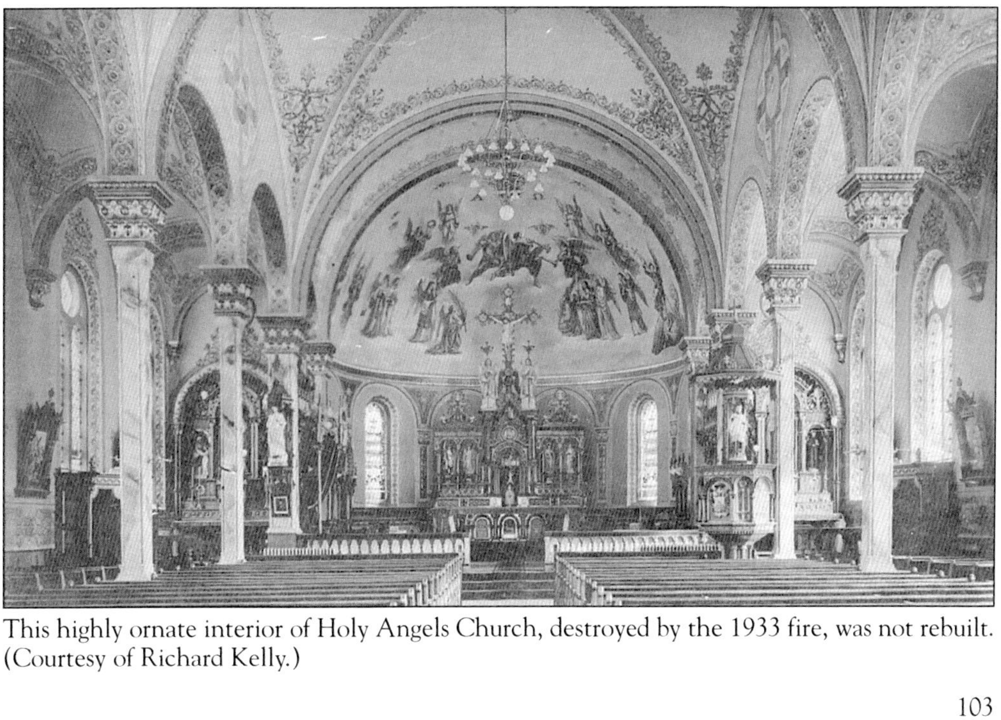

This highly ornate interior of Holy Angels Church, destroyed by the 1933 fire, was not rebuilt. (Courtesy of Richard Kelly.)

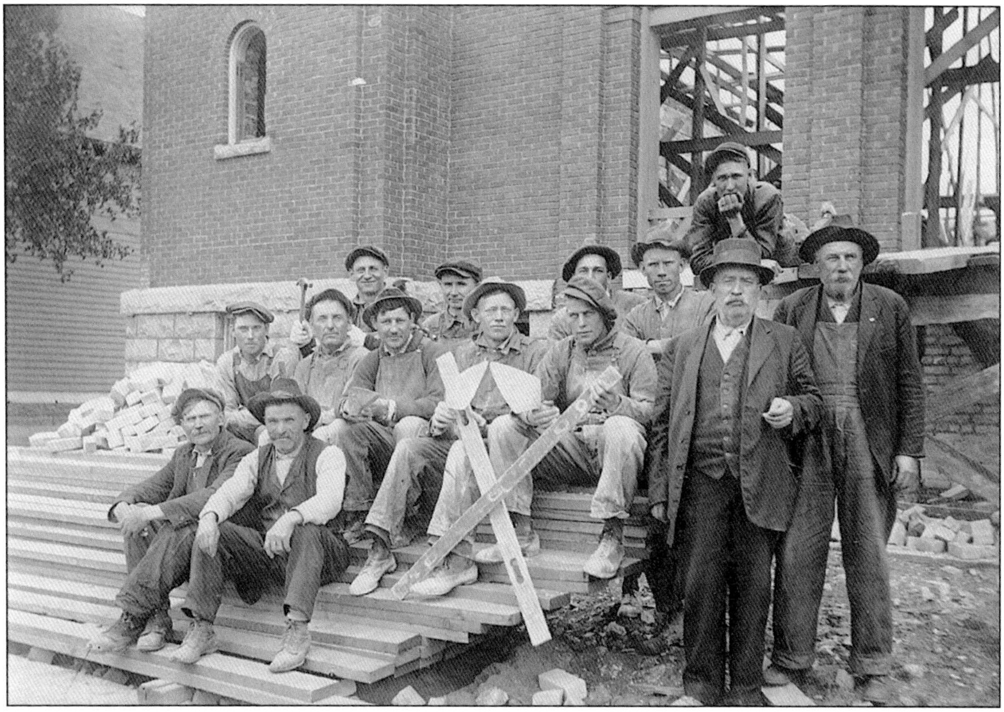

Workers are shown above in 1933 during the rebuilding of Holy Angels Church. The stained glass windows were not replaced, nor were the columns. (Courtesy of David Lindmeier.)

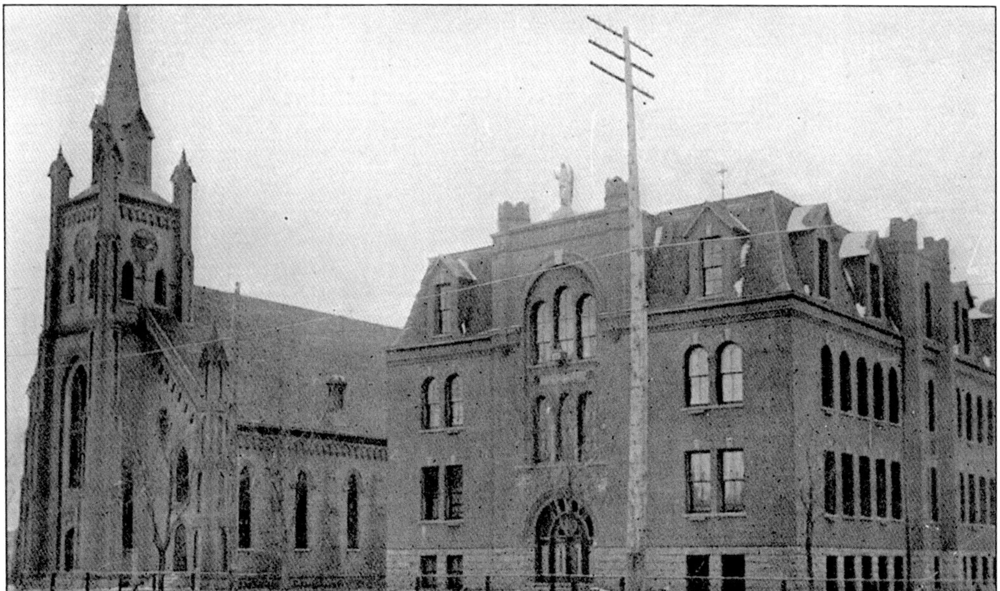

Immaculate Conception Church and St. Mary's School, St. Cloud, *c.* 1915, was destroyed by an electrical fire on August 25, 1920. (Courtesy of Richard Kelly.)

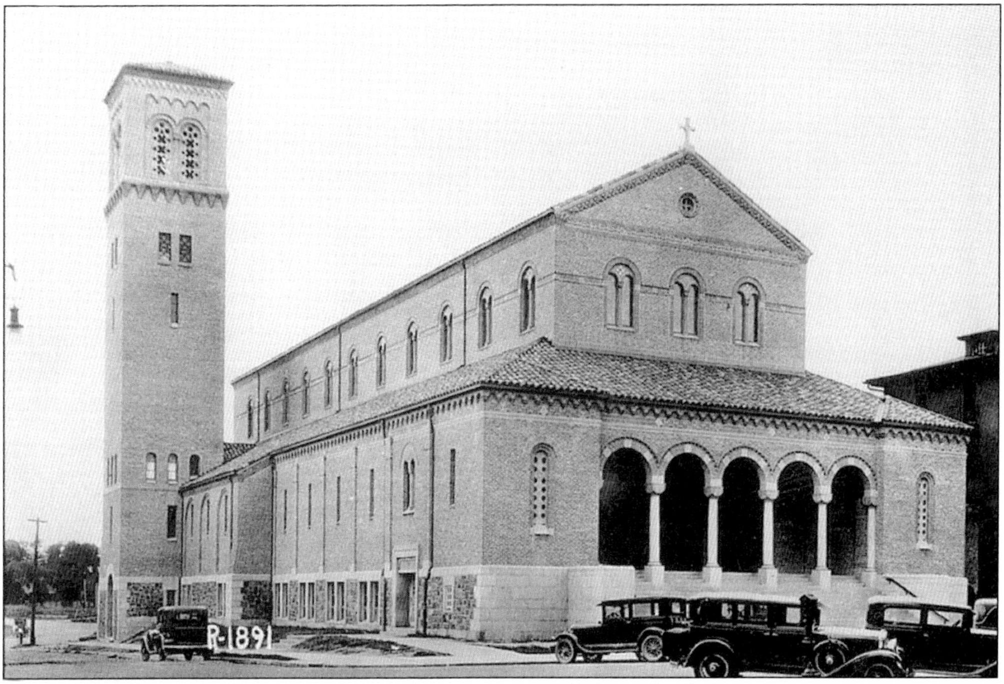


The Cathedral of St. Mary's on Seventh Avenue South St. Cloud, *c.* 1935, began construction in 1920 and services were held in the completed basement as early as 1921. The superstructure was completed in 1931. In 1937 the Vatican gave its blessing for the church to serve as the cathedral for the St. Cloud Diocese. (Courtesy of Richard Kelly.)

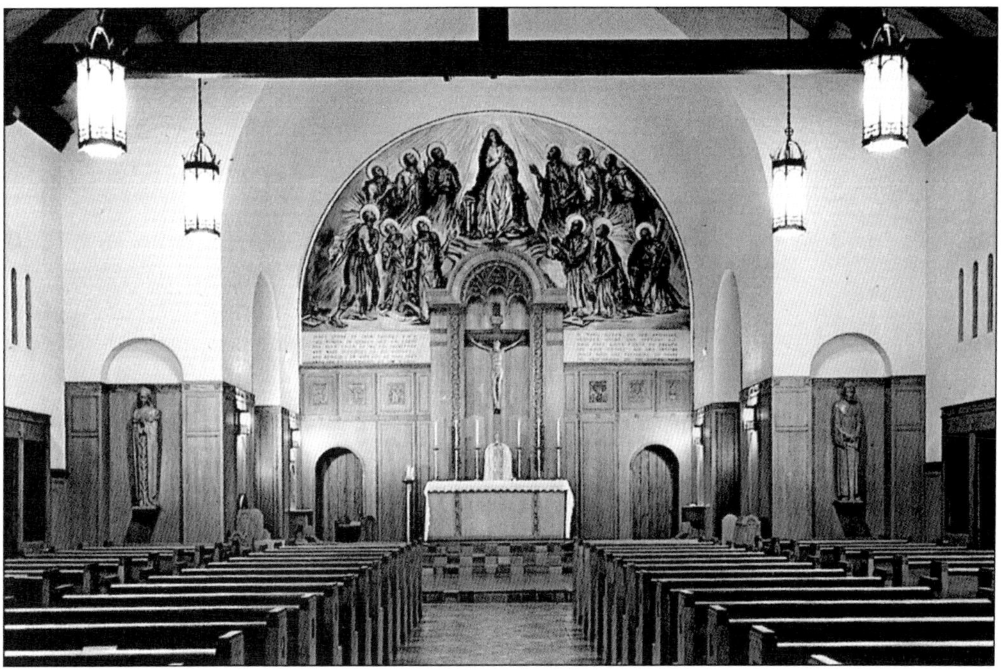

Queen of the Apostles' Chapel at St. John's Seminary of the Diocese of St. Cloud, Collegeville, pictured in 1960. (Courtesy of the Central Minnesota Historical Center.)

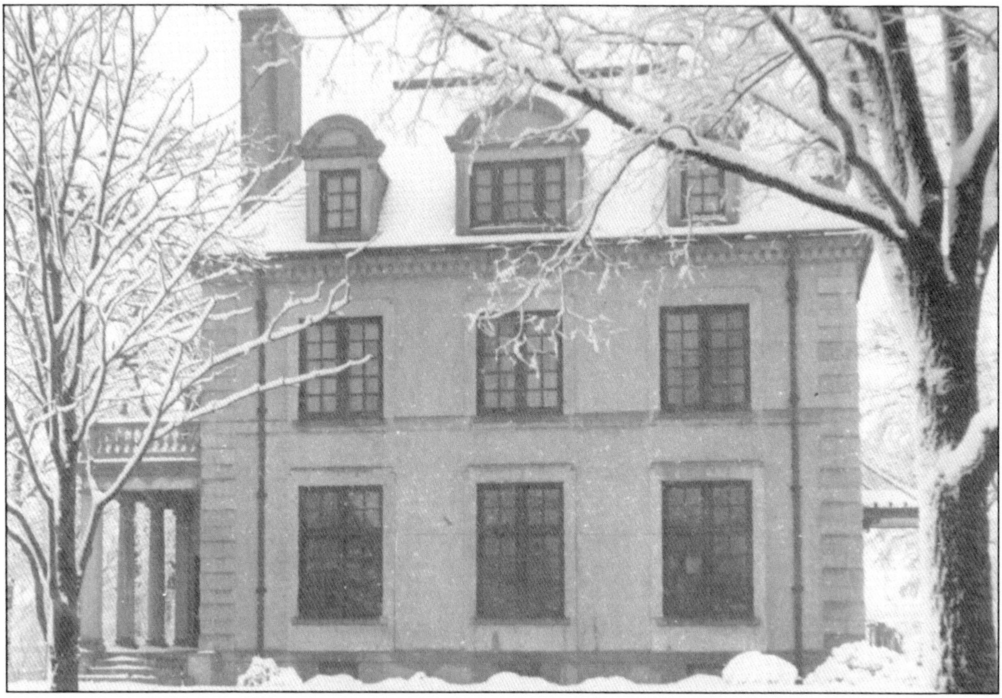

Above is a side view of Bishop Busch's house on Second Avenue South, St. Cloud. Busch used his own family money to build the residence in 1916. He lived there until his death in 1952. The house contained living quarters, a chapel, and space for a chancery office. Today the building solely houses the chancery office. (Courtesy of the Central Minnesota Historical Center.)

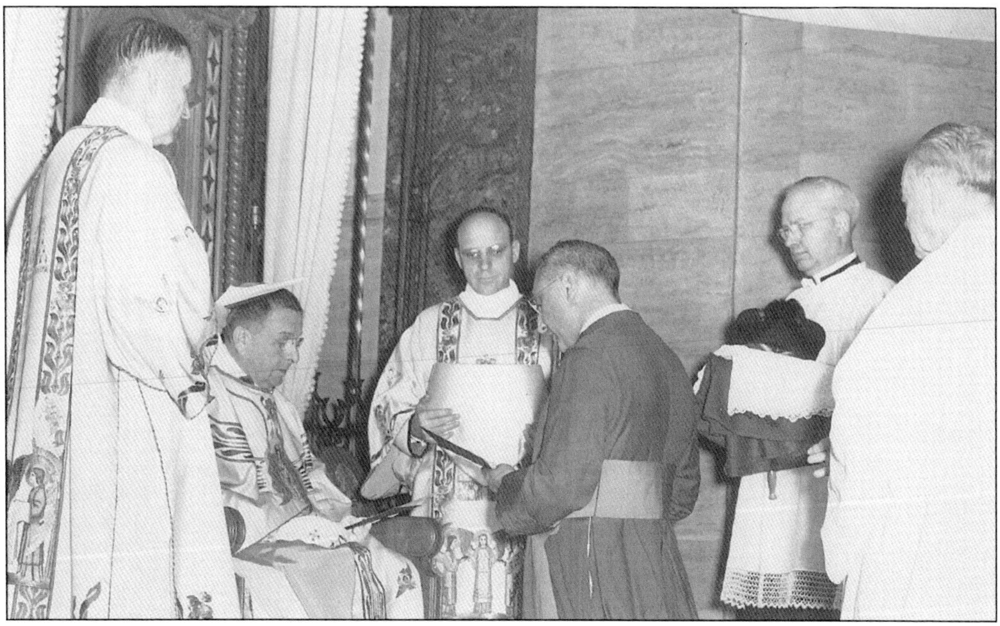

Bishop Peter W. Bartholeme (seated) presides over the investiture of Monsignor Peter Lorsung in 1952. Father Vernig stands between Bartholome and Lorsung. (Courtesy of the Central Minnesota Historical Center.)

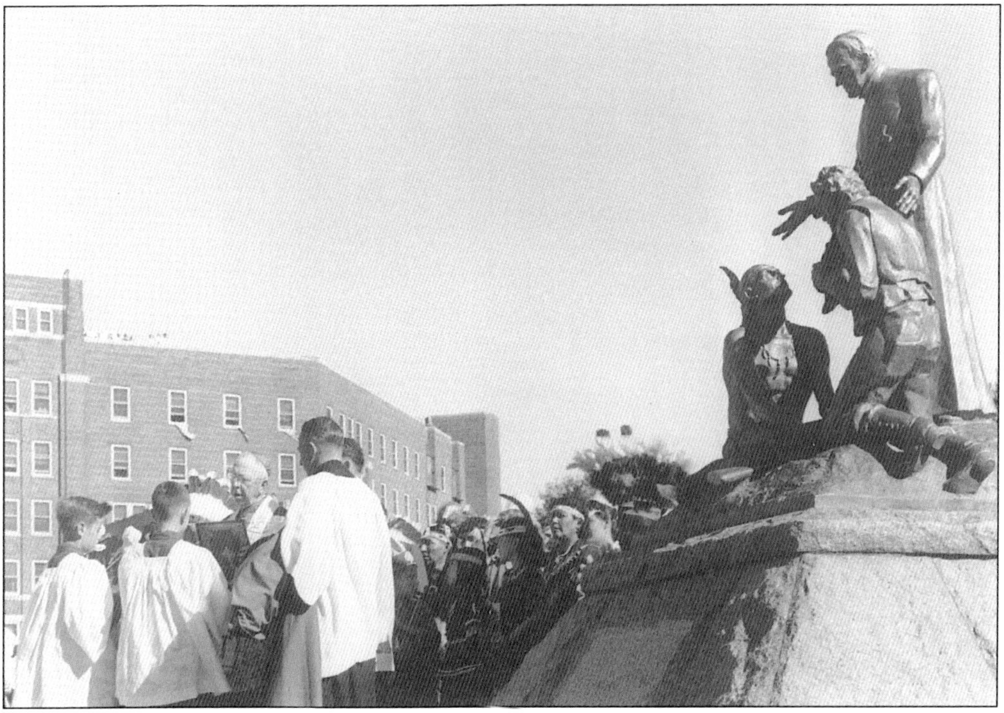

As part of the centennial celebration of the arrival of Father Pierz in central Minnesota, Cardinal Mooney, the Archbishop of Detroit, dedicated a statue honoring Father Pierz at the St. Cloud hospital. After dedicating the statue, dignitaries and guests marched down to the Cathedral where Cardinal Mooney spoke to over 10,000 spectators, 1952. (Courtesy of the Central Minnesota Historical Center.)

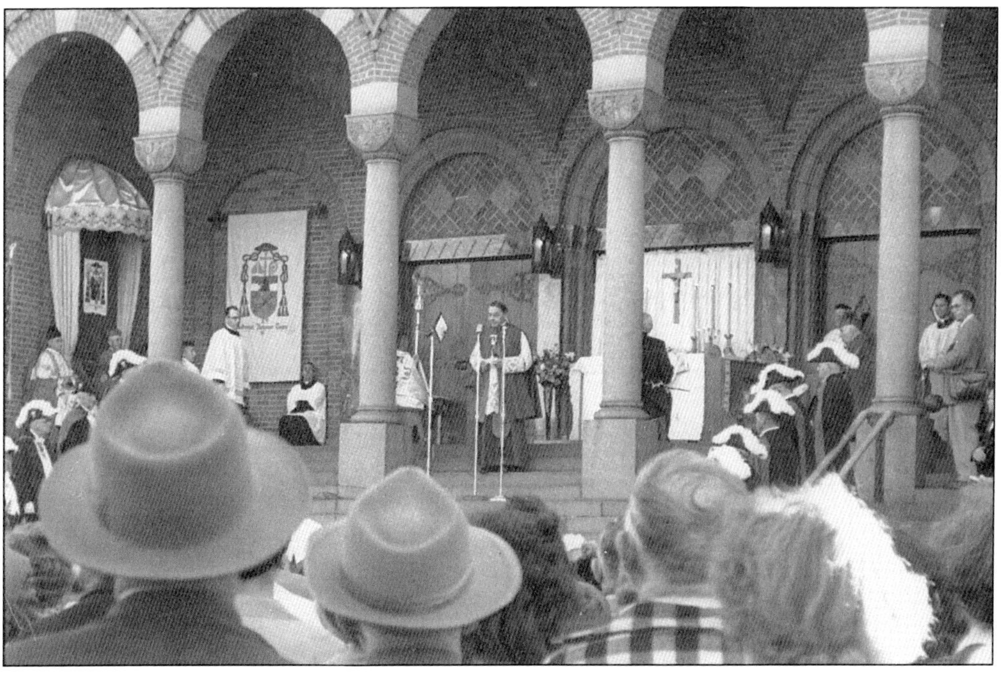

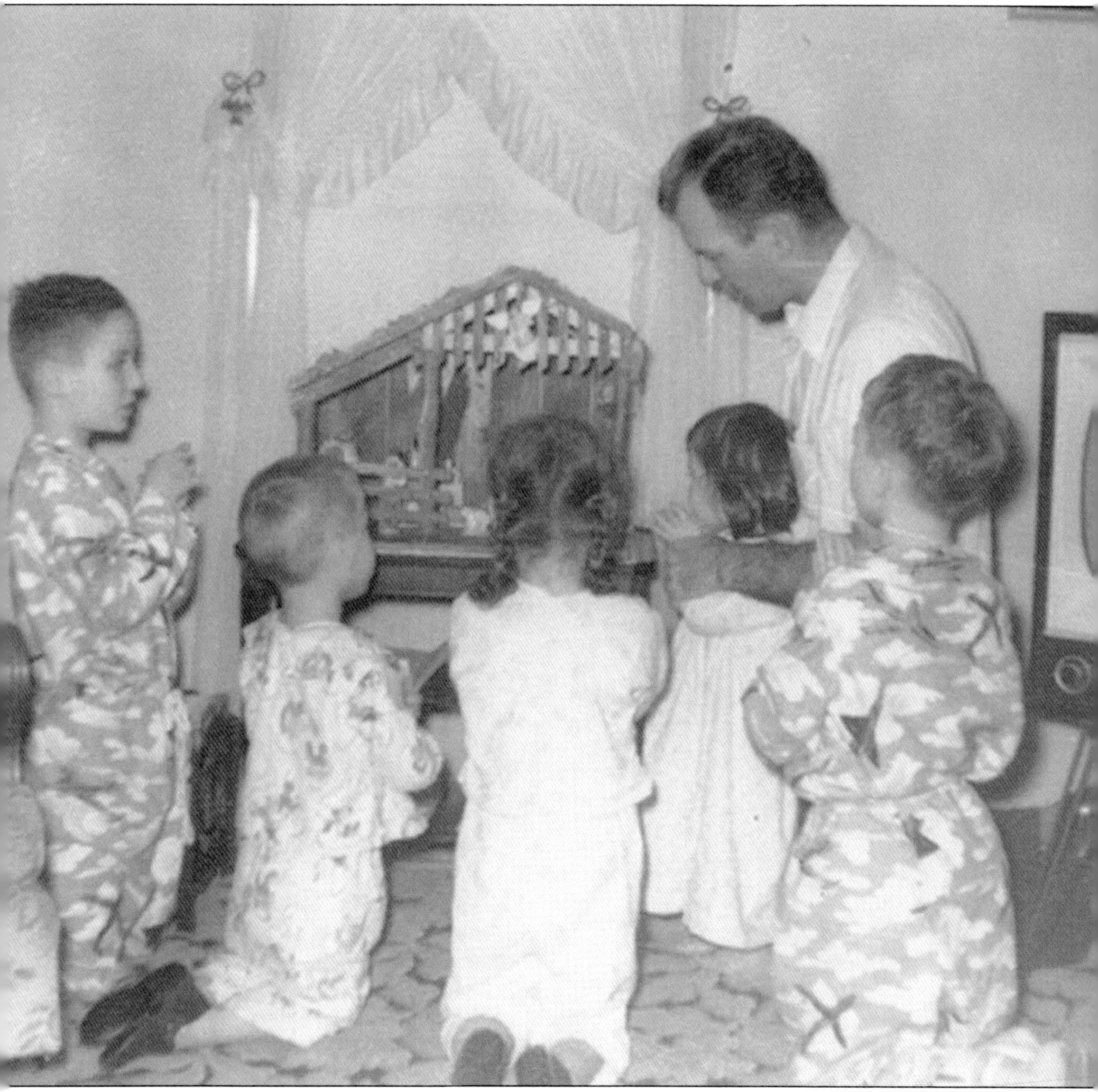

All of this religious activity did filter down to the lay people of Stearns County. Like most Catholic families, Christmas was and still is an important time of year. Here the Brixius family took time out to worship as a family in front of a Nativity scene. Pictured, from left to right: Albert A., Paul, Barbara, Andrew, Albert C., and Zita. (Courtesy of Kari Brixius.)

# *Eight*

# TO PROTECT AND TO SERVE

Between 1830 and 1930 cities in America experienced a century-long period of economic and population growth that fundamentally altered the way we relate to city government. Prior to this century, city government had been minimal, regulatory, or responsive. But during this phase, city government began to take on new tasks. Cities became promotional. Working in combination with Chambers of Commerce, Boards of Trades, and social organizations, cities had to sell themselves as modern service cities. In addition to the basics of sewers, water, and power, cities had to provide services like fire and police protection. Citizens needed to feel safe and secure before they would invest in a community. Stearns County cities fell in line with this national movement and the county seat, St. Cloud, became a leader in protecting and serving county residents.

While all Stearns County cities provided services to their residents, St. Cloud also had to provide county services and even state services. Even in a county dominated by Christians, crime and delinquency and disputes over property and other matters were a problem from the founding of the county. Some place had to be built to try cases and settle disputes. On July 8, 1856, citizens began the process of building a courthouse. The original red brick, stone foundation courthouse was completed eight years later. It continued to serve the needs of residents. It was demolished and a new building was erected at the same location and dedicated in 1922. Today the county courthouse has been expanded by the addition of a second court facility and a law enforcement center. The 1922 building is still in service and is registered as a national historic landmark.

As a law enforcement center, St. Cloud also houses the Stearns County jail—a state correctional facility known locally as the reformatory. Opened to first-time offenders in 1889, the facility was built by prisoners from local granite. The 22-foot high, 4-foot thick granite wall enclosing the 55-acre tract is the longest granite wall in the world. Two pictures of this facility are included in this chapter. The first shows the building under construction, and the second shows it in operation.

St. Cloud also serves as a medical center for the county and for greater central Minnesota. The Sisters of St. Benedict opened the first hospital for the community at the location of the present state reformatory. Finding it too far out of town, the Sisters moved the hospital to Ninth Avenue North. They anticipated the need for a larger facility and wisely purchased property on the banks of the Mississippi north of town. The hospital has become a premier heart center and recently began Life Flight service to the Twin Cities.

These services in St. Cloud affect the entire county and the city government of St. Cloud has had to work closely with county and state government to integrate these county-wide services into its city plan. The city has also taken advantage of these services to sell itself as a modern service city that is safe and secure. The images that follow show a variety of buildings that have served the residents of Stearns County. City Hall, the courthouses, the reformatories, the hospitals, the orphans home, and other buildings have helped Stearns County residents find aid in times of need. This chapter is dedicated to the hard working men and women who have served the county.

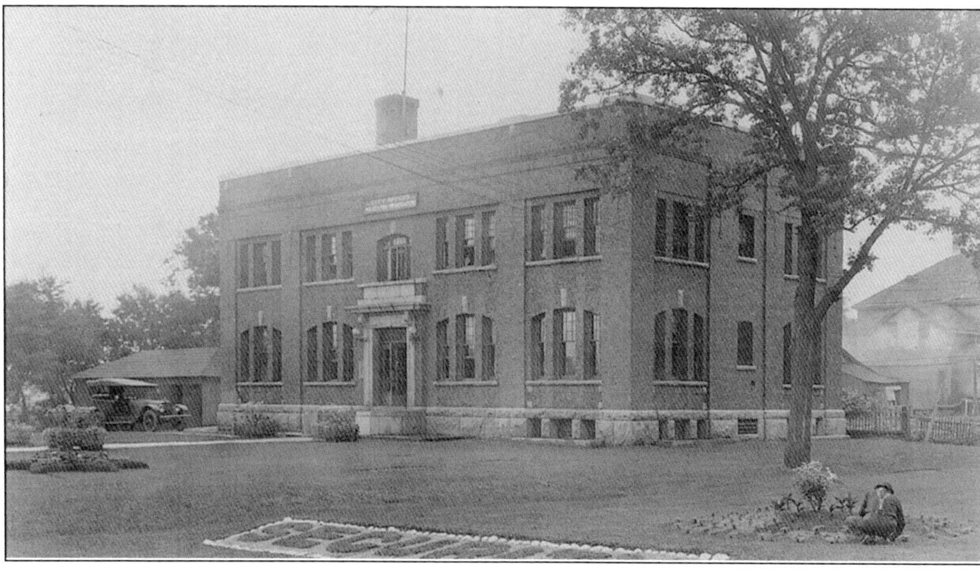

St. Cloud City Hall, located at its original site on the banks of the Mississippi, c. 1930, housed city government, the police department, and the fire department for ten years until the fire department moved to new quarters in 1928. A squad car, like the one parked on the right, once rolled into the river. The "security" flower arrangement was an advertisement for the Security Blank Book and Printing Company. The building was torn down in 1980 to make way for a new civic center. (Courtesy of Richard Kelly.)

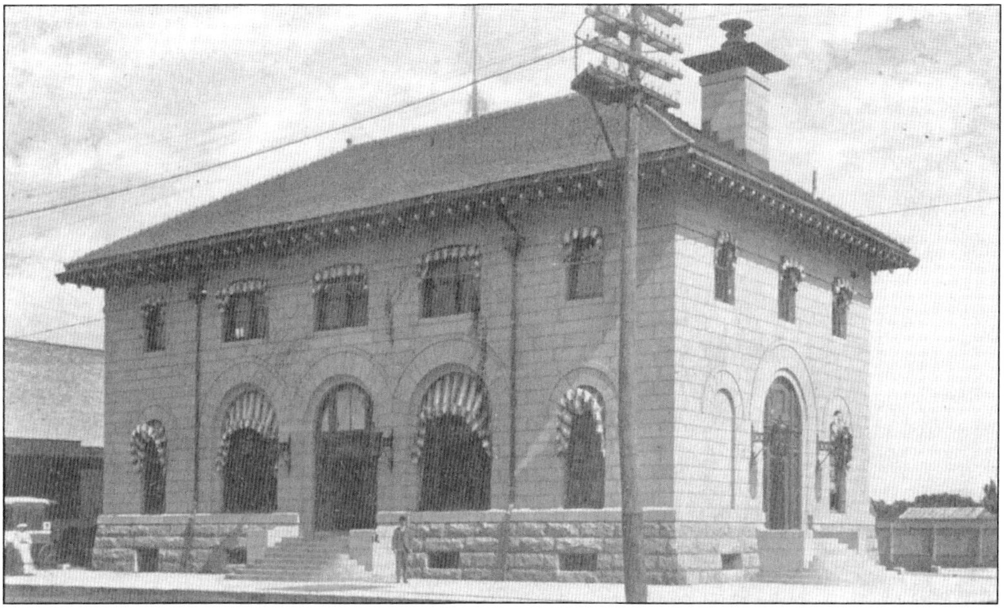

The Federal Building as it looked in 1930 and as rebuilt in 1945. In the mid-1930s the original building was moved down St. Germain Street by horse-drawn skids to the banks of the Mississippi River. It was torn down in 1980 to make way for a new civic center. (Courtesy of Richard Kelly and the Central Minnesota Historical Society.)

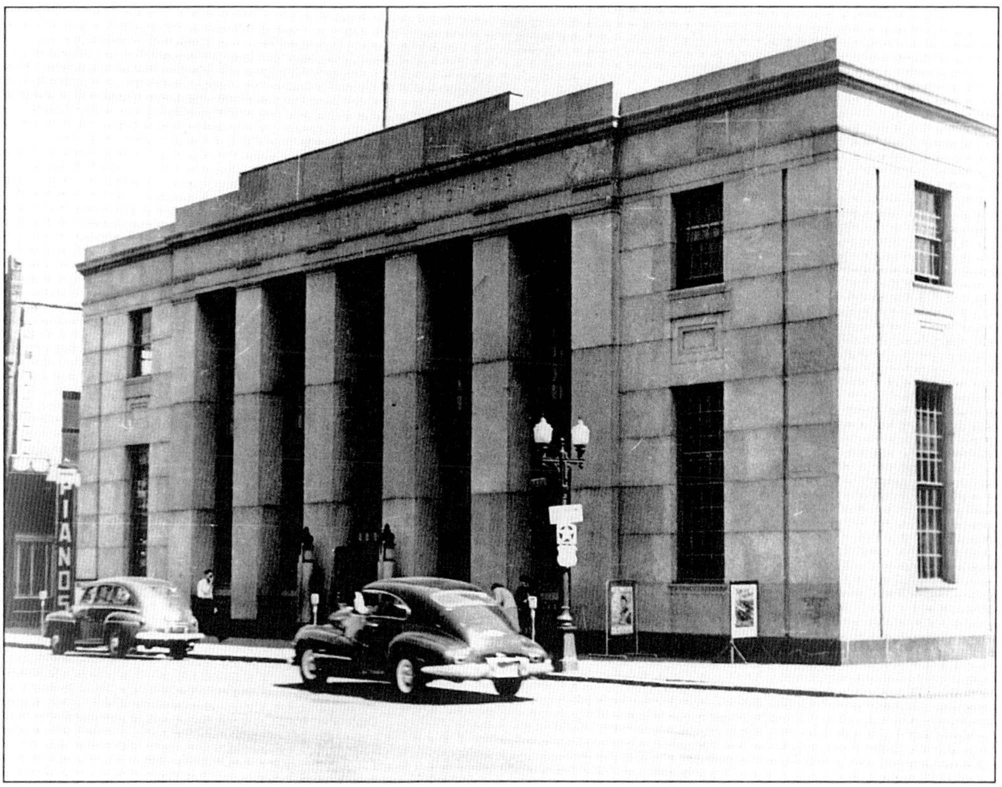

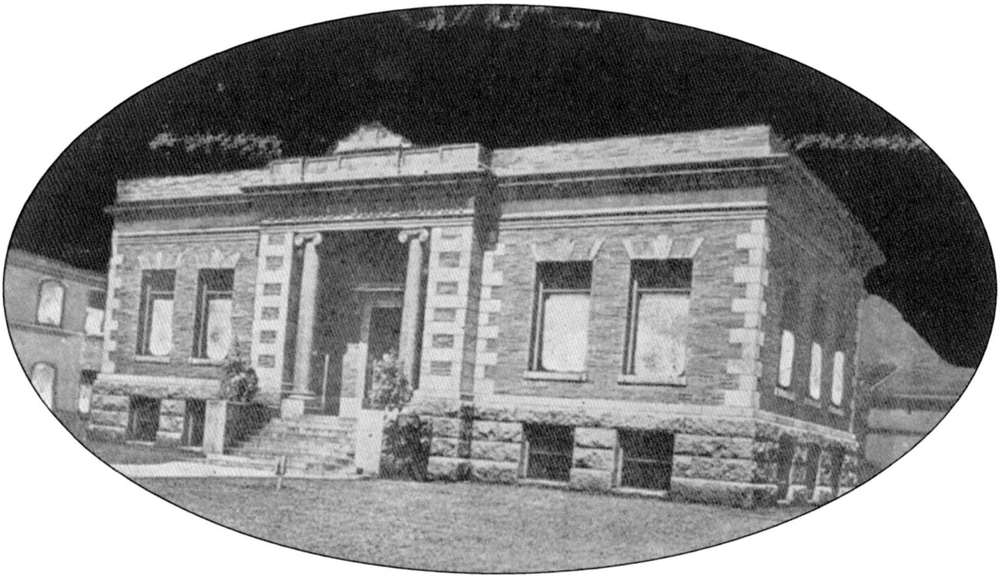

The public library on Fifth Avenue South, St. Cloud, 1915, was registered as a national historic landmark, but still demolished in 1980. The pillars were saved and now stand in front of the Stearns County Courthouse and Administration Building on Seventh Avenue North. (Courtesy of Richard Kelly.)

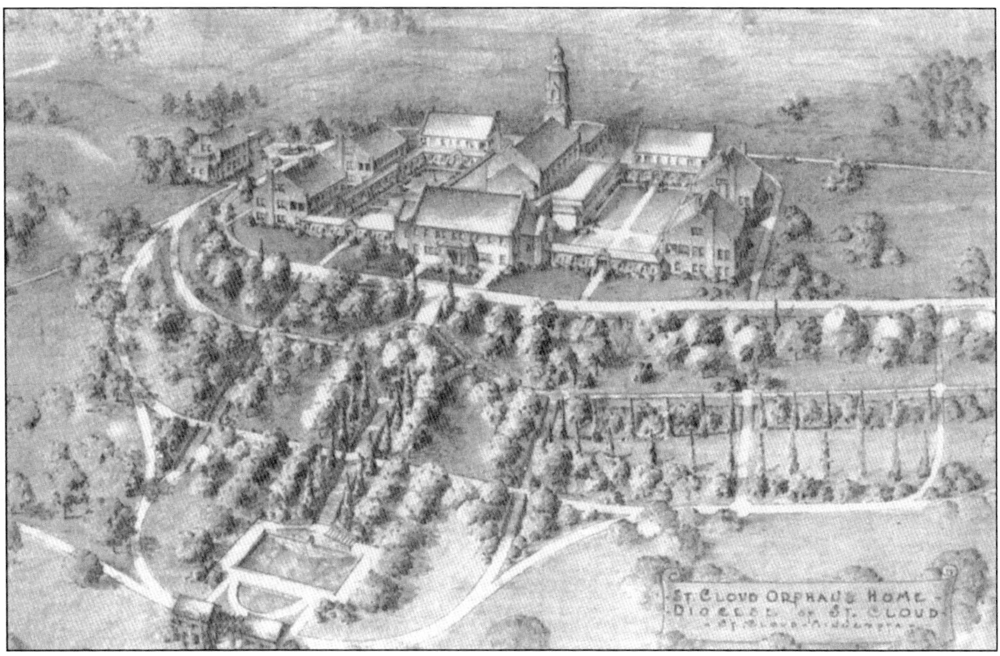


The St. Cloud Orphan Home, *c.* 1925, was founded in 1892. Completed in 1924, the home continues in operation today. (Courtesy of Richard Kelly.)

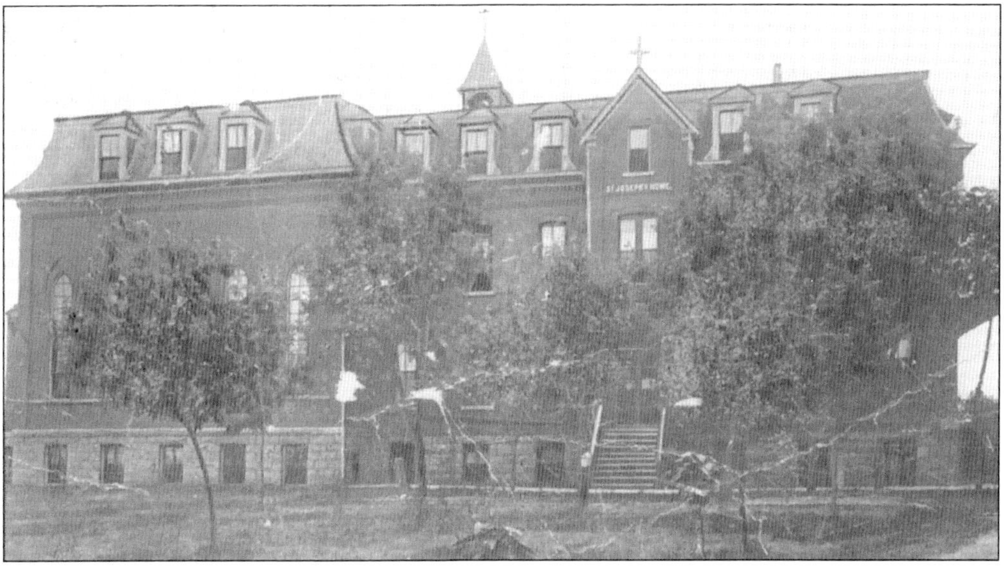

St. Joseph's Home, St. Cloud, 1911, was built by the Sisters of St. Benedicts in 1890. This building served as the first St. Raphael's Hospital near the site of the present day state reformatory. Because of its location, people had trouble finding the hospital so the sisters moved to a location on Ninth Avenue North. This building later served as a senior citizens home, and now, under the name St. Scholastica's, serves as a home for retired Benedictine nuns. (Courtesy of Richard Kelly.)

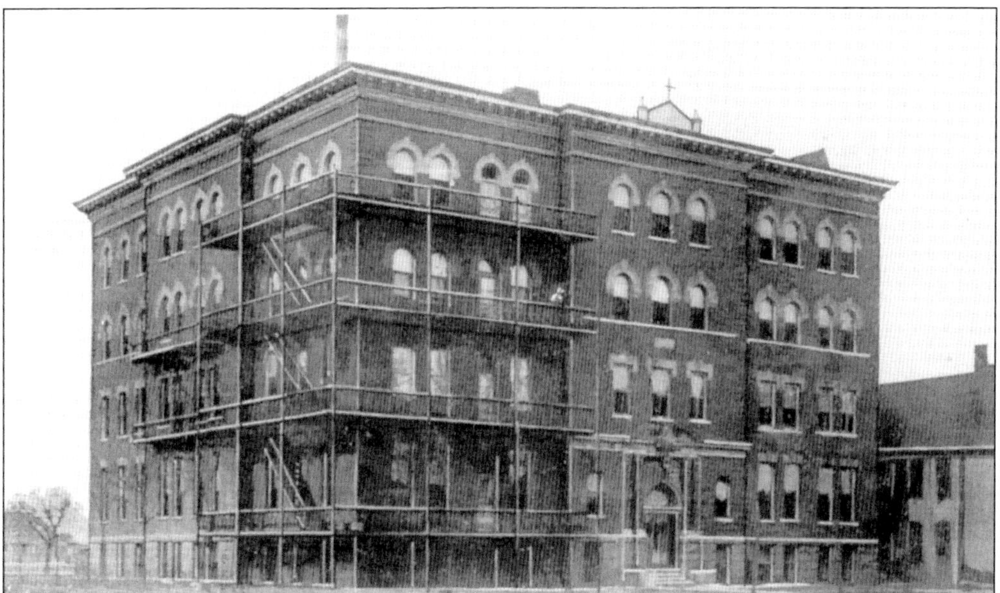

Pictured above is St. Raphael's Hospital on Ninth Avenue North St. Cloud, c. 1915. This building was later turned into a convent and is currently being renovated as a Christian retreat center. (Courtesy of Richard Kelly.)

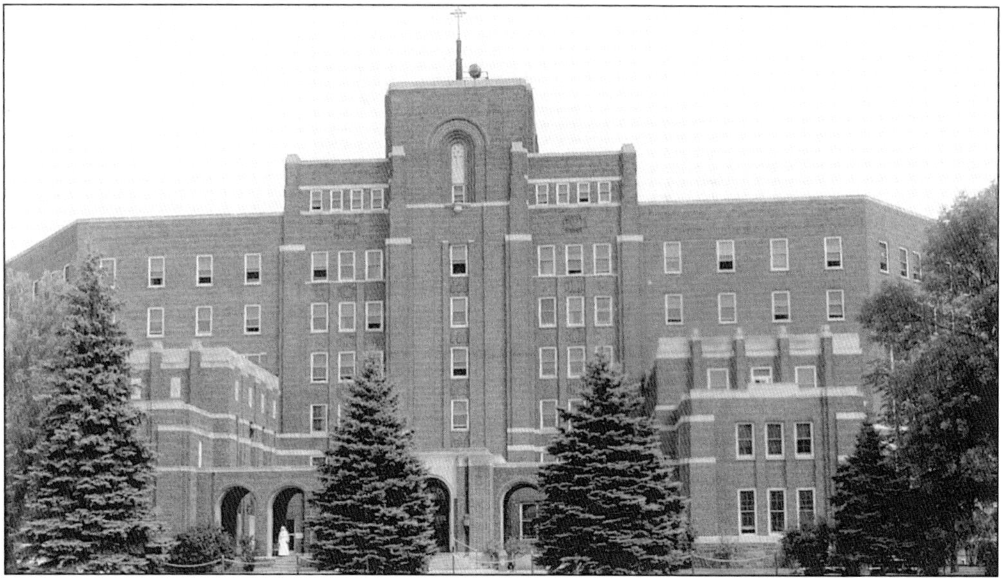

St. Cloud Hospital, 1200 Sixth Avenue North, appears above c. 1930. Anticipating the need for a larger facility, the Sisters of St. Benedicts purchased the land for this site in 1916 and began building in 1927. (Courtesy or Richard Kelly.)

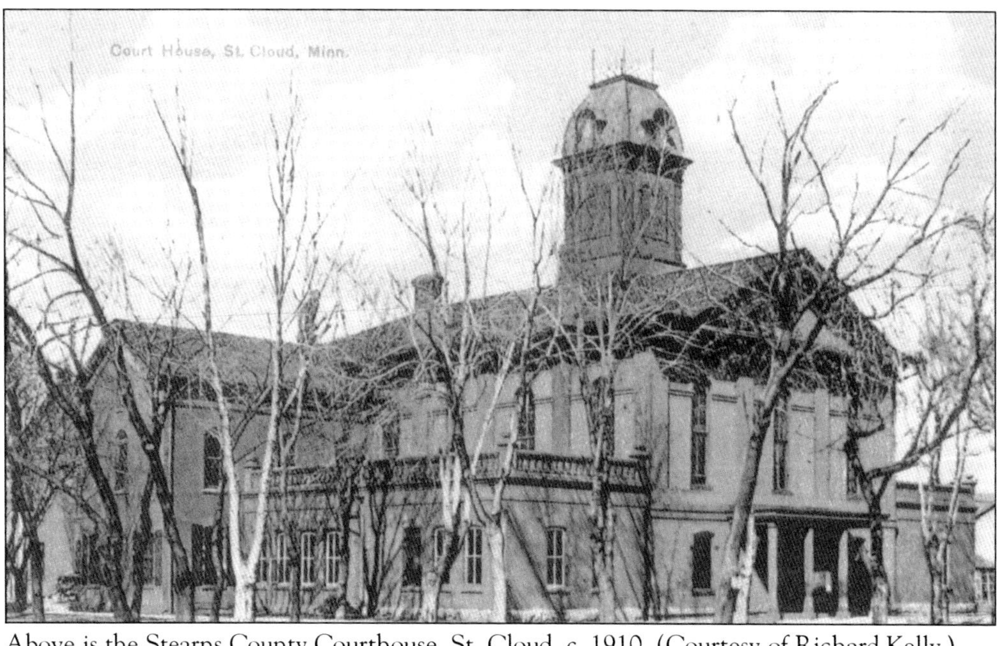


Above is the Stearns County Courthouse, St. Cloud, c. 1910. (Courtesy of Richard Kelly.)

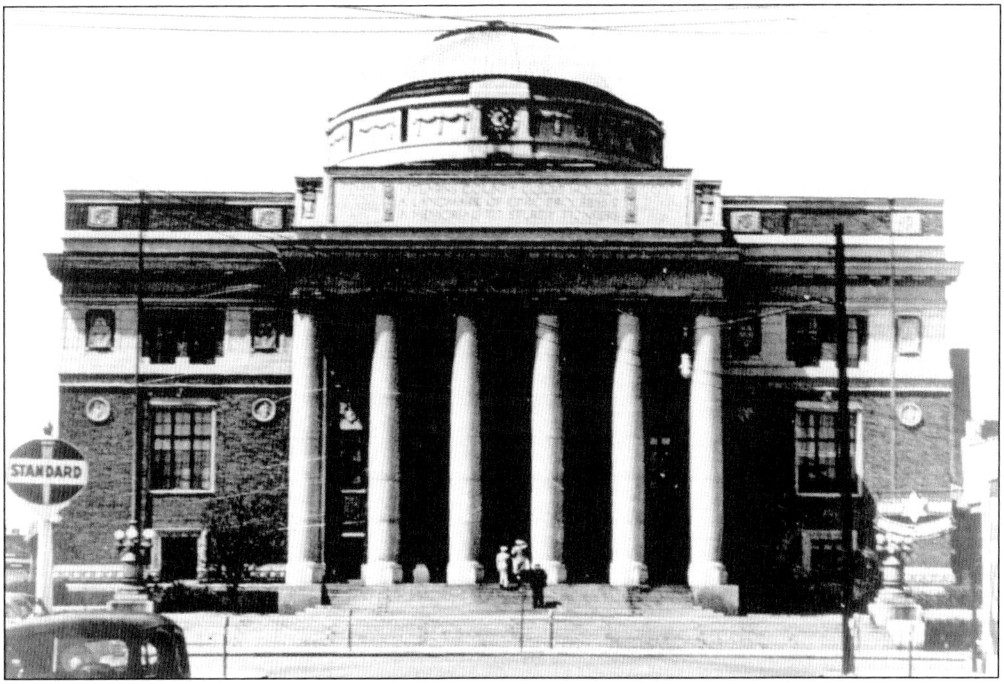


The new Stearns County Courthouse, St. Cloud, appears in the above *c.* 1930 image. (Courtesy of Richard Kelly.)

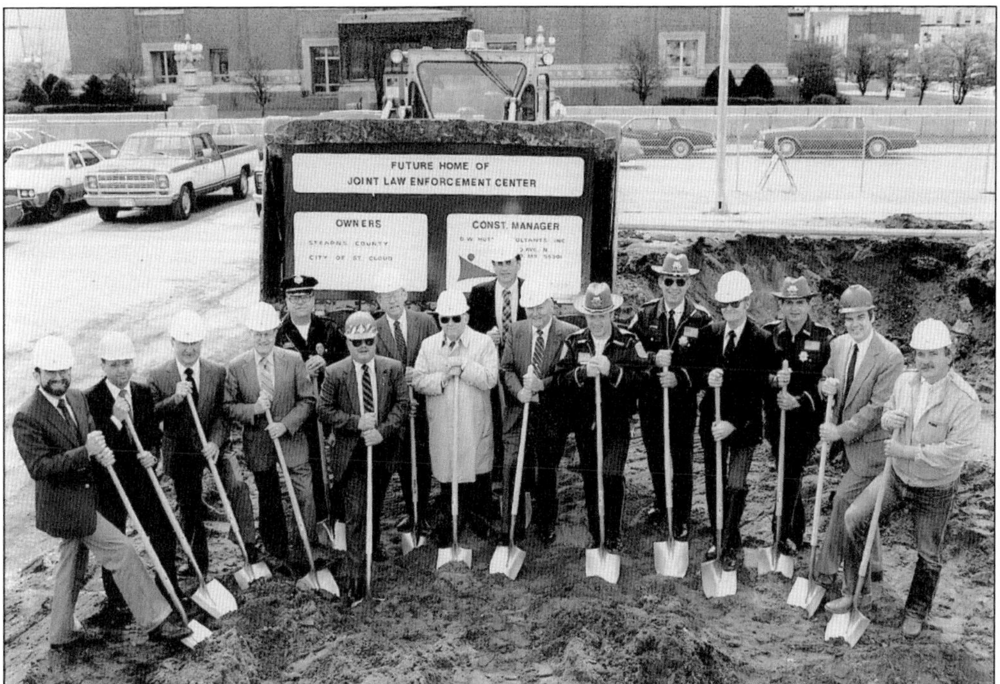


Groundbreaking for the new Stearns County Law Enforcement Center in St. Cloud, 1985. Sheriff Charlie Grafft is fifth from the right. (Courtesy of Charlie Grafft.)

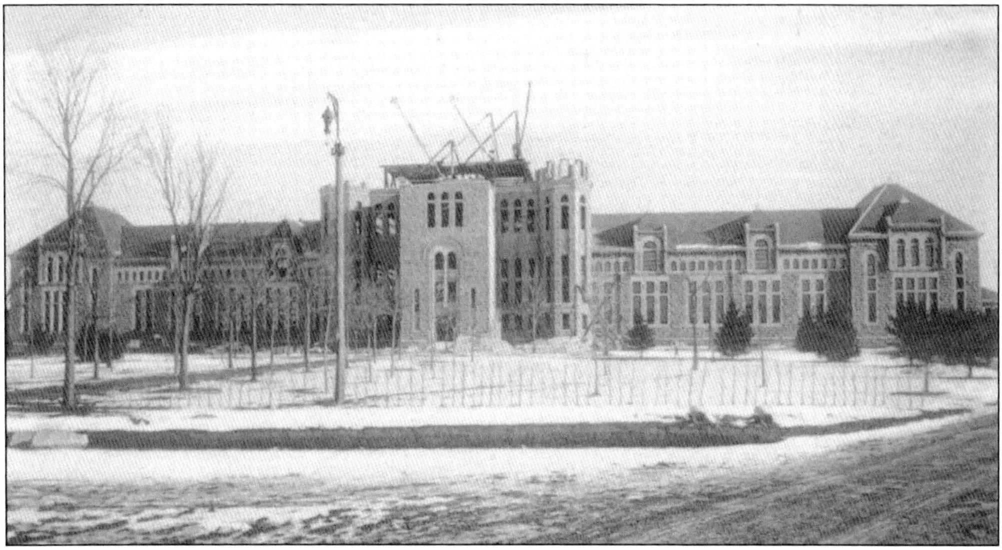

The state reformatory at St. Cloud is shown here under construction. The reformatory was built using prison labor. The wall surrounding the facility is the longest continuous granite wall in the world, with all of the granite coming from local quarries. (Courtesy of Richard Kelly.)

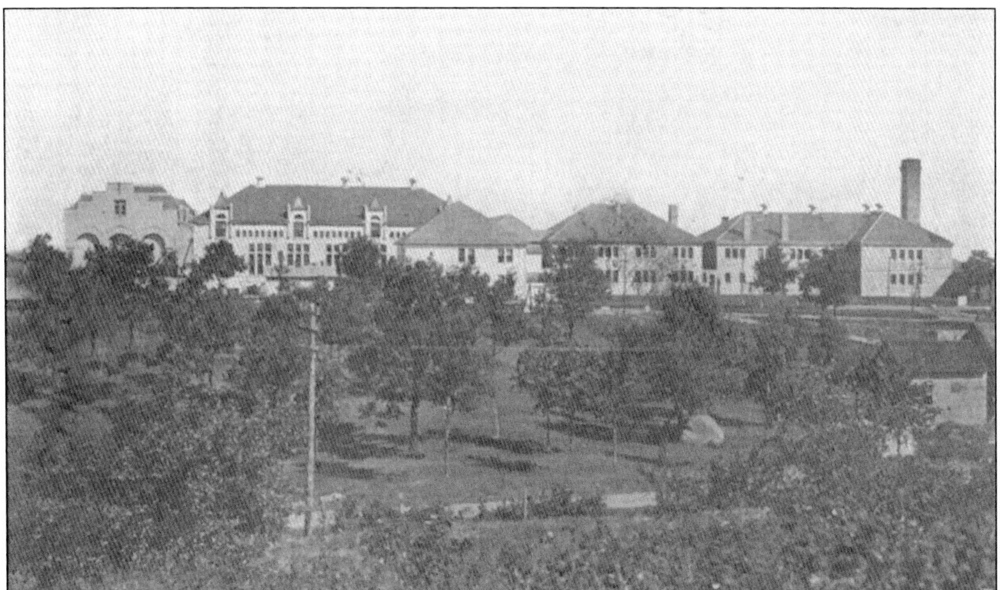

The state reformatory at St. Cloud as it stands completed. (Courtesy of Richard Kelly.)

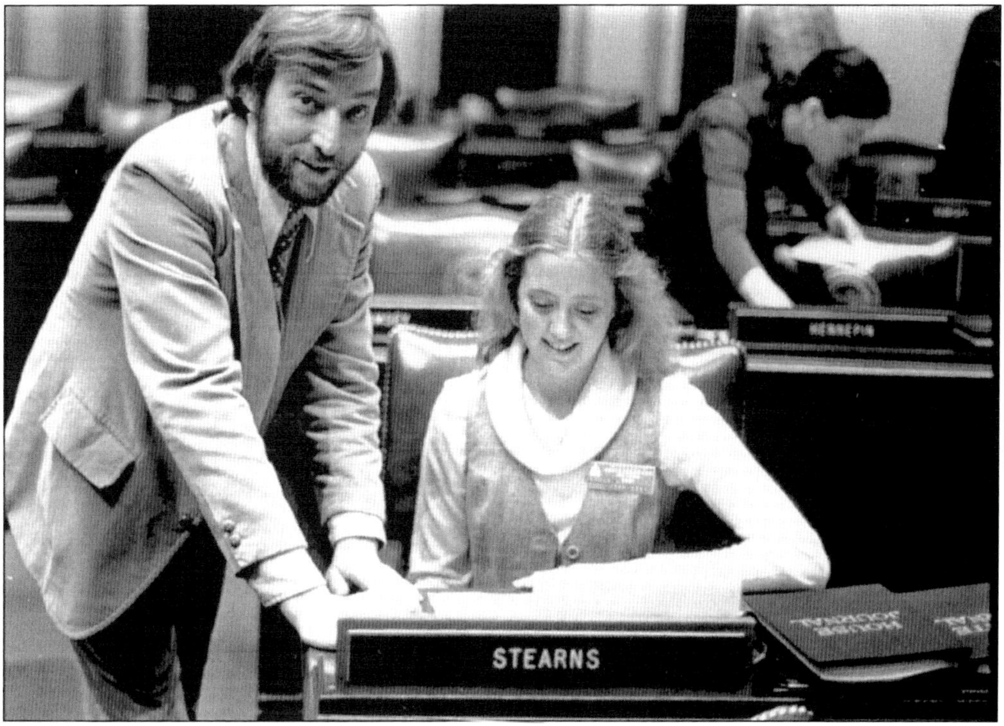


Minnesota State Representative Jim Pehler representing Stearns County in 1986. (Courtesy of the Central Minnesota Historical Center.)

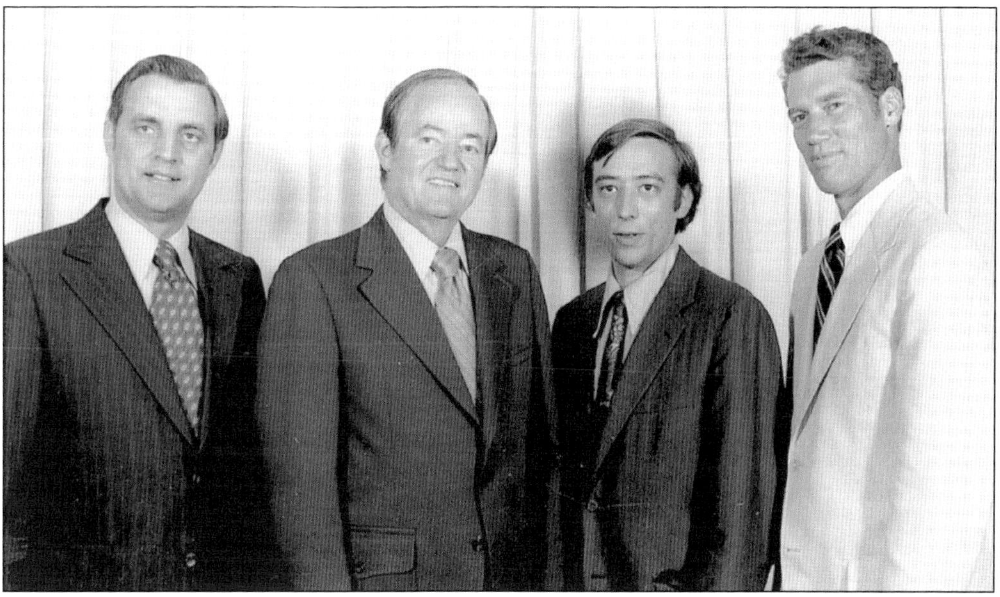

Minnesota State Representative Jim Pehler stands with Walter Mondale, Hubert Humphrey, and Minnesota Governor Wendell Anderson in 1986. (Courtesy of the Central Minnesota Historical Center.)

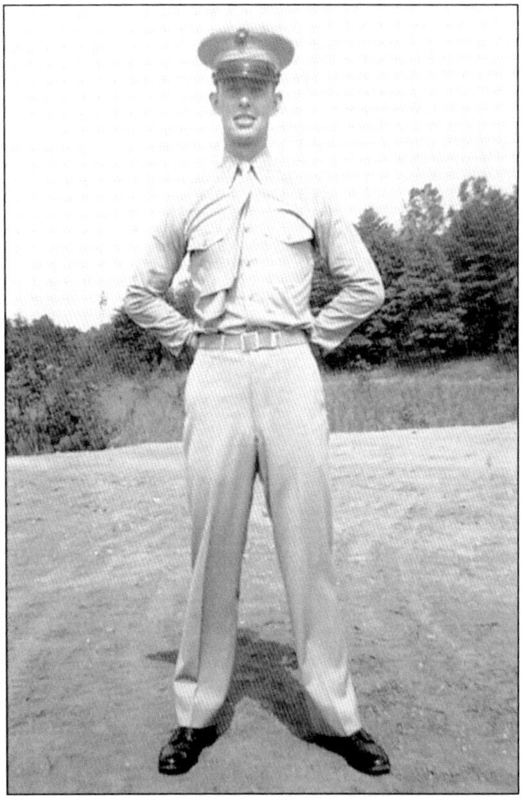

Since the days of the Civil War, Stearns County residents have answered their country's call to service. Richard Rawlings poses in his air force uniform and at the Yuma Air Base. (Courtesy of Jenny Giambruno.)

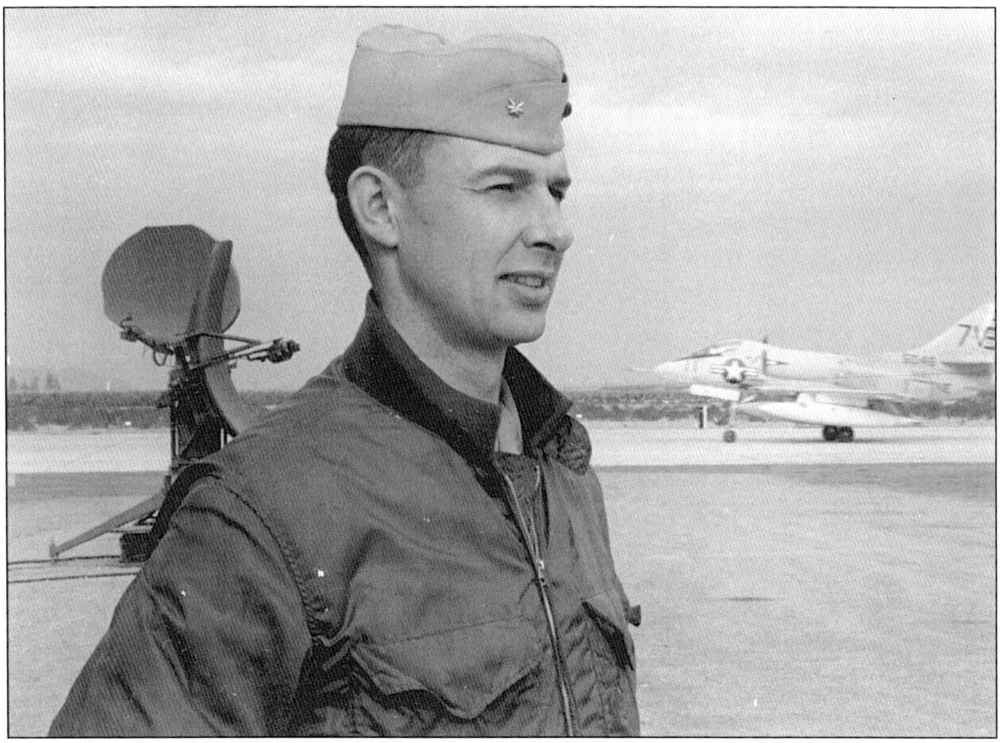

# *Nine*

# THE NATURAL ENVIRONMENT

Like most of the state of Minnesota, Stearns County's history is intimately linked to the natural environment. The county is bounded on its northeast corner by the Mississippi River and is drained by the Watab, the Sauk, the Crow, and the Clearwater Rivers. The county contains its fair share of lakes, which have served as recreational havens as well as agricultural sources for food and water. Eighty large lakes and about 125 smaller lakes dot the landscape. Of the county's 851,241 acres, 37,021 acres are covered by water.

In summertime, these water resources offer residents and visitors exceptional opportunities for swimming, fishing, boating, water skiing, sailing, and lazy days on quiet riverbanks. In winter, frozen waterways provide opportunities for ice-skating, hockey, ice fishing, and snowmobiling. The same waterways can also mean danger. The history of the county is marked by stories of drownings and floods. A winter with heavy snowfall coupled with a sudden thaw can raise river levels to hazardous flood stages. Such was the case for Cold Spring and Waite Park in the spring of 1997 when the Sauk River rose to flood levels. The river crested at 8.5 feet above flood stage and rose 1.5 feet in 24 hours before it receded, flooding nearby homes and businesses. The river is notorious for flooding at least once every 10 to 20 years.

Mother nature has sent other natural disasters to Stearns County. One of the most common natural disasters experienced in Minnesota during spring and summer is a tornado. The destruction left by a tornado in 1886 altered the history of both Stearns and Benton Counties. St. Cloud in Stearns County and Sauk Rapids in Benton County were hard hit by an April storm that killed 58 and injured 140 people. The tornado jumped over the business district in St. Cloud and hit Sauk Rapids with exceptional force. Over 109 public and commercial buildings were destroyed or damaged in Sauk Rapids. While Sauk Rapids worked to rebuild the community, St. Cloud became the prominent business district. Sauk Rapids lost its stature as the dominant community.

Perhaps the most famous natural disasters to hit Stearns County were the grasshopper plagues of 1857–1858 and 1873–1877. Swarms of grasshoppers descended on the county, eating everything in their path. The insects devoured crops, gardens, clothing, trees, and shrubs. Even fences, houses, and barns were damaged by the voracious plague. The devastation was so severe that residents experienced serious food shortages during the following winters. Many farmers returned to the East or had to travel many miles to find work, leaving wives and children to manage the homesteads. The end of the plague in 1877 led to the building of special chapels in Cold Spring and Luxemburg to commemorate its miraculous end.

In spite of the ravages of floods, fires, tornadoes, and grasshopper plagues, Stearns County residents have endured. They are a hearty lot who, through an abiding faith in God and a willingness to assist each other, have overcome the odds to create a prosperous community that has experienced sustained economic growth.

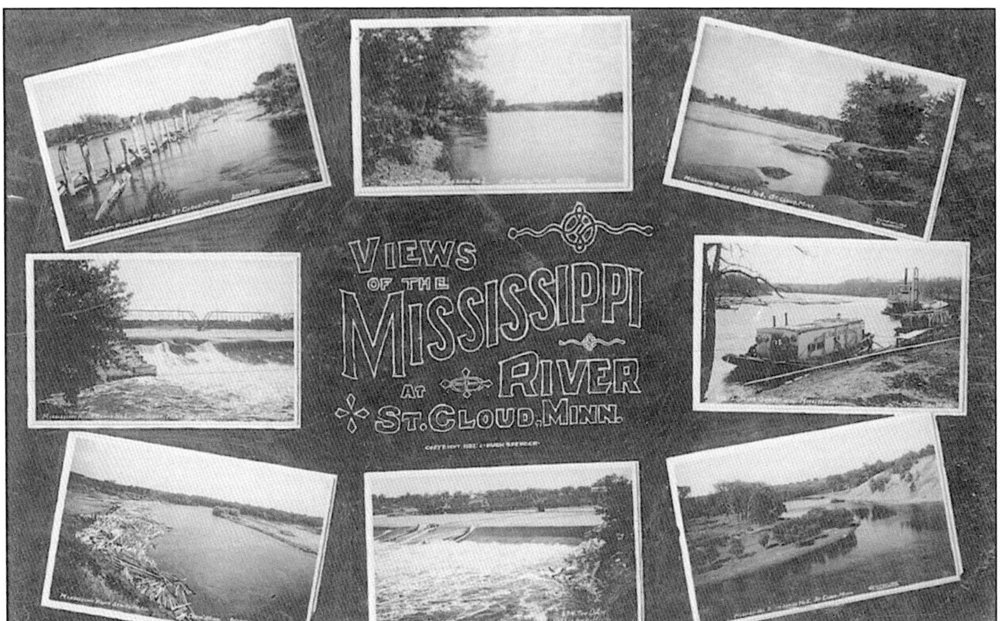


The Mississippi River is one of the major natural features of Stearns County. This collage shows the importance of the river to marketing St. Cloud, 1910. (Courtesy of Richard Kelly.)

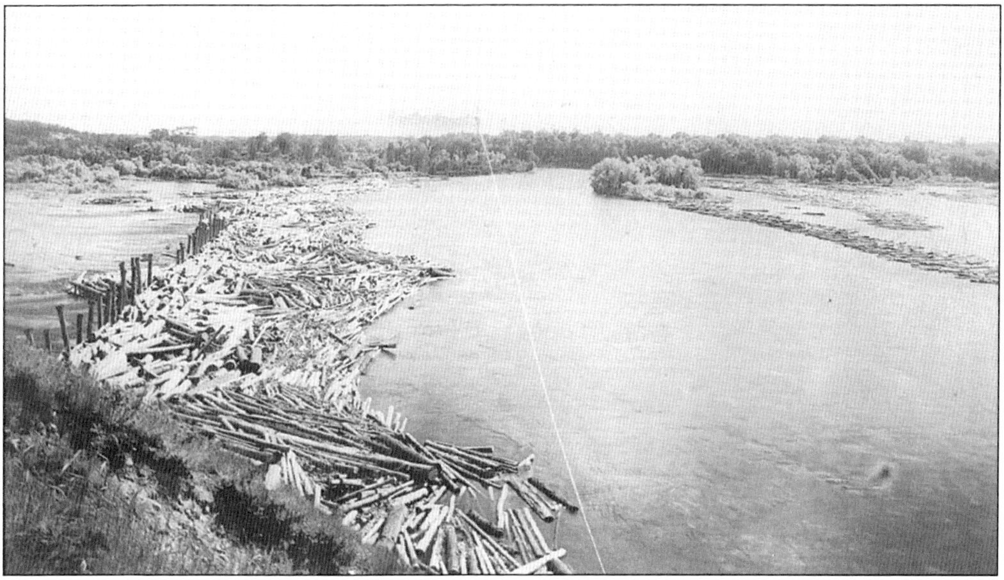

Pictured above is a logjam on the Mississippi, near St. Cloud, 1910. (Courtesy of Richard Kelly.)

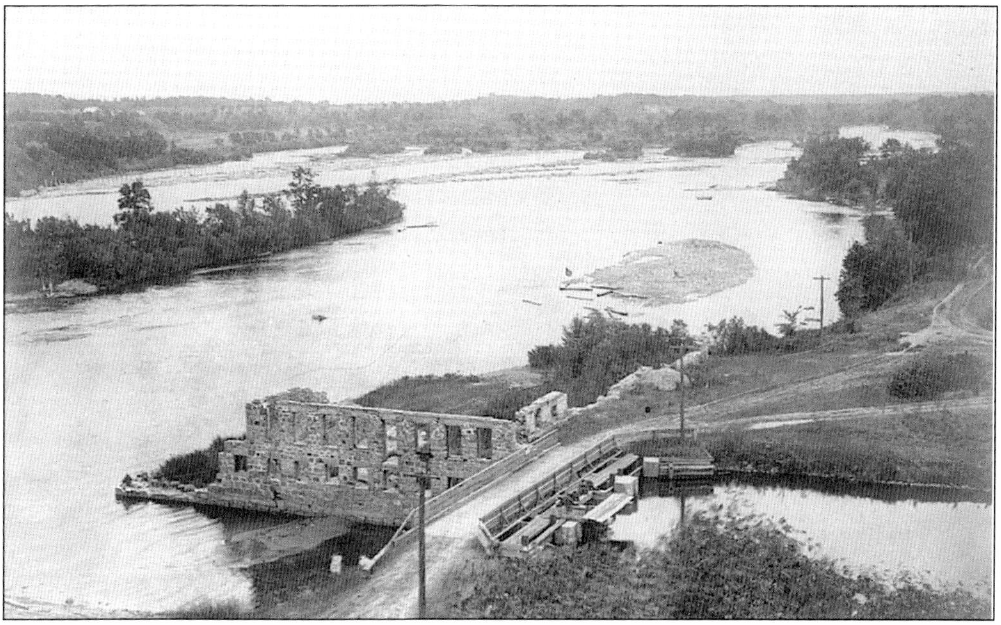

Ruins of a burnt out paper mill appear near Beaver Island, south of St. Cloud, 1910. The lower millrace is in the right foreground. (Courtesy of Richard Kelly.)

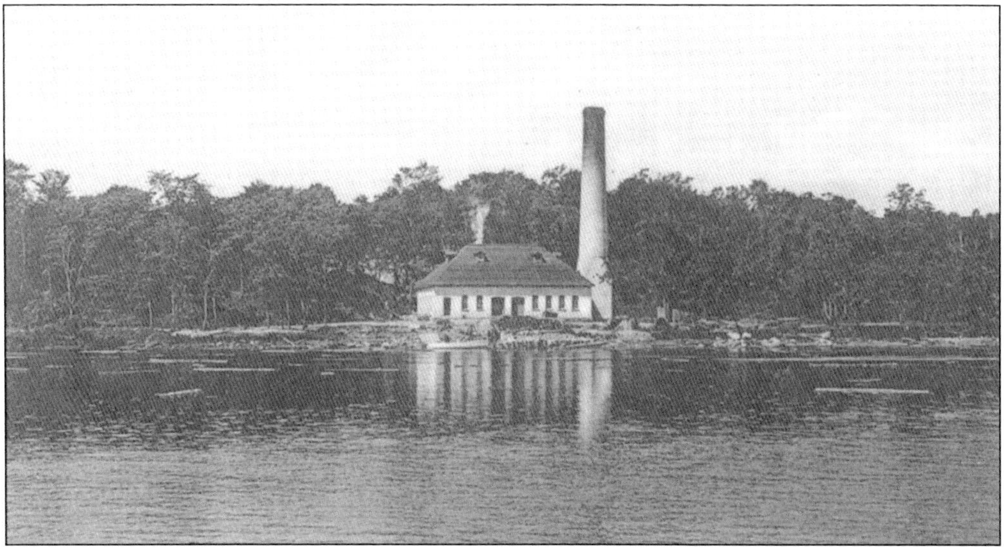

This is one of the first incarnations of the St. Cloud city water service at Hester Park in 1910. At this time the facility did not produce potable water, but only water for putting out fires. (Courtesy of Richard Kelly.)

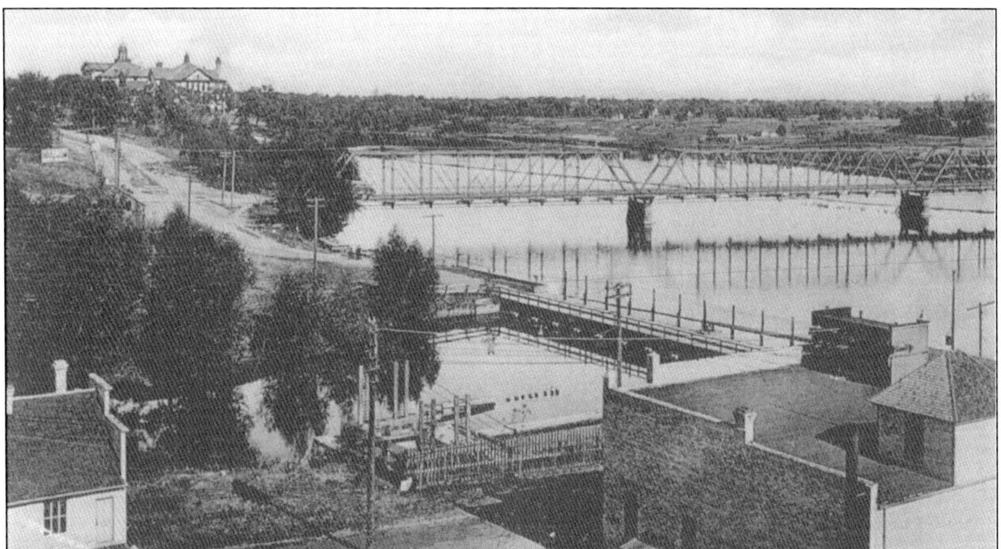

Pictured is the power station at the dam just south of the State Normal School, St. Cloud, *c.* 1910. (Courtesy of Richard Kelly.)

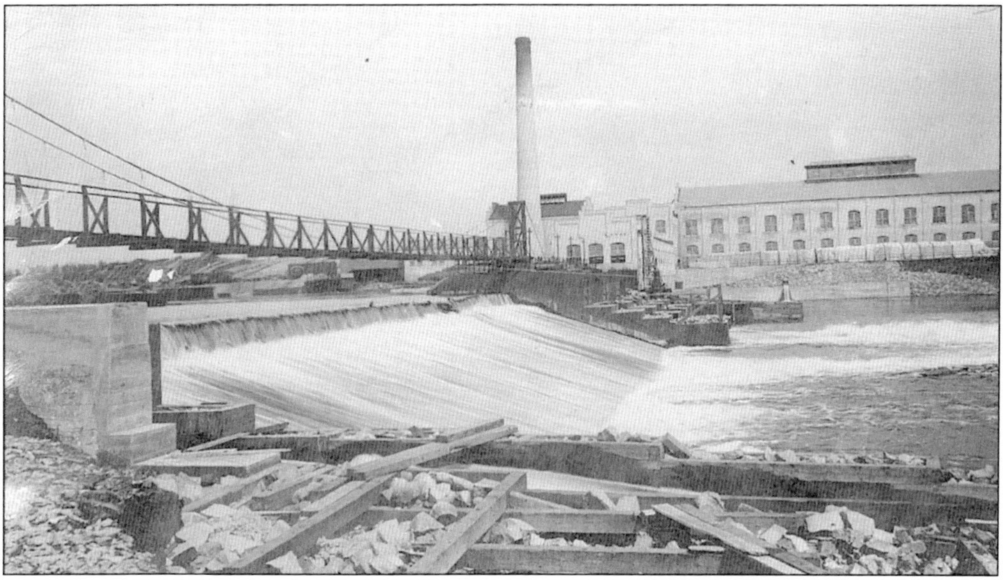

The Watab Dam at Sartell, 1911, provided power for the Watab Paper and Pulp Mill. (Courtesy of Richard Kelly.)

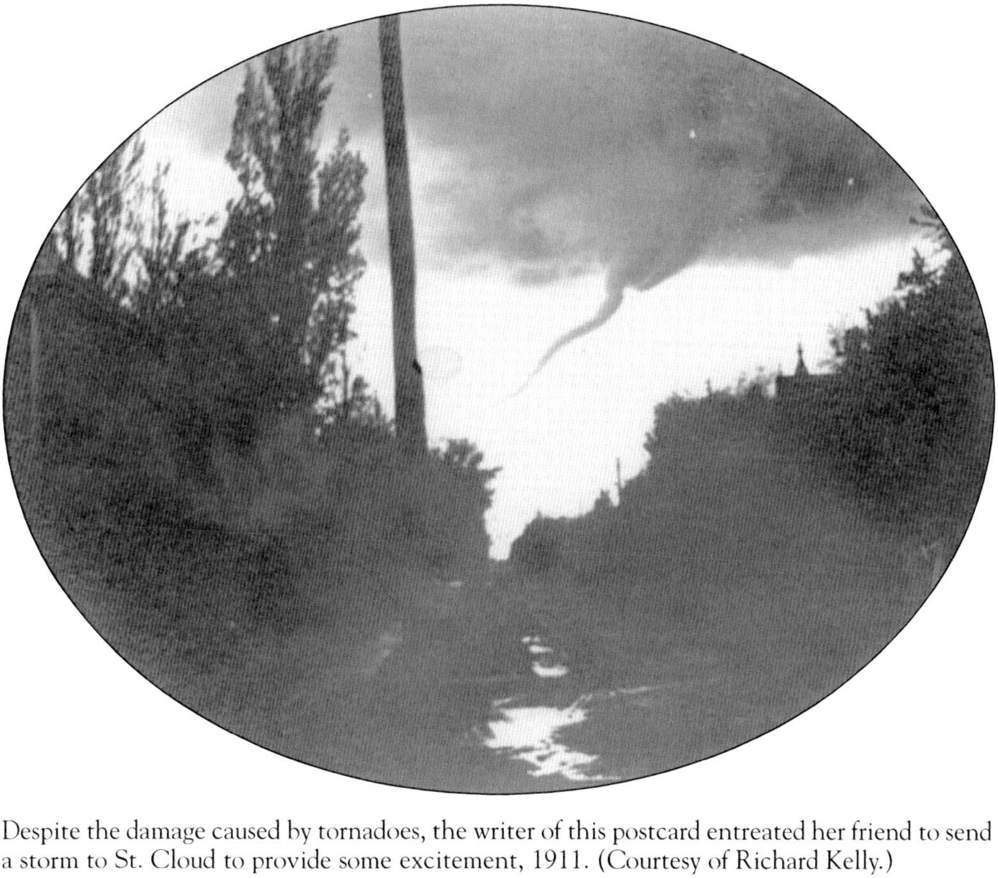

Despite the damage caused by tornadoes, the writer of this postcard entreated her friend to send a storm to St. Cloud to provide some excitement, 1911. (Courtesy of Richard Kelly.)

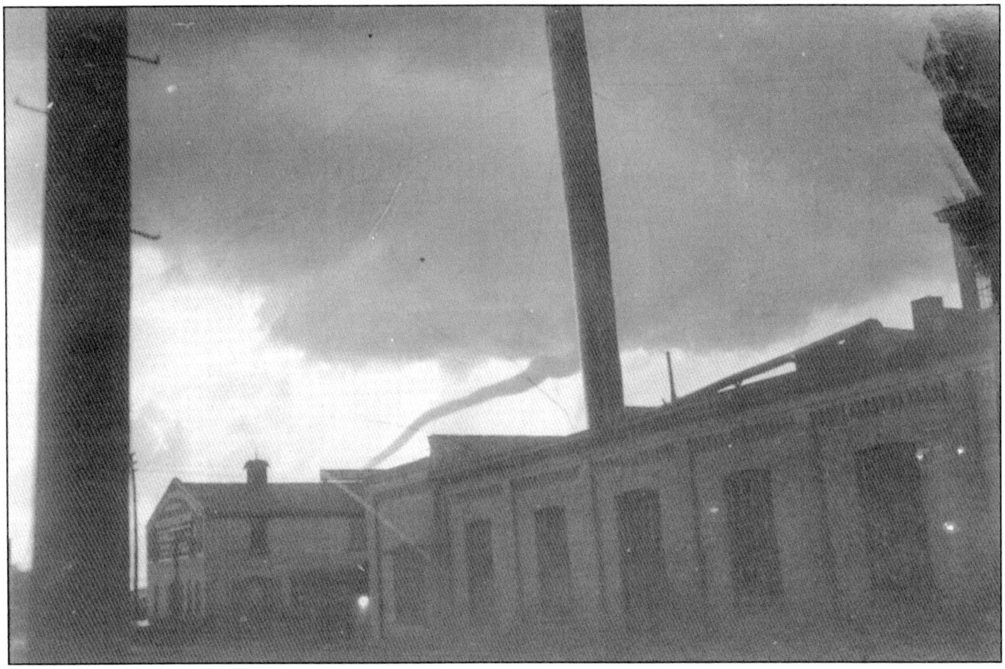

A tornado hit St. Cloud on May 30, 1909. (Courtesy of Richard Kelly.)

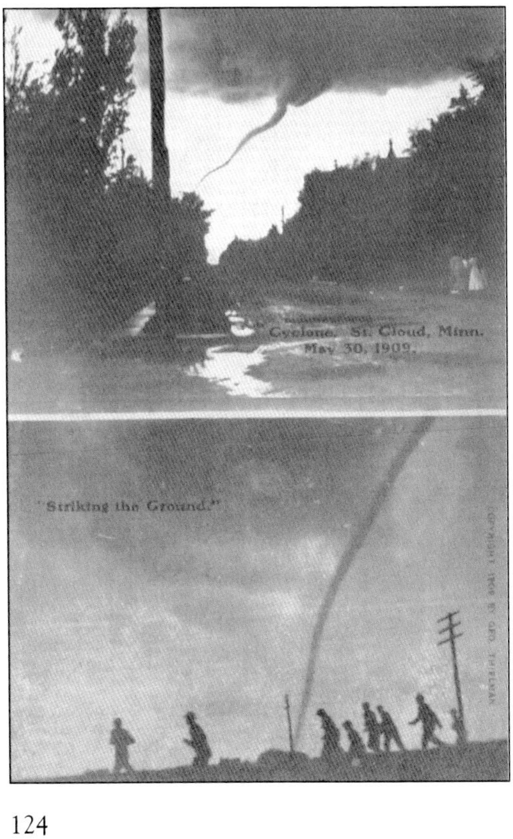

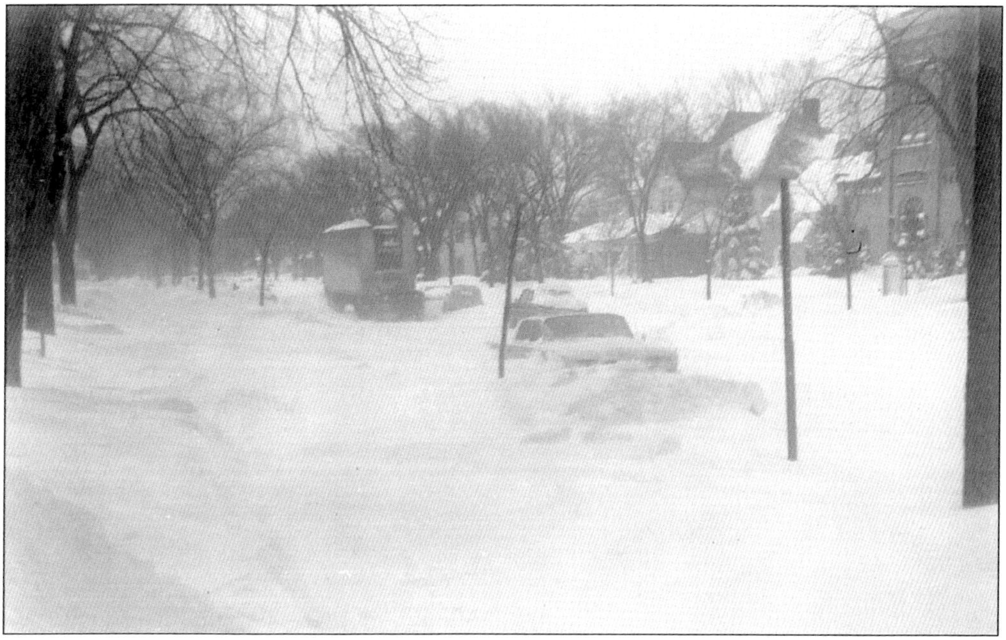

The heavy snow of 1965 slowed, but did not stop traffic on Fifth Avenue South, St. Cloud, (top). The snowplows cleared the road leaving drifts of 4 to 6 feet. (Courtesy of the Hunstiger family.)

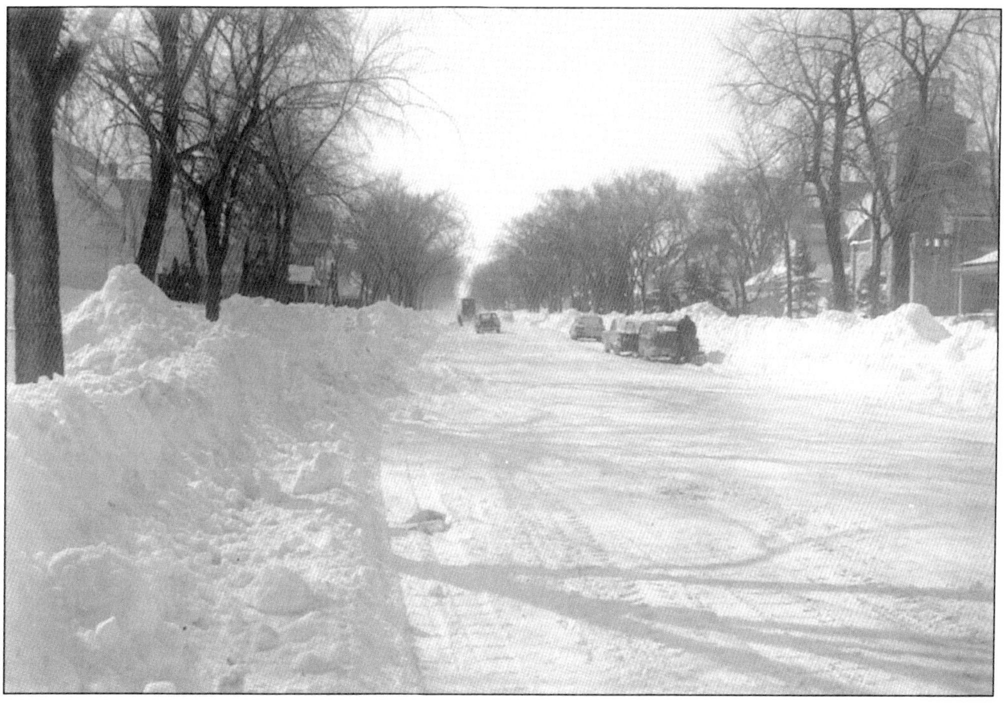

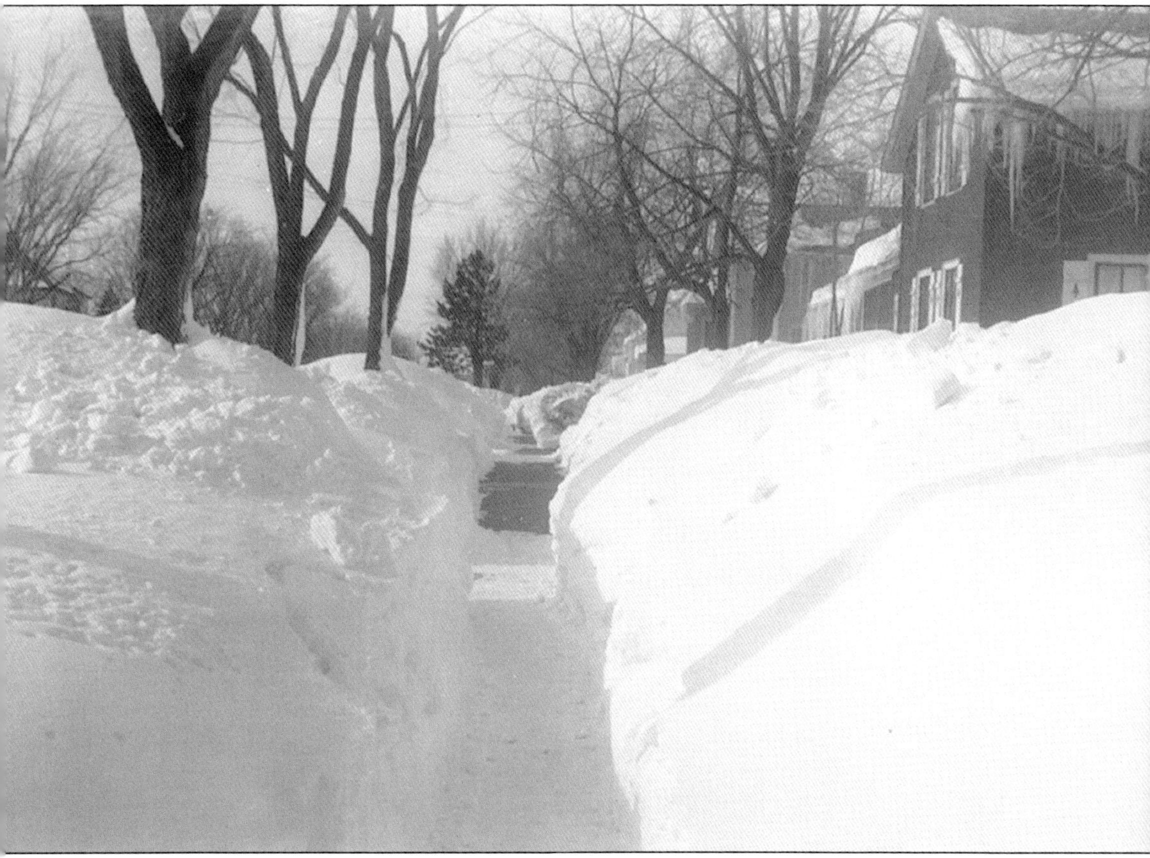

For pedestrians, walking between drifts could feel like walking through a tunnel. The area cleared on sidewalks grew progressively narrower as the snow got deeper. This is Fifth Avenue South, St. Cloud, 1965. (Courtesy of the Hunstiger family.)

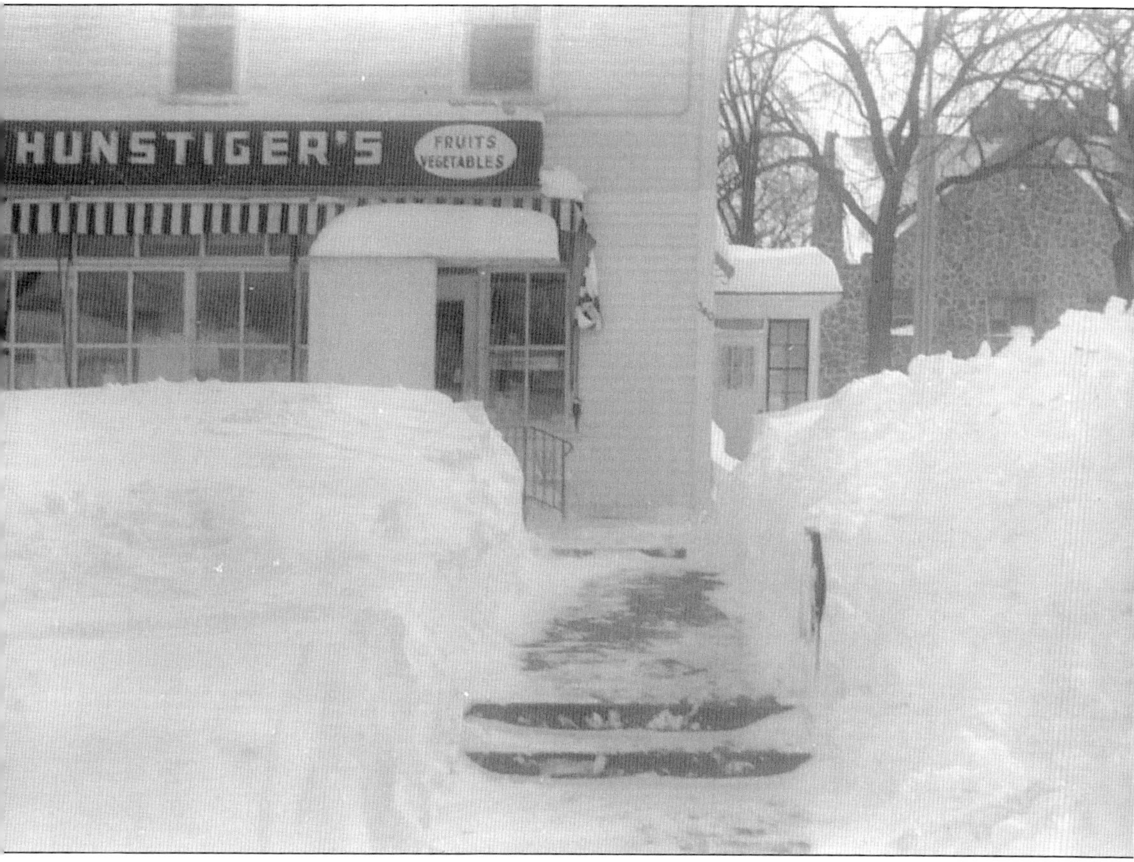


Businesses could be particularly hard hit by snow. In 1965 snow practically covered the front entrance to the Hunstiger Meat Market on Fifth Avenue South, St. Cloud. (Courtesy of the Hunstiger family.)

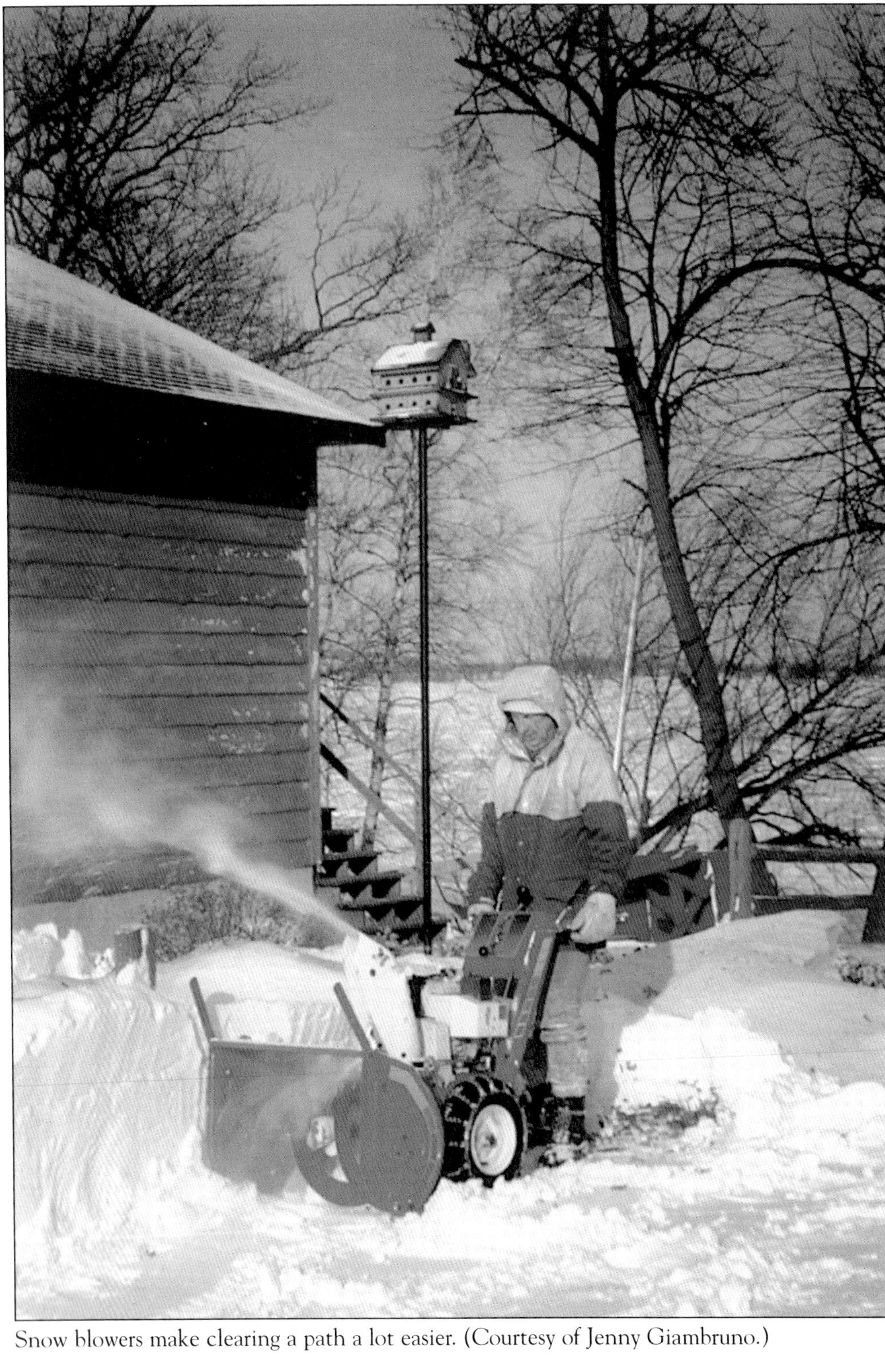

Snow blowers make clearing a path a lot easier. (Courtesy of Jenny Giambruno.)